Sociology's Models of Man

*The Relationships of Models of Man to Sociological
Explanation in Three Sociological Theories*

William L. Skidmore

GORDON AND BREACH

New York   London   Paris

Copyright © *1975 by*

Gordon and Breach Science Publishers, Inc.
1 Park Avenue
New York, N.Y. 10016

Editorial office for the United Kingdom

Gordon and Breach Science Publishers Ltd.
42 William IV Street
London W.C.2.

Editorial office for France

Gordon & Breach
7–9 rue Emile Dubois
Paris 75014

Library of Congress catalog card number 75–24593. ISBN 0 677 04780 0. All rights reserved.
No part of this book may be reproduced or utilized in any form or by any means, electronic or
mechanical, including photocopying, recording, or by any information storage or retrieval
system, without permission in writing from the publishers. Printed in Great Britain.

Sociology's Models of Man

to
My Parents

Preface

This work consists of a contextual analysis of the logical relations between the models of man and explanations of social order in the three main sociological theories of North America.

In examining exchange theory, the works of George Homans are considered. His hypothetico-deductive theoretical style is examined for consistency. The theoretical postulates advanced are found circular and the concept "value" unspecified; the statements are deemed unfalsifiable, and thus outside positive discourse. When values are not generally specified, *ad hoc* assumptions about particular values describe the substantive model of man. The relationships of the major categories of variables are relevant. These imply the existence of a norm of rationality. This norm, setting the conditions under which the theory applies to behavior, is in direct contradiction to the stated position of the theory regarding norms.

Parsonian functionalism is found to contain a fundamental dualism regarding models of man. Depending upon the focus of the system analysis, man emerges as a structureless atom with the abilities to be infinitely adaptable, or a specifically constituted being with a full complement of structured personality and needs. Depending upon the focus and the model of man, social organization is explained alternately as voluntaristically organized or structurally determined.

Symbolic interaction theory is examined through the works of G. H. Mead and some of his followers. The models of man and society in this theory are characterized by the same central concepts—symbol and language. Man is seen as a self, having internal components rooted both internally and externally, linking self to society, while not violating its autonomy. Mind is characterized by internal processes analogous to interhuman communication. The concepts "symbol" and "language" are examined. It is found that the "symbol" concept is inadequate to account for "language" as the term is used in symbolic interactionism. The implications of this are found to be that psychologically based explanation of social organization is inadequate.

In the conclusion, some of the main arguments are reviewed, and the models of man and their relations to social organization are compared. Wholly psychological explanations of social organization are deemed insufficient. Problems of the theoretical motivation of action, internal and external determinism and voluntarism are examined. The three models of man are compared, paying special attention to the strengths each possesses.

Thanks are due to the Killam Foundation for support received during the research and writing of this piece. Similarly, I am indebted to the Sociology Department of the University of Alberta for their cooperation and assistance, and to Dr. G. Nettler for several suggestions concerning my original draft.

William L. Skidmore
University of New Brunswick

Table of Contents

Part III   Symbolic Interaction

List of Figures

Introduction

Dennis Wrong offers what is essentially a critique of the Parsonian approach to sociological theory in his "The Oversocialized Concept of Man in Modern Sociology".[1]* His objective is not to spell out Parsons' assumptions about the nature of man, but rather, to criticize Parsons' method of dealing with the "problem of order" or the "Hobbesian question". It is Wrong's opinion that Parsons, by adopting certain propositions about man, destroys the "problem of order" as an answerable question. Instead, Parsonian theory places heavy stress on internalization of norms, solving the Hobbesian question by fiat.

Wrong does not describe Parsons' model of man, but makes it clear that he believes sociological theory in the Parsonian manner neglects some aspects of man which bear upon the problem of order. Wrong argues, in effect, that for the sake of Parsons' theory of social organization, he has had to make man "fit in" by concentrating on the sociological concept "role"—making man only a collection of his individual roles with no "nature" except plasticity. Wrong suggests that the term "oversocialized" is appropriate to this implied model of man, since it connotes complete social formation of persons.

Wrong's criticism of Parsonian theory suggests questions that may be appropriately asked of the field of sociology. Two of these are: what are the various, perhaps competing views of man explicit or implicit in modern sociological theories, Parsonian as well as others? What impact do these assumptions and assertions about man have upon the answers to sociological questions derived from these theories?

The purpose of this book is to systematically examine the relationships of the models of man in three sociological theories to the explanations of social organization given by the same theories. This work will thus deal with the controversy over whether or not sociological explanations need make use of psychological constructs and data, and if a "psychological" approach is sufficient to explain social action.

The broad questions guiding the analysis are: (1) concerning patterned human action to be explained by a sociological theory, to what extent must explanations at the sociological level rely on or be reduced to psychological ones; (2) to what extent may sociological explanations be regarded as standing alone and apart from psychological ones?

---

* Numbered footnotes are found at the end of each part.

1

Answers to these questions are worked out in the following pages by examining three theories for their explicit or implicit propositions (or models) about man. If the theories are logically sound, the model of man (essentially a psychological notion) ought to have some bearing on the explanation of sociological material. That is, there should be a logical relationship between the model of man and the kind of explanation given to sociological questions in each of the sociological theories. In the course of this essay, the extent to which sociological explanations may be seen to stand alone, and the extent to which psychological explanations provide an adequate theoretical account of social order will be shown.

Since this book deals with both the psychological and the sociological levels of explanation, it requires an examination of the theories regarding their accounts of a distinctly sociological problem. Particularly appropriate in this context is the examination of the problem of social organization. Sociology studies many things which are all concerned with social order or change at various levels of analysis. But the fundamental problem of socio-logical theory is precisely to account for patterned normative behavior, i.e., social organization.

Thus, within the frameworks of the three separate sociological theories, there are three kinds of material assembled and related. The model of man in each of the theories concerned has a prominent place. It is with models of man in sociological theory that this book is especially concerned. The ac-count of social organization is also made clear in an analysis and explanation of each of the theories' general accounts of social order. Finally, the relation-ships between the models of man and the explanations of social organization are explored. Particular attention is given to how the assumptions about man in each theory relate to the account of social organization advanced.

The choice of theoretical frameworks which are to be examined for their implicit descriptions of man, and for the impact of these views on the results of theorizing, was made using two criteria: (1) the importance of the theoreti-cal framework judged by the amount of further research and writing it has stimulated, and (2) the varieties of theory current in Northern American sociology.

Using these criteria, three theoretical frameworks were chosen for examination. Davis[2] argues that all sociologists are functionalists, and that functionalism is synonymous with sociology. When making the above observation, Davis fails to make clear what he means by functionalism; and since it is some of the assumptions and propositions of functionalism that are to be examined, Davis' argument is too vague to be accepted. Modern functionalism in sociology has been developed most systematically and fully by Talcott Parsons and his collaborators. For purposes of clarity and to avoid dealing with differences of interpretation among functionalists, the section on theoretical functionalism is limited to consideration of some of the writings of Parsons and his collaborators.

A second major theoretical framework to be examined is symbolic interactionism. Often, symbolic interactionism is confused with functionalism because of the apparent similarity between functionalists' treatment of "double complementarity" and symbolic interactionists' propositions about interpersonal behavior. Basic differences exist between the theoretical frameworks, especially relative to the genesis of society. These differences make symbolic interactionism distinct as a theoretical formulation.

Symbolic interactionism presents particular problems of choice regarding which statement of its general principles and insights ought to be examined. Like functionalism, it has many adherents who do not always agree on exactly what symbolic interactionism is. It is clear, however, that the fundamental principles of this branch of theory were laid down by George Herbert Mead and the adherents of "social behaviorism". Since this is the case, and since it is the basic principles of the theory that are of particular concern in this book, Mead's works will be given considerable attention. It is true also that Mead's works do not present a fully developed picture of the theory, especially as it is applied to the problem of social organization. Mead's followers have attended to this aspect of symbolic interactionism more systematically than Mead himself (although Mead is not silent on the question). Thus it has been necessary to supplement Mead's works with those of others who freely acknowledge him as their mentor. It must be emphasized, however, that it is Mead's work which sustains the exposition of symbolic interaction theory throughout.

Growing from a critique of functionalism, exchange theory, which is the third major theoretical orientation to be examined, has taken on a clear identity, principally owing to Homans' clarification of his objections to functionalism. Homans' direct style and the fact that his works tend to be complete statements rather than fragments make the delimitation of exchange theory as a distinct branch of sociological theory much easier than in the case of symbolic interactionism. Since Homans' works have formed the basis of exchange theory, and because he has developed this theoretical perspective so extensively, the examination of exchange theory in this book is limited to Homans' relevant works.

This book is a logical and explanatory reconstruction of three of the most influential sociological theories in North America. It is thus important from the standpoint of its subject matter alone. An examination and analysis of what sociologists are doing with their theory and what they expect from it is of considerable worth to those who would critically explore the sociological enterprise. This work will demonstrate that, rather than the three sociological theories being logical sets of propositions with determinate models of man and explicitly derivable accounts of social organization, in fact they contain unjustified logical leaps and unwarranted deductions. In short, while sociological theories are acknowledged to be indispensable in ordering data and thinking about man and social organization, they have not always been well-ordered, logically arranged insights.

The models of man in these three modern sociological theories have not been previously drawn together and analyzed with reference to their implications for the problem of explaining social organization. These models have often been forgotten or ignored in sociological work. It is emphasized throughout the following pages that the models of man, far from being only minor or unimportant aspects of sociological theory, constitute sets of premises foundational to sociological accounts. It is therefore imperative that sociologists be aware of the models which they are implicitly accepting when they employ theoretical schemes as explanations, advise on social policy, or voice predictions concerning events to which sociological theory is relevant. Just as scientists in the social studies can not fail to take account of the assumptions on which their statistical and methodological techniques are based, they ought not to allow themselves to remain unaware of the models of man they are implying when they use sociological explanations. By taking account of these models in the sociological theories currently in use, the theorist of social organization is better prepared for his analytical work.

This project has presented certain methodological problems. One can not begin such work with a set of definitions concerning man, social organization, or even sociological theory. Rather, one must initially take each theory on its own terms. Thus, in dealing with Homans' exchange theory, formal deductions are traced out and analyzed; in Parsonian theory, the implications concerning his typological framework are considered, and so on. Several styles are current in sociological theory, and if one is to gain a perspective on North American theory and characterize it, one must begin by dealing with the various branches of theory in their present forms.

Implied or stated within these works are the tenets upon which the theories are built. In order to make an analysis of the theory in question, it is necessary to assume temporarily the theorist's perspective on his own work. If this is not done, one theory might be analyzed from the perspective of another and the analysis would reduce to an argument concerning whether or not a theorist's procedures and conclusions are "right". Thus a strategy of contextual criticism has been chosen. The theories have been examined "from the inside" for their models of man and the relations of these to the explanation of social organization. For example, in the case of Homans' exchange theory, it will be seen that the theorist has taken a particular perspective on what constitutes a theory and how one ought to operate in explaining behavior. Criticizing this view from another perspective would be of no value. It would not allow the analysis to penetrate to the implications of Homans' own view of theory for the problem for which his analysis was intended. Hence Homans' own perspective has been assumed by taking his hypothetico-deductive style as a point of departure and following out the deductions as he does. It is in this process that we find, for one reason or another, that several of his deductions are unwarranted and that his model of man is, in part, incompatible with his theory of social organization.

In dealing with the three theories in this way, it is necessary to conceptually pare down the theories to their fundamental tenets about man and the basic assumptions implicit in their accounts of social organization. Penetrating to the roots of the theories in this way both simplifies the problem of relating the models of man to sociological analysis and makes such a relation more meaningful and clear. Once the fundamentals of a theory are in view, and the elements of the models of man have been built up, it is an easier task to relate the two together and show the relevance of such a relation than if the theories were not first laid bare.

The following expositions of the three theories and their accompanying models of man will constitute relatively independent parts of the total work. That is, each of the three theories is analyzed by itself; the analysis is made as complete as possible from the point of view of the theory alone. In the conclusions, we return to the fundamental questions concerning the logical and conceptual relations between the models of man and sociological explanation. It will be seen in each of the expositions that certain incompatibilities exist among the models of man and sociological explanations current in modern sociological theory. In the conclusions we can note several points of contact between the three theories with special reference to the models of man. It will be suggested that the three theories, rather than being taken as complete in the sense that they have given adequate explanations of the social order and man's relationship to it, ought to be considered strong in some aspects of this explanation and weak in others. A fundamental complementarity among the three will then be noted, which, while not suggesting that the three theories are logically compatible, will point out ways in which the three may be understood to illuminate certain aspects of the problem of the relationship of man to the social order. Finally, some suggestions for further conceptual research in the theory of sociology will be offered.

Notes

1.   Dennis Wrong, "The Oversocialized Concept of Man in Modern Sociology", *American Sociological Review*, **XXVI**, No. 2 (April, 1961), 183–93.

2.   Kingsley Davis, "The Myth of Functional Analysis as a Special Method in Sociology and Anthropology", *American Sociological Review*, **XXIV**, No. 6 (December, 1959), 737–71.

Part I
Exchange Theory

CHAPTER 1

Introduction to part I

This book is concerned with models of man as they are related to explanations of normative, or ordered, behavior. In the writings of George Homans, the account of social behavior that has been dubbed "exchange" theory will be examined.[1] In undertaking this examination, it will be necessary to do more than draw out the models of man and the sketches of group behavior in order to show their interconnectedness. Doing this alone would leave the work incomplete because what Homans understands by "theory" and "explanation" would be left unstated. The reader would have no basis for appreciating or criticizing the specific pictures of reality that Homans shows us. It will be necessary to examine the structure of Homans' theory to determine if he in fact follows the ideal of explanation that he espouses.[2] We shall also have occasion to examine the consequences for social science of following such ideals.

In this examination of Homans' work, we are fortunate in two respects. Homans has written much that is specifically called "theory"; he has also made himself quite clear regarding what he *means* by "theory" and "explanation". He has been clear in his argument and explicit in his philosophy of science. His concern for the structure of theory and the logic inherent in it has helped to suggest the appropriate kinds of analysis.

We shall turn first to Homans' understanding of the term "theory". Since theory can take alternative forms, and the term by no means connotes the same things to different people, it is appropriate that Homans' meaning be understood before advancing to an examination of his theory of social behavior. Homans stresses that "theory" is not simply a term for abstracted and general formulations. The form these generalizations take must meet requirements. Homans' understanding of the term "explanation" will then be discussed, showing its intimate connection with the meaning he gives to "theory". Pointing out this connection will help in understanding the criticisms that are to follow and the significance of Homans' model of man for his theory of social behavior. The analysis will then turn to the theory itself, examining it from the vantage points of its major postulates. We are again fortunate that Homans' has been so explicit in his formulation.

9

His postulates and corollaries are clearly stated, facilitating orderly analysis of them.

At this point, it will be necessary to introduce some requirements that Homans' himself (as well as others) suggests for the writing of scientific postulates. We will deal with the two kinds of concepts Homans discusses in his own writing on social science—"operative" and "inoperative" concepts. It will be shown here that Homans refers to the same general problems that Popper discusses relative to "falsification" for scientific theory, and that other philosophers of science have discussed in other terms.

In the light of the discussion concerning the necessary requirements for concepts in a theory of the type Homans intends to write, Homans' own concepts will be examined. It will be shown that his concepts do not always meet these scientific requirements, and that the consequences are in some ways disastrous for the theory as a scientific work. The model of man in Homans' theory will then be spelled out, and later, the relations between this model and the theory will be made clear. Set in the context of the examination of theory, explanation, and scientific concepts, it will become clear that the model of man assumed by Homans in his theory of social behavior is fundamental to the social picture he is able to draw in his theory. It will be necessary to view the intellectual roots of Homans' man in experimental psychology and elementary economics. In this connection, the difference between induction and extrapolation will be mentioned, and later, questions can be raised concerning whether Homans' work represents a deductive theory of general propositions inductively arrived at, or a framework and interpretive system through which human behavior may be viewed.

Homans' sketch of ordered social interaction will be examined. His exchange propositions concerning conformity, leadership and status in group performance will be analyzed not from the point of view of plausability, or from the perspective of other theories of the same general phenomena, but from the background of the foregoing examination of Homans' theory. This exposition of the theory as it accounts for order in groups will be an examination of the problem of order from the viewpoint of Homans' theory itself, stressing the logical possibilities Homans' had in accounting for order, given the type of theory he was writing and the sketches of man he drew into his fundamental propositions.

In the course of the exposition, the connections between the model of man and the theory of social behavior (the problem of accounting for social order in groups) will have been worked out. We should then be at the point of summarizing the connections as they appear. This summary will demonstrate several difficulties with the theory, especially those of circularity, generality, and the problem of developing scientific concepts about human behavior.

An empirical evaluation of the theory of social behavior is not called for.

In this book we are not concerned with research findings that have been interpreted as supportive of Homans' theory. But, as will be shown, the model of man implied and expressed in Homans' theory has impact on the theory itself in a formal as well as a substantive sense. The formal sense will be focused on in the final statements of this section. It will be argued that Homans' is not a "theory" in the way he wishes us to understand that term, but a framework, a conceptual lattice, which when applied to human behavior seems to be plausible; it is suggestive of ways in which we may hope to understand human action and seminal in its attempt to summarize a wide range of behaviors. But no real deduction is possible from this framework. Rather, it is simply suggestive of ways to interpret behavior.

CHAPTER 2

Homans' view of "theory" and "explanation"

As noted above, it is necessary in this examination of Homans' theory of social behavior to understand what he means by "theory" and by "explanation". It is from the point of view of Homans himself that his theory is to be judged, and it is necessary that it be perfectly clear what kind of theory Homans intends. An understanding of this kind of theory, and an examination of Homans' own theory, will lead to an assessment of the possibility and efficacy of such theoretical attempts.

Homans is concerned with *deductive* theory and explanation.[3] In this regard, he is interested in developing theory which has a certain form as well as a specific content. The form of a deductive theory consists in the arrangement of propositions in hierarchical order according to their generality with respect to inclusiveness.[4] At the bottom of this ordering of propositions stands the hypothesis or prediction derived from the theory. This must be an empirical statement connecting two or more concepts in a determinate hypothetical relationship to each other. The testing of theory is carried out at this level, when this hypothetical statement is compared with experience to determine whether or not it seems to describe the world.

An hypothetical statement of this kind is made up of two or more terms that have empirical referent. These terms may be an operationalization of theoretical terms, but there must be an agreed way in which the terms relate to concrete properties, such that their use in empirical test results in independent definitions of the terms themselves. This means that an hypothesis, to be useful, must be made up of terms that are defined and operationalized independently.[5] Thus (A) could not be defined as an upward trend in (B) when an upward trend in (B) was defined by (A). If this were the case, no empirical use could be made of the statement using (A) and (B), since it would be impossible to empirically separate (A) from (B), thus reducing the statement containing (A) and (B) to one containing only one term, (AB), or simply one or the other.

At the level of the hypothesis, or lowest level of a deductive system, the terms making up the statement are of a specific nature. That is, they pertain to specific properties of the world which they are put forward to explain.

Thus, in the example above, (*A*) and (*B*) would refer, if they were indeed independent terms, to specific properties. The hypothesis containing them would form a prediction about identifiable aspects of reality. For example, mental illness and social class may be related theoretically, but the hypothesis needed to test this relationship must contain independent knowledge of certain peoples' social class positions and insanity rates, where insanity and social class are defined independently of each other.

In the above example, the notion of a theoretical relationship was introduced, from which the particular hypothesis about given people was deduced. This theoretical relationship of concepts to each other was of a general nature. In it, social class and mental illness were related as units. That is, all mental illness was related to something known as social stratification. These general concepts defined classes of attributes which described the world in more general terms than the ones used in the suggested hypothesis.

This illustration shows the ways in which general propositions are related to more specific ones. Propositions of still greater generality might be discovered which could link other general statements together, under which the statements concerning mental illness and social stratification could be subsumed. If this were the case, a deductive chain would have been formed which contained three distinct levels of generality. It is this kind of deductive system that Homans is attempting to create in his theory of social behavior. His theory contains propositions which are of such generality that they are said to cover a very wide range of behavior indeed. Under Homans' propositions, he argues, extremely diverse behaviors can be subsumed and the deductive links shown. To Homans, this kind of deductive exercise constitutes an explanation.[6]

"Explanation" has been used to mean many things, but it is clear that Homans has a specific meaning for it. To construct a deductive theory of an event or class of events is to *explain* that event or class. The act of explanation is the actual deduction of an objective piece of reality from more general propositions about realities of that kind. "To deduce successfully is to explain".[7]

The logic of Homans' theoretical strategy should now be clear. His aim is to derive propositions about human behavior which are very general and can be fitted together in a theoretical system. In order to fit, propositions may not contradict each other,[8] or have internal conflicts that would impede deduction from them. Taken together, the propositions form a small number of highly generalized statements under which, Homans argues, the social behavior of humans may be subsumed. His propositions are thus held to constitute a theory of human behavior. He argues that he is writing statements of "elementary forms"[9] of behavior. He holds that all behavior, whether elementary or not, is built up from forms of behavior that may be described by a few general propositions. Homans calls this generation of statements the process of induction. More about this process should now be included to clarify the nature of the general propositions.

Homans argues that in *The Human Group*, his goal was to describe five specific instances of human group life (although the size of the groups as well as other factors varied) in an attempt to arrive at some general statements which could characterize all the groups, and from which all of the group life being explained could be derived deductively.[10] Homans was able to formulate several propositions, general statements about the relationships of abstract qualities of group life, which he argues could serve as starting points from which all his data could be deduced. This was the process of induction. Beginning from what should have been predictable, Homans shows how, through the use of certain propositions, that which should have been predictable (group life of certain kinds) in fact could be predicted. There are no logical rules for the generation of such general statements.[11] This is in part because it is never possible to know that one has observed all the varieties of group life that may require deduction. Nevertheless, it is argued that if the propositions are general enough, and subjected to enough testing empirically, the poorer propositions will be weeded out. The remaining ones will constitute those propositions which hold good to the present time, given the degree of detail and comprehensiveness of knowledge about group life. Statements of this kind might be called "empirical generalizations".

Homans further argues that empirical generalizations are not enough in themselves to constitute a theory, since they only describe, but do not explain. Homans' attempt in both editions of *Social Behavior* is to answer the question "why" the propositions found in *The Human Group* obtain.[12] As was seen above, he holds that subsuming these empirical generalizations under more general propositions constitutes explanation of them. It is thus the work of *Social Behavior* to provide explanation, that is, give a theory of human group life.

The very general description of deductive theorizing that has just been given sets the stage for the analysis of Homans' theory of social behavior, but it omits some of the more specific requirements for deductive theory. It will be well now to examine some of these requirements so that Homans' theory of social behavior may be later evaluated and discussed in more detail.

As was suggested above, the propositions which make up the highest levels of a deductive system contain two or more terms. These terms, or concepts, are linked together in a determinate way. That is, the statement must take the form of "*x* varies as *y*". This statement means that as the value of *x* increases, the value of *y* will also increase. Thus a specific example of *x* and one of *y* would be hypothesized to act in the following way: as the value of any *x* increases, the value of any related *y* also increases.[13]

This kind of statement requires that some determination of the values of x and y be possible. Thus the terms must be in some sense quantitative, if the statement linking the classes to which they belong is to make any sense. This requirement means that before we can speak of relationships such as increase, decrease, expand, contract, there must be some measure of the dimensions over which these changes are to be observed. Qualitative concepts have less power, in that the measurement of their properties in terms of quantity is limited. Thus the use that may be made of qualitative terms in propositions such as "x varies as y" is strictly limited.[14] This is especially the case when another proposition, such as "y varies inversely as z" is also relevant. When x varies as y, but y varies inversely as z, and when all three terms are qualitative with respect to measurement, it is impossible to derive any specific prediction about the behavior of any one x, y, or z when all three are varying in indeterminate amounts.[15] What is needed to give this kind of statement power is ratio measurement, in which it is possible to know how much each varies, and the ratios in which they vary with respect to each other. Then, when measures of each are possible, specific deductions about the behaviors of any x, y, and z may be made even though they are all varying. Thus it can be seen that if a deductive system makes use of qualitative terms, it may be robbed of its usefulness for theory construction and prediction.

The statement "x varies as y" was given above as an example of a determinate proposition. This statement indicates direction of variations which occur together, but does not indicate how much variation is to be expected. A more powerful statement about x and y would be the following: $x = (a)y$. In this statement, the term "varies as" is replaced by an "equals" sign, and the factor (a) was introduced. This statement gives the exact amount of variation in y to be expected for a given variation in x, since in this example, (a) is taken as a constant. In this more powerful general statement, the same requirements hold true regarding ratio measurement. The increase in precision resulted in the increase in the determinacy with which the two terms, x and y, were said to be related.[16]

The above discussion has been concerned mostly with the form of the statement relating x and y. The notion of qualitative and quantitative concepts (x's and y's) was introduced to facilitate differentiation between powers of statements linking concepts. The concepts themselves are important in the formation of statements for use in a deductive system. As noted above, the form of the statement may be the linking of concepts in a conclusive way $[x = (a)y]$ or in a less conclusive way (x varies as y), but the concepts themselves required measurement, (even if, in the least precise way, the measurement could take only one of two values). As the complexity of the propositional system increases, ratio measurement may be mandatory if any deductions using the concepts are to be made. The definitions of the concepts themselves become very important with respect to both their qualitative or quantitative nature, and their relationships to each other in propositions linking them.

Definitions of qualitative concepts rely upon no measurement. Thus a qualitative concept might be "animal". In "animal" there is an agreed-upon essence which is linked to other concepts, such as "life" or degree of "consciousness", none of which may be measured, but which do relate to other aspects of experience. If "animal" were related in a proposition to another qualitative concept, such as "plant", the second term would have a qualitative definition, setting it off from "animal", but still relating it to experience.

Concepts are defined in terms of other concepts. This truism limits the kinds of concepts that may be linked together in a proposition. Two concepts that are defined independently of each other may be related in some fixed way in propositional form, since the definitions of each are separate, and the proposition directs us toward diverse aspects of experience that may or may not have the relationship hypothesized in the proposition's linking terms. Concepts that are defined in terms of each other may not be linked together in propositions; such a proposition would make no empirical sense. If (A) is defined in terms of (B), and (B) in terms of (A), then (A) and (B) can not be said to be related "directly", since their relation is a truism derived from the definitions of (A) and (B) and not from examination of experience. The concepts can not direct us toward two different aspects of experience. If a proposition were made linking (A) and (B), no judgment could be made about the accuracy of the proposition's linking terms, and it would reduce to no proposition at all. This is the problem of circularity in proposition formation.[17]

It will be useful now to introduce the difference between empirical generalizations and explanatory propositions. These terms have been used more or less synonymously up to this point, but the differences become crucial when "explanation" is the problem. An empirical generalization states a regularity in general terms. Thus, "the higher the traffic density on a given street, the higher the number of accidents per hour", is an empirical generalization. In it, no information was given about "why" the regularity should occur. It simply stated a fact, in a general way. From empirical regularities, deductions can be made, but not deductions of an explanatory nature.

Explanatory propositions, on the other hand, have an explanatory function. One of the terms in such propositions "explains" why the regularity described occurs as it does.[18] In this kind of proposition, cause is either stated or implied. Homans' proposition No. 2, from the first edition of *Social Behavior*, illustrates the form of these explanatory propositions: the more often within a given period of time a man's activity rewards the activity of another, the more often the other will emit the activity.[19]

In this proposition, the frequency of emission of an activity is being "explained" by the rewarding of the activity by another. The second half of the proposition, the statement about frequency of emission of an activity, is being accounted for by the first half of the statement, i.e., the part stating the conditions under which the second occurs.

We will see in examining Homans' theory that his propositions link behavioral terms to explanatory terms in this way. The explanatory terms will combine with the linking terms to delimit Homans' implied "nature of man". Since the "nature of man" so implied is fundamental to each proposition, and since the propositions are offered as the general explanatory statements that constitute a sociological theory, the "nature of man" is fundamental to the account of sociological reality that may be deduced from the propositions.

CHAPTER 3

Homans' propositions in the theory of social behavior

Homans has recently published a revised edition of *Social Behavior*. Therefore, this chapter will give the 1961 versions and compare these to the 1974 versions. This will point up how the two editions differ and demonstrate that, on the whole, they are substantially alike. In a later section, we will consider the theory as a whole and its derivative corollaries; some deductions from Homans' theory will be examined.

1) *If in the past the occurrence of a particular stimulus-situation has been the occasion on which a man's activity has been rewarded, then the more similar the present stimulus-situation is to the past one, the more likely he is to emit the activity, or some similar activity, now.*[20]

Homans spends very little time developing the above proposition but gives it, recognizing a "very great inadequacy".[21] This inadequacy is the problem of the discrimination of stimuli. Indeed, there is no reason to expect Homans to develop explanations of generalization and discrimination of stimuli. These are notions that may be borrowed from the experimental psychologists, if the borrowing is done carefully. Borrowing from psychology raises a problem for Homans' style of theory building in a formal sense as well as a substantive one: the problem is that of the difference between induction and extrapolation.

Homans argues that he is inducing propositions.[22] He includes in this kind of activity the borrowing that he does from economic theory and experimental psychology. Popper has argued that since induction can not be justified satisfactorily, we should provisionally admit any statement into scientific tests, provided that it meets the criterion of falsifiability.[23] If Homans has "induced" his first proposition by borrowing it, does it meet the falsifiability criterion for a scientific statement?

It seems that the statement gives no indication, as Homans admits, of how to tell a similar stimulus-situation from a non-similar one. Thus his proposition is immediately, and by his own admission, put in doubt of falsification. There is no real definition of reward, a problem that psychologists have solved more by fiat than by empiricism. Thus the proposition states a regularity between some situation and some later one, but the characteristics of these situations are unknown. Homans' argument is that if a man is "rewarded" in the prior situation, his behavior in the later situation is likely to resemble his prior behavior. It is not clear, nor can it be, how the activity is to be similar, what aspects of behavior may be taken into account in the observations, and how the situations in which they occur are to resemble each other. Reward is left undefined.

It is relevant to point out how behavioral psychology has solved some of the problems enumerated above. In the Skinner box, the characteristics of prior and subsequent situations are made as similar as possible by the reduction of spurious stimuli to a minimum—only the experimental stimuli (pecking a key or some other simple activity as bar pressing) is available. Since there is very little else going on in the Skinner box to distract the experimental animal, it is reasonable to assume that the activity in which the animal engages is the activity which in fact gains rewards for him. No such simple situations exist in human behavior. There is nothing to convince us that it is in fact the activity of the other which is rewarding. Extraneous attributes of the situation may hold the reward.

Behavioral psychology usually uses the technique of fixed times of fasting before "rewarding" an experimental animal with food. Thus it is easy to make the assumption that motivation from hunger exists and moves the animal to action. Hunger is controlled and "known" to exist in the animal. No such assumption concerning motivation can be made for man. The rewards suggested by Homans are presumed to be less fundamental than those of food, and conceivably, the range of possible rewards is infinite. In short, no assumption about the motivation level of a man to emit activity can be safely made.

In behavioral psychology, that which is rewarding is commonly defined as that which increases behavioral emissions, usually with respect to time. Thus propositions containing statements of activity and reward are circular. This does not seem to be a problem for the behavioral psychologist, since it was seen that the experimenter's control over the situation and the rewarding nature of food and water make it safe for him to formulate propositions in which the definition of rewarding activity is identical with the definition of the behavior which is rewarded. Homans is not justified in making these kinds of circular propositions. In proposition No. 1, no indication of the nature of reward is given. It is left inferred that the activity which is more likely in a later situation is the activity referred to in the beginning of the proposition, in which situation and reward were linked. In short, the proposition is hopelessly circular.

It is reasonable to ask in what way this proposition explains. It can explain only in a *post hoc* manner, and it is difficult, because of the problems of circularity and vagueness pointed out above, to tell what distinctive predictions might be drawn from it. Since the terms in it are essentially qualitative ones (although they are couched in pseudo-operational language), it is impossible to tell to what amounts or frequencies of behaviors the statement refers. Thus, we must wait to observe a behavior in man, and then "explain" it by reference to this proposition. We invoke some suppositions about the man's past behavior; we presume that he has been "rewarded" (whatever that may mean) in similar circumstances (in whatever aspects may be relevant to the present behavior). Little deduction is at work here. The train of thought is not from the general proposition to the specific behavior according to the rules of deduction; rather, it is from observation to general proposition. This proposition is made to explain the action by loading its terms with whatever meaning "seems reasonable" with respect to the present behavior.

In fairness to Homans, it must be said that the qualifications he himself puts on his propositions have been left unstated to this point. He recognizes that his propositions are made up mostly of qualitative terms. He acknowledges that the measurement possible in most social research does not reach the ratio level. But he hopes to state propositions that point to regularities in covariance, although not to the exact amounts of variation.[24]

The consequences of this kind of theorizing may, however, have been overlooked by Homans. The definitional problem which he does not seem to recognize is that the circularity, through definition of the inferred properties from observed behaviors being explained, reduces the proposition to essentially a non-working statement, removing it from scientific discourse. It was seen that propositions useful in deductive systems must link concepts that have independent definitions. Since this is not the case in Homans' proposition No. 1, it is difficult, as has been shown, to use it in a deductive way. In Popper's terms, the proposition would not satisfy the criterion of demarcation of scientific statements from metaphysical ones since it may not be falsified.[25] Thus it is unfit for use in a deductive explanation or theory.

In the recent edition of *Social Behavior*, the same basic proposition appears as the "stimulus proposition".[26] It says:

If in the past the occurrence of a particular stimulus, or set of stimuli, has been the occasion on which a person's action has been rewarded, then the more similar the present stimuli are to the past ones, the more likely the person is to perform the action, or some similar action, now.

Of course, this proposition is liable to the same difficulty as the earlier one: the delimitation of what constitutes a situation. Similarly, the vagueness of the key term "reward" gets in the way.

In defense of his work, Homans implies in another connection in the second edition of *Social Behavior* that there is really no problem here. In the first place, he argues that there is some social behavior that comes in "countable units".[27] He has in mind something like factory piece work, in which a man's pay is directly related to his productivity. Of course, it is questionable whether or not there is really very much social behavior of this kind outside the factory. But there is also another defense offered. It is that since in reciprocal social behavior, one man's reward is another man's activity, there is no problem about what constitutes activity and reward—they come to the same thing. "Situations", similarly, are no problem, since all we need count are "units of reward". We match them with units of activity between interacting persons.

But there is more to be said. If situational similarity is no problem for Homans' reasons, then the measurement of "units of reward" and "units of activity" are all the more important. This is definitely left unsolved in the second edition of *Social Behavior*, so it must be concluded that the problem remains.

Homans does explicitly recognize the question of similarity of situations in explaining his "stimulus proposition". But here, the defense is less impressive. He discusses the psychological questions of stimulus generalization and stimulus discrimination as these processes may occur in the actor. The argument runs to the effect that as the actor himself more finely discriminates situations, so the rewarding properties of them are more closely discriminated. And again, as the actor generalizes situations of reward, so succeeding situations may not have to be similar to past ones in so many ways.

The trouble with this is that these propositions are supposed to be explanatory statements in a general theory. It is fine to know that stimulus generalization and discrimination differ among persons, and at different times and places for the same person. But this is not much help in formulating descriptive generalizations. In fact it is a hindrance. What Homans has done is to point out two good reasons for questioning the general applicability of the stimulus proposition as stated, and he has shifted the focus of the proposition. By raising stimulus generalization and discrimination he has pointed to another psychological variable which, being particularly hard for the outside observer to evaluate in any concrete case, reduces the confidence one might have in the proposition as an empirical generalization or theoretical proposition.

Homans states his second proposition as follows:

2) *The more often within a given period of time a man's activity rewards the activity of another, the more often the other will emit the activity.*[28]

The second proposition is susceptible to some of the criticisms outlined for the first. It seems obvious that there are no measures of a man's reward from an activity which are independent of the changes in amount or frequency of that activity. The rewarding aspects of behavior are strictly inferential, and thus the proposition is circular. The explanatory power of this proposition is doubtful, as is its possibility of falsification.

Introduced in this proposition is the idea of frequency of activity. It is argued that it is frequency which makes the propositions usable in theory construction and deductions, since it is on the basis of frequency that the essentially qualitative terms take on a measurable dimension.[29] Homans says:

Real propositions do appear in the literature of social science, and so do definitions of the terms that occur in them, the equivalents of the definition of pressure that accompanies Boyle's Law. These I call "operating definitions", because we actually work with them. An example might be a definition of the term "frequency" to accompany the proposition: The more valuable a man perceives the result of his action to be, the more frequently he will perform the action.[30]

Actually, the proposition seems to indicate that we should impute more "value" to the activity of a man, the more often in a given period of time he emits the activity. But there is nothing in the addition of frequency to the discussion that makes the proposition any more acceptable as a scientific statement. Since, in proposition No. 2, activity, "which rewards the activity of another" is undefined, the addition of the term "frequency" adds little.

Suppose, however, that we did understand something concrete by the idea of rewarding behavior. That is, suppose we knew which activities were being denoted by the application of this proposition to a specific situation. We would have to make an unreasonable assumption about each "activity" with regard to its value. Since there would have to be some standard unit of worth in order for the inclusion of "frequency" to be meaningful, we would need to know not only which activities were rewarding, but *how* rewarding each activity was.

Finally, exactly what are the bounds of "an activity"; when does one leave off and the next start? Is a date with a girl which lasts six or seven hours one activity; or is it a series of activities, each of which has a reward value; or is it to be considered part of a larger activity called "courtship"?[31]

It must be concluded that the addition of frequency in the discussion of propositions built up from qualitative terms adds little of significance to the use that may be made of the propositions. Since in proposition No. 2, as in No. 1, the two concepts being linked have in fact only one empirical referent, and the major explanatory concept (reward) is qualitative and inferred from the behavior being explained rather than observed independently, the proposition must be regarded as circular. Since it is true by definition and the terms are hopelessly vague, it does not belong in a deductive system.

Homans has restated this proposition as the "success proposition" in the second edition of *Social Behavior*. It says:

For all actions taken by persons, the more often a particular action of a person is rewarded, the more likely the person is to perform that action.[32]

Being principally a restatement of the old proposition, the new one is susceptible to the criticisms of the old, but Homans has anticipated some of the critical points in his new edition. In addition to claiming that some activity comes in countable units, as we saw above, Homans has added the distinction between "activities" and "acts or actions".[33] By this distinction, he means to call grosser units of activity by the term "activities", and the smaller units "acts" or "actions". But this renaming does not solve the problem. There must be criteria for telling an activity from an act, and we need to know if the proposition in concrete use is to describe acts or activities. Proposition two, or the "success proposition", has intuitive appeal, as all the propositions do; but the logical difficulties outweigh these if the objective is conclusive deduction. An example of the problem would be the following: among the things Homans considers to come in discrete countable units are words. By counting the frequency of these messages as they are directed among the members of a group, it might seem that a measure of "activity" is available. But the proposition says that activity is to be linked to reward, so we need to know the reward value of these words. On *ad hoc* grounds, perhaps a rough idea could be had from listening, but on objective grounds alone, since it is unknown how rewarding which communications are, the reward value must be surmised from speech frequency—hence, the success proposition is as circular as the old proposition No. 2.

Homans' proposition No. 3 links the ideas of frequency and value in a single statement:

3) *The more valuable to a man a unit of the activity another gives him, the more often he will emit the activity rewarded by the activity of another.*[34]

The failure of the theory to be stated in terms that are useful quantitatively is most telling at this point. Homans suggests that by considering both propositions No. 2 and 3, it is possible to establish the "rate of exchange" between two persons in interaction[35] and answer the question of the extent to which one man's activity is proportional to another's.

Homans argues that the frequency of interaction between Person and Other depends upon the frequency with which each rewards the activity of the other and on the value to each of the activity he receives. Now, to make sense of the notion of reciprocity in exchanging activities, the activities themselves must be known, delimited quantities of behavior observed to be emitted by one prson and rewarding to another. Since this is not the case in Homans' theory, it is hard to see how he can make the following statement:

By the present proposition [No. 3] the rate of exchange between approval and help [in the example Homans is using] should tend to equal the ratio between the value Person puts on help and the value Other puts on approval.[36]

It should be clear by this time that no ratio can be meaningfully spoken about with respect to value and help (a kind of activity). Thus the interesting formulation concerning the "rate" of exchange between people loses meaning. Since help is not calculable in terms of value to Other, or in terms of its intrinsic worth (whose viewpoint would be taken in such a calculation?), no "ratio" can be calculated. The concepts of value and help (activity), being qualitative, do not allow ratio level measurement. Thus the statement that the ratio of approval and help should tend to equal the ratio of value of help to value of approval can mean nothing, since none of the concepts is measurable in the sense necessary to establish ratios. The ratios spoken of are indicative of a method of conceptualization of the interaction process, but have only a suggestive quality. In short, they do not form a corollary derivable from propositions No. 2 and 3 as Homans suggests, nor do they add anything to the theory in its attempts to establish the reciprocal nature of human interaction.

In the second edition of *Social Behavior*, proposition No. 3 is found in the form of the "value proposition".

The more valuable to a person is the result of his actions, the more likely he is to perform the action.[37]

Homans makes clear that he is talking about both reward and punishment here, and that it is a matter of relative reward or punishment which establishes value. The lesser of evils can be "valuable" in this sense.

Apart from the reiteration of his earlier position that some values are innate (a curious position to be followed up later) and that some are learned, there can be no specification of what men value or for what reasons. Homans makes a claim related to value that sets out his position on this. He denies that the theory is hedonistic. Arguing that altruistic values work just as well in the theory as egoistic ones, his claim remains that no constrictions on values are being theoretically made. This direct claim serves to reinforce the criticism here against the theory: that no independent knowledge of value can be had apart from the behavior that it is supposed to explain.

4) *The more often a man has in the recent past received a rewarding activity from another, the less valuable any further unit of that activity becomes for him.*[38]

In the second edition this proposition is almost unchanged, and is named the "deprivation-satiation proposition".

The more often in the recent past a person has received a particular reward, the less valuable any further unit of that reward becomes for him.[39]

This is almost a literal translation into Homans' terms of the economic law of diminishing returns. It will not be necessary to restate the criticisms concerning circularity and vagueness of meaning of the concepts, although in the main, these apply to this proposition as well as to those already considered. Of interest is the problem of how this proposition may be used in conjunction with proposition No. 2 which states: "The more often within a given period of time a man's activity rewards the activity of another, the more often the other will emit the activity".[40] Proposition No. 2 seems to indicate an increasing function between reward and activity, while No. 4 seems to indicate the opposite. Homans recognizes the problem. It will be our task to evaluate his answer:

This proposition [No. 4] may mask the truth of Proposition No. 2, which says that the more often Other rewards the activity of Person, the more often Person will emit the activity. For if Other rewards him often enough to begin to satiate him, his own activity will tend to fall off in frequency. This is the sort of thing we refer to when we say the propositions hold good only with "other things equal".[41]

The key to Homans' explanation is the phrase "other things equal". It is probably not possible to hold other things equal in human affairs to the extent he requires.

Explanations making assumptions about the variables being explained are of reduced value in serious theorizing; yet this is what Homans is arguing for. With no useful measure of the reward value of activity, we must make a choice about whether the rewards being gained under proposition No. 2 either are or are not sufficient for satiation to set in. The addition of this *ad hoc* choice can account for either increasing or decreasing frequency of activity,[42] depending on the choice made. The theory seems to have a built-in mechanism for explaining either the decreasing or the increasing frequency of activity in any given situation. When propositions Nos. 2 and 4 taken together predict both an increase and a decrease in frequency of activity, and with the impossibility of telling when each proposition should be in force, both an increase and a decrease in activity can be "deduced" from the theory relative to the same reward. It is as if (x) stood for frequency of activity of a given kind, (y) stood for value placed on that activity, and (z) stood for the satisfaction which accrues as that activity is emitted. If either (y) or (z) is held constant, it is possible to make predictions (conceptually) about what will happen to (x). But with all allowed to vary at the same time, it is not possible to tell what value of (z) will be necessary to "mask the truth" of statements relating only to (x) and (y). Similarly, it is not possible to tell when one should invoke proposition No. 4 to predict the effect on (x) when (y) and (z) are allowed to take several values.[43]

Obviously a science, when using ratio level measurement to establish propositions, can handle three and more variables in a set of propositions applied to a given situation involving laws. Since most concepts in the human sciences are not rigorously quantitative, it is impossible for Homans to make more than suggestive statements about human behavior with the qualitative concepts available to him.

Homans states his fifth proposition as follows:

5) *The more to a man's disadvantage the rule of distributive justice fails of realization, the more likely he is to display the emotional behavior we call anger.*[44]

In developing the last proposition, Homans introduces some variations that must be understood here in terms of the primary concepts of the theory: value, reward, and activity. To begin with, it is necessary to understand what he means by "cost" and "profit". He argues that since men have alternatives in social behavior, they knowingly must bypass some activities in favor of others. The reward that these bypassed activities might have yielded is defined as the cost of the activity actually carried out.[45] Homans argues that it is legitimate to use an admittedly inferred concept in his theory (cost), since the same kinds of activity from which values and rewards are inferred are involved in the inference of costs.

Profit, the psychic variable which is also introduced in his discussion of distributive justice, is the difference between rewards and costs.[46] That is, for any activity, there is a reward (which may have either a negative or positive value) and a cost (the value of reward foregone). The difference between these may take on either positive or negative value; thus, profit may be either positive or negative (a loss). Homans then argues, quite plausibly if we have followed him this far, that no exchange continues to take place between people unless both persons (or all persons) in the relationship are making a profit. This follows from propositions No. 2 and 3. It is not clear how proposition No. 4 fits into this picture, since it was shown above that no determination of when proposition No. 4 will "mask the truth" of No. 2 is possible.

Distributive justice refers to the distribution of rewards and costs among persons in the exchange.[47] The problem is one of allocating to the satisfaction of each participant in the exchange the amounts of profit that each deserves. Homans argues that to determine the amount they deserve, it is necessary to understand each participant's "investments". These are facets of each individual's history, presumably known to each member of the exchange, that entitle him to a greater or lesser share of the rewards. Homans argues, finally, that:

A man in an exchange relation with another will expect that the rewards of each man be proportional to his costs—the greater the rewards the greater the costs—and that the net rewards or profits of each man be proportional to his investment—the greater the investments, the greater the profit.[48]

It is difficult to see how the proposition concerning distributive justice really explains. By this time, it has become clear that no real proportionality can be calculated between such notions as rewards, costs, investments, or profits, when these terms refer to psychic inferences that may be invoked *post hoc* to explain behavior, but may not be engaged predictively to reconstruct action. Since the terms in the propositions take on meanings particular to the situations in which they are employed (as they must to be general propositions), it is impossible to pin down which aspects of behavior they really refer to. This is simply to say that the definitions of the terms are quite open. Even if the terms were precisely defined in a qualitative sense, it would be impossible, as demonstrated above, to measure the variables so that the calculations suggested by the proposition would be meaningful.

The distributive justice proposition is altered considerably in the second edition of *Social Behavior*. It is in two parts, and is called the "aggression-approval" proposition. To avoid repetition, we can collapse the two parts of the new proposition together, using brackets, and paraphrase as follows:

When a person's action receives (does not receive) reward he expected, or receives reward (or punishment) he did not expect, he will be pleased (be angry); he will become more likely to perform approving behavior (aggression), and the results of such behavior become more valuable to him.[49]

Seemingly gone from this treatment of the distributive justice proposition are the rates of exchange and the concept of "investment". The new formulation is better, since it is more compatible with previous propositions. Homans accounts for the routinizing of unexpected rewards or punishments by saying that over time these become habitually expected. This idea seems to play a similar part to the idea of "justice" in the old proposition, but without the moralistic overtones. Nevertheless, the formal and logical difficulties remain, or are intensified. The tighter integration of the new "aggression-approval" proposition with the previous ones makes clearer than ever the fact that this proposition is afflicted by the same problems as the others. To this extent, it is liable to the criticisms about reward, activity, value and so on outlined above.

The old distributive justice proposition had one great value, however. It clearly suggested that a time dimension entered Homans' theory. Rewards could be had now for past efforts. Investments made now could be expected to have rewards in the future. The distributive justice proposition not only suggested a comparison among individuals receiving rewards, but comparisons at different times for the same person. This direct implication of time is gone from the new "aggression-approval" proposition, but Homans has added a less systematic discussion[50] to make up for its loss. In this he says that, primarily because of the reliance on individuals' histories to establish value and appropriate activity, the theory is meant to actually retain the time perspective.

In this section, it has been shown that the theory of social behavior has several faults. These center on the explanatory concepts and the ways these concepts are linked with behavioral observations and concepts. It was shown that the explanatory concepts and the linking terms in the propositions were the points through which the model of man in Homans' theory enters the explanatory system. We have seen that it is just these points which are most problematic to Homans' explanation of behavior. Thus, the model of man implied in Homans' theory is crucial in that it forms the keystone of explanation—it suggests the concepts that are taken as explanatory. But the questions we ask about man are at least partially qualitative. Theory which attempts to objectify and quantify man's "nature" for use in deductive systems therefore runs into difficulties. This suggests that such theory may be inappropriate to social studies.

CHAPTER 4

Reconstructing Homans' logic—an example

This brief section will examine Homans' method of explanation in operation. It has been shown that Homans' propositions include terms having questionable empirical referent except for the behavior they are invoked to explain. Often, concepts crucial to the propositions do not point at regularities in the world other than the regularities being explained in that system. This definitional situation renders the propositions themselves circular; the behavioral and explanatory terms within given propositions share the same closed meaning. Also, the explanatory power of the system was shown to be drastically reduced. Homans ends up with a group of statements which fails to meet the criteria of "falsifiability". Most of the terms in the theory are qualitative rather than quantitative; therefore, the deductions Homans wishes to make from his propositions may be impossible, since the effect of any one variable can not be determined where more than one independent variable are involved.

Despite Homans' protestations that he has written a deductive theory applicable in the social studies, it is usually asserted by philosophers of science that no theory of the deductive type exists for these fields. Homans appears to agree with Mill that in principle, the laws which "govern" human behavior are discoverable and deductive theory is applicable to them.[51] He might also agree that it is unlikely that the laws of human behavior are discoverable and describable in sufficient precision to make the human sciences more than inexact. He would not accept Winch's idea that "the notion of a human society involves a scheme of concepts which is logically incompatible with the kinds of explanation offered in the natural sciences".[52]

Let us examine an example offered by Homans. It is given in support of his general theoretical perspective, and is said to be a sketchy but accurate product of his method of explanation. Since this example is so simple, it may seem trivial, but it exemplifies the problems of definition of key terms and other related logical issues.

Homans offers the following deductive argument to explain why William the Conqueror never invaded Scotland. Notice that, since explanation and prediction are of the same logical structure in deductive theory, if the example pertained to a possible future event, the same "explanation", (which would in that case be called a "prediction"), would be given for the event. Homans' explanation of why William I never invaded Scotland is as follows:

1) *The greater the value of a reward to a person, the more likely he is to take action to get the reward.*

2) *In the given circumstances, William the Conqueror (a particular person) did not find the conquest of Scotland valuable.*

3) *Therefore he was unlikely to take action that would win him Scotland.*[53]

The first premise is not literally one of Homans' major propositions from his theory of social behavior. It is, however, very much like all his propositions in structure and format concerning reward, value, and the like. The first proposition in this example is similar to Homans' proposition No. 1 discussed above.

Proposition No. 1: If in the past the occurrence of a particular stimulus-situation has been the occasion on which a man's activity has been rewarded, then the more similar the present stimulus-situation is to the past one, the more likely he is to emit the activity, or some similar activity, now.[54]

In less abstract terms, but in a distinctly social setting, Homans' main proposition in the example is very much like his proposition No. 3.

Proposition No. 3: The more valuable to a man a unit of the activity another gives him, the more often he will emit activity rewarded by the activity of the other.[55]

It may be seen by comparing the proposition at the head of the example's deductive system with the propositions cited from the theory of social behavior that the example pairs intensity of value and likelihood of action, whereas in the propositions from the theory cited above, the pairing is, on the one hand rewarding occasions and similar occasions at a later time, and on the other, intensity of value and number of emissions of a behavior. Thus, it is seen that the first premise of the example, while not exactly like those of the theory of social behavior, might have been a part of it, since it relates a psychic variable, reward (or value) with action in an increasing function—an increase in one is associated with greater likelihood or greater similarity of action.

In Homans' example, the second premise makes two assertions, which in accordance with the rules of deductive logic, establish the minor premise as a subset of those aspects of reality covered by the major premise:

1) William the Conqueror was a man, " *(a particular person)*," goes with the first phrase of the major premise, " *The greater the value of a reward to a person* . . . ."

2) The conquest of Scotland was not rewarding to the particular man in question. This goes with the second phrase of the major premise, the one setting forth the action in general terms—". . . *the more likely he is to take action to get the reward.*"

Homans concludes that since the minor premise denied the value of Scotland to William the Conqueror, this low value on the particular reward would lead one to expect, according to the major premise, that the likelihood of action to gain the reward of low value would also be low. Thus, Homans concludes:

3) *Therefore he was unlikely to take action that would win him Scotland.*[56]

It has been argued that the terms used in explanation of behavior in this theory are defined by the activity they are meant to explain. The example before us is a particularly good one to point out the consequences of this. It seems to be a reasonable assumption (and one we will make for the moment) that Homans has no evidence, other than the fact that William failed to attack Scotland, that William set no value on the conquest of that country. Thus it seems that Homans, in arriving at the sentences he has presented in a deductive format, used something like the following logic:

1) *I need to explain why William the Conqueror never invaded Scotland.*

2) *People do those things that they find rewarding. "The greater the value of a reward to a person, the more likely he is to take action to get the reward."*

3) *Therefore, William must not have found the conquest of Scotland rewarding, and this is my explanation for his not invading it.*

4) *Now, rearrange the propositions into a deductive system which places the thing I am explaining at the bottom of the system, instead of the top. Take out "therefore" from the beginning of the third statement, make that statement the minor premise, and I have a deductive explanation for William's failure to attack Scotland.*

In short, it seems that Homans could have come to his explanation of William's behavior regarding Scotland in no other way. He thus affirms the premise concerning the relation of valuable reward and action (a logical flaw) instead of the consequence, William's behavior. Homans did this, it would seem, since he had no independent measure of William's value regarding Scotland. That is, he had no way of making sense of the term "value" except as an inference from the behavior being explained. This situation reduces Homans' major premise to a tautology (value of a reward and the action associated with it being different "observations", different inferences, from the same behavioral event.) Since the major premise contains no external linking of the theoretical term "value" to the world, the minor premise, drawn up as a particular case of the generality stated in the major premise, contains nothing other than the reassertion of the major premise in particular form. Since that premise was shown to be vacuous, the conclusion reduces to simply a peculiar way of stating the historical truth that William the Conqueror did not take action to win Scotland. Subsuming this fact under the general statement Homans offers as an explanatory principle has therefore produced nothing new, nothing falsifiable, and nothing suggestive, since the theoretical terms of the major premise form an identity. It is asserted here that this is the case with each of Homans' general propositions found in the theory of social behavior.

What this example does show, however, is that Homans' concept of man (a valuing creature who takes action according to his understandings of his possible profits and costs) determines the statements that will be offered in the theory as explanatory ones. Placing the attributes of valuing and calculating action according to value standards at key points in the general statements in the deductive system ensures that the explanation of social behavior derivable from the theory will be built directly upon the suppositions about man's nature and qualities. Certainly other suppositions about man substituted into Homans' explanation of William the Conqueror's activities would have yielded a different explanation of his behavior regarding Scotland.

CHAPTER 5

The model of man in Homans' theory

It was shown above that Homans' theory is designed to be of the deductive type and that some of the concepts used in its construction are qualitative. It is just these kinds of concepts, ones which are not readily applicable in a rigorous deductive theory, which are the explanatory ones. It has been argued that Homans' propositions are circular in that there is no empirical referent for the explanatory concepts, other than the behavior being explained. Finally, the system as a whole seems to work in other than a deductive way to explain.

It has been necessary to focus on the type of concepts in Homans' theory and the logical flaws in the explanation in order to set the background for the understanding of Homans' theoretical model of man. It is now time to show the part played by this model in more detail.

In Homans' theory, each proposition was shown to link two concepts (or more than two) in a somewhat determinate way. Thus the propositions took the following form as the paradigm for their construction:

$C_1 --- C_a$; where C_1 and C_a are concepts and "---" is a relationship. It was shown that C_1, the concept explaining behavior, was, in every proposition, a qualitative concept (one which could not be handled adequately by mathematical ordering of its properties) and an inferred one. This concept was either borrowed from the explanations given in economics or experimental psychology, or extrapolated from propositions from these studies. Circularity was evident. C_1 was invoked to explain C_a through the relationship noted by the proposition. C_a was the empirical concept (behavior or activity,) referring to actual observable behavior.

When the propositions are examined in this way, we see:

Concepts		Propositions	
inferred	behavioral	1st ed. No.	2nd ed. proposition
C_1	C_a	1	"stimulus"
C_2	C_b	2	"success"
C_3	C_c	3	"value"
C_4	C_d	4	"deprivation-satisfaction"
C_5	C_e	5	"aggression-approval

Using terms from the first edition of *Social Behavior*, C_1 through C_5 are the following: reward; reward; value; reward; distributive justice. C_a through C_e become the following: activity; activity; activity; activity; anger. If each of these propositions is circular, as was asserted above, in each of them an inferred term, (reward, value, and the like), explains a behavioral term, (activity). It has been shown that the inferred terms are the points at which the model of man enters the theory. Since the theory places so much weight on the concepts C_1 through C_5, and these are the inferential concepts concerning the nature of man, these terms should be focused upon in the discussion of the model of man. It is clear that the deductive pattern of explanation invoked by Homans rests squarely on his model of man, i.e., his assumptions about individuals' behaviors.

Of necessity, a deductive theory depends upon assumptions. The point to stress, however, is not that a set of assumptions is acknowledged and used in the development of Homans' theory, but that the assumptions enter the theory at the crucial point (the explanatory concept) in each proposition, and that the theory is useless apart from the assumptions that actually explain behavior. Explanation is more by fiat than by deduction, and Homans' failure to justify his assumptions by more than a passing acknowledgment that some assumptions exist must be regarded as serious.

These assumptions are part of the idea of the "elementary form" of behavior. Homans argues that he is explaining what men *actually do*, rather than what they are supposed to do or some system of regulation conceived to be exterior and prior to man. The elementary forms are those kinds of behaviors that are the basis of all human action. They are summarized in a system of propositions. From these propositions, it is said to be possible to derive the diverse activities of man. When the form of behavior has been subsumed under one or more of the general propositions and deduced from it, the behavior is explained. Since the theory is conceived this way, and the model of man in Homans' theory is indicated by the explanatory concepts and the theoretical terms by which they are linked to the behavioral concepts, an examination of the explanatory terms and the linking terms will give an indication of the nature of man in Homans' theory.

The elementary forms are "believed" to be human universals.[57] Homans sees human behavior as a function of "pay-off".[58] That is, he employs the fundamental paradigm of behavioral psychology (i.e., motivation leads to behavior) in an attempt to explain all human behavior in the general theory. As can be seen from the propositions, Homans suggests that the motive in human affairs is described in terms of value, reward and reinforcement. His model of man is in these terms. The linkages between the explanatory and behavioral terms suggest other attributes of man. For example, choice and choosing behavior are fundamental. Calculation of value and reward among alternatives is another. It will be useful now to examine some of these fundamental attributes and processes in detail to better sketch in the model of man.

VALUE

Perhaps "value" is the most important term in Homans' theoretical scheme. The term refers to the degree of reinforcement (or negative reinforcement—punishment) a man gets from a "unit" of activity. Without criticizing this formulation for the moment, it is apparent that Homans' man is a valuing creature. He calculates, either consciously or not, the "value" of the acts he will perform, and he behaves in ways that gain the valued aspects of the environment (human or non-human) which most please him. The question of where values come from is immediately suggested. Homans argues that to understand a man's values we study his history.[59] This involves circularity just as much as inferring values from present behavior would. If values are inferred from past behavior rather than present, it still involves the assumption that man demonstrates his values by his behavior ("put out more units of an activity within a given time to get a more valuable reward than he will to get a less valuable one", as Homans puts it).[60] This principle of human nature becomes a first step in the reconstruction of the model of man in Homans' theory. Man is a valuing creature and the desire to obtain that which he values motivates him to act in ways he has learned might get him the valued objects.

This placement of value in the theory shows that the theory puts a great emphasis on man as a singular atom, working toward the fulfillment of his own desires. Nowhere in Homans' analysis does it seem that the man involved followed a norm about anything initially. Norms are not given to the actor; he is controlled by nothing except his own reading of the situation relative to the things he values and his estimation of how to get those things. His fellows, doing presumably the same thing (attempting to gain for themselves that which they value) seem not to matter to the individual in Homans' theory. Thus, for the individual from whose viewpoint the theory is being discussed for the moment, every other individual is a means to be employed in the pursuit of ends. This is why it is very unlikely that Homans' would have concerned himself primarily with norms, as such, or more generally, the concept of culture. For Homans, culture and normative systems have their genesis in the working-out of men's desires in the world. As desires and/or men change, the systems of regulation they build in relation to their own behavior changes accordingly. More will be said about this in the section on Homans' account of normative behavior. It is mentioned here to emphasize that the actor in Homans' theory (the major part of it, at least) is an atom that is capable of action without reliance on culture at the present time. Certainly Homans allows for culture; a man's history is the determiner of his values. But the history of each individual is truly "in the past". Once the actor has gained a system of values and has built up a stock of kinds of activity that seem to gain him rewards, he seems not to be bound by culture to utilize the actions at his disposal in the "culturally prescribed" ways that he may have learned in his past.

There is no systematic inventory in Homans' work of the things which persons value. His theory, as has been shown, is based on valuing and acting, but the theory has little to say outside of its examples to suggest what is valued by humans. This is an important problem. It is discussed below in connection with the origins of institutions. Homans makes no suggestions of what the circumstances are under which a man will act in certain ways. The theory tends to reduce to its paradigm when this is the case. Since it is supposed that man will act to gain himself the thing that he values, and that to escape circularity (perhaps) it is necessary to examine a man's history to see what he values, the theory seems simply to affirm that man is very likely to act in the present as he has acted in the past. It can not even be argued that the theory sets down the circumstances under which the present activity will resemble the past. Since this is the case, there seems to be no way in which we can suggest what things will be done to gain which ends. Therefore, we can only assume at this point that the ends of action are completely random among group members in a social arrangement. It may be that each man wants the same things as every other man, but this is an empirical question. Up to this point, the theory itself gives no reason to assume anything about the ends of action of each actor or of a system of actors working in some sense "together".

The discussion of value has avoided the use of the term "reinforcement", since value and reinforcement are very similar; it is this term that forms the next aspect of Homans' model of man.

REINFORCEMENT

The concept "reinforcement" is central to several of Homans' propositions. Although the term is not used specifically, the concept is employed in the construction of the propositions themselves. Reinforcement refers to the properties of a reward or situation that make the emission of the behavior associated with these properties more likely in the future. It is obvious that Homans assumes man is an animal who follows the laws of reinforcement. In his propositions No. 1, 2, 3, and 5, the relationship between reward and rewarded activity is a direct one. From this we infer that the man being described is capable of learning from the situations in which he acts which aspects of the world are pleasing to him.

The term "reinforcement" helps to indicate why the terms that link the concepts in propositions link them in direct relationships. A property of man, as man, is his response to positive reinforcement. From only the terms "value", "reinforcement", and "activity", we see that Homans' use of them draws a picture of man responding to his environment by judging its atributes according to a value system and actively engaging himself in satisfying personal desires by acting to gain certain aspects of the environment. This does not seem particularly startling, but it does show that choice and selectivity are fundamental aspects of Homans' model of man. The exact way that choice and choosing behavior operate should be the next topic.

CHOICE

Considerable discussion has been spent on the point that a rational man is assumed in Homans' theory. Homans himself says, "Indeed, we are out to rehabilitate 'economic man'."[61] He means by this that economic man is one who uses his resources to some advantage; but Homans argues that the "economic man" concept is not wholly appropriate to general social science because it implies a narrowly limited range of values. Homans would allow his "economic man" in sociology to have any values whatsoever. As was suggested in the section on values, this causes some problem for the theory, since there can be no indication of what a man's values *qua* man might be. But assuming for the moment that this formulation of an expanded economic man is viable, what does it imply?

The crux of the choosing problem is the statement that economic man (and by implication Homans' expanded economic man with his wider range of values) uses his resources to some advantage. The obvious problem here is how to tell when a person is using resources advantageously. Homans is obscure on this point. For instance, it is not clear whether Homans means for us to understand that the man in his theory uses the social resources at his disposal to some advantage, or that he merely uses those resources somehow. It is clear, however, that choice on the part of Homans' theoretical man is a central part of the theory. Man has alternatives. Formulations about cost[62] would make no sense outside of a situation where alternatives exist. Thus Homans' man is a choosing creature. His choices are guided by his understanding of what things are most worth his effort. That is, he makes some judgment of alternatives in terms of reward, cost and profit. The person in Homans' theory thus seems very close to the classical economic "maximizer".

In order that this maximization of rewards scheme have meaning, there must be some understanding of the individual's criteria for making choices. Since Homans does not wish to set down the criteria by which persons value their activity, it is impossible to be precise regarding the specific choices we might expect man to make. It does seem reasonable, however, to suggest here that we have found a chink in Homans' conceptual armor. There is no way of knowing which things will be valued by men, but we believe that individuals will be maximizers of their rewards; and since values can be anything (by Homans' admission), it seems that Homans' theoretical man is following at least one "norm", that of "efficiency" or "maximization". Since the theory can make no sense unless we assume that persons do those things which gain them valued rewards, and since it would be impossible to create propositions that did not state some variation of this premise, then the norm of efficient use of means to valued ends must be a central concern for each of Homans' actors. It is far from clear whether this norm is given through cultural transmission or is inborn. However, it is clear that Homans' actors do not create *all* the norms by which they live according to their own caprice and short-run satisfaction.

RATIONALITY

Sooner or later the problem of how choice is made in Homans' theory comes down to the question of rationality. Is Homans' man a "rational" being? There are several avenues of approach.

Homans' man does not seem to need consciousness or highly sophisticated reflective behavior to fit the theory. The theoretical terms are based in reward and punishment. These terms do not presume a conscious individual. A man, as proposition No. 1 suggests, might emit similar activities in similar situations without being aware of it. However, Homans' first edition proposition No. 5 seems to suggest a degree of consciousness when a man's awareness of unequal distributive justice will anger him. Homans says that "a man in an exchange relation with another will expect that the rewards of each man be proportional to his costs ... and the net rewards be proportional to his investments ..."[63] The terms "will expect" seem to show an assumption of consciousness in this sentence; but on the whole, it does not seem that consciousness is needed for the theoretical man Homans is describing.

It was suggested above that Homans' man is a calculator of alternatives; this attribute might suggest rationality, since the calculation of expected rewards entails dealing with means and ends. However, there is no suggestion of a criterion for the calculation of these rewards. Thus, the man involved may not be considered rational in the sense of logically rational, since from the point of view of the theory, there is no set of rules by which an individual can be judged rational or not.

It seems that the crux of this problem is in the means–ends relationships confronting each man in each situation. Indeed, the men in Homans' theory may act "irrationally" in that they might choose the "wrong" alternatives in calculating their action, and yet still come within the purview of the explanation given. This is because action can always be conceptualized in terms of means and ends. Since means and ends may be anything for any actor, and no criteria for "rational" choice can be suggested in a general theory, it seems that any behavior falls within the rhetoric of "rational" action.

The best that can be said of the theory is that it seems to suggest a "rationalistic" view of man. This view may be summarized in the following way. Persons act to gain themselves those things and behaviors of others that are valuable to them. Since men theoretically have choices, the various actions open to men must be decided upon according to some criteria. Homans would have us believe that each person is sufficiently different that it is either not possible or not wise to suggest a universalistic criterion upon which judgments about certain kinds of actions would be made.[64] The criterion of judgment for each man must be searched for in his past experience, that is, in the experience of each man with the kinds of situations which face him in the present. Knowing the past behaviors that are relevant, we may infer the criterion by which the man made his choice. Knowing the past behavior also allows us to infer the values of the man in question. Thus we can infer a man's values from his past experiences. Knowing both past behavior and past values (inferred), we can then apply the following kind of reasoning:

1) *past situation (A) led to an inference of past value (a).*

2) *present situation (A') resembles past situation (A) in some way. (Homans is unable, in the theory, to tell us how this situation may be similar.)*

3) *past situation (A) has led us to the inference of past value (a); thus we may assume that present value (a') will lead person to act in present situation (A') similarly to his way of acting in situation (A) where he held value (a).*

This would seem to be the understanding Homans means to give in his first postulate. Further, the more, and the more often, past situation (A) rewarded the person, the more and the more often we can expect him to act in a similar way in present situation (A'). This last statement is a central one to the discussion, since it is the point at which the rationalistic criterion of choice of present behavior enters. Because of the reward gained by the person in the past situation, the present situation is likely to find him acting in a similar way, since he has chosen the past situation's behaviors as a model or type of behavior which he will perform in the present with the expectation of reward.

This discussion of rationality and choosing behavior shows that rationality is a property of the theory under discussion, but not necessarily a descriptive term for the men involved. Since the theory proposes a rationalistic relationship between the values of men and the actions they take, it is impossible to impute anything different than a faculty for rationality to the men themselves. But since it is to arrive conceptually at actions and reasons for actions of man that theory is invoked, the men being explained must conform to the requirements of the theory rather than to their own empirical ways of acting. Thus rationality is imputed to men to solve the problem of choice. The actor is *conceived* to be rationalistic, i.e., choosing between means in order to maximize returns relative to some end. But since it is only the continuance of history that actually is being predicted, the rationality of man in Homans' theory is at once central to the workings of the theory, and irrelevant to its results. That is, the formal system places man first; man's actions and normative behavior are derivable from man's nature. To solve problems of choice, which must be solved for man to have alternatives, man himself theoretically must have properties allowing him to make choices. The problem with the theory thus far, and the one that has led to the suggestion that the formal system has placed the major emphasis on the fundamental rationalistic and free-choice nature of man, is that the theoretical men have been allowed to hold any values they wish, and they have been allowed, with no common criteria, to go about trying to realize their aims in all possible ways. Thus, in a very real sense, the theory reduces to a formal system with no explanation of man or of society except the one that is implicit in the meanings with which one chooses to load the major concepts of "value" and "rewards". Man, in general in Homans' theory, has no substantive nature. He has, rather, an operationalistic nature. He is conceived in terms of certain performances of which he is capable, certain mechanisms that are envisioned to take place in the process of acting in the world in pursuit of gain. These processes have been suggested above. Basically, they amount to the capacity to discriminate between valued and non-valued aspects of the environment and the ability to contrive activities that will lead to the gaining of valued ends while avoiding the non-valued. When concepts such as "value" and "reward" are loaded with the meanings that seem appropriate to the particular situation being explained, the men involved take on "natures" defined by the meanings of the concepts so defined.

In the second edition of *Social Behavior*, Homans approaches the question of rationality with a suggestion of a proposition. He does not state this as a part of his theory, but it appears to come from some of his other propositions. This proposition is derived from the concepts of choice, alternatives and value, as the above criticism was; but Homans' conclusions are different. His proposal is:

In choosing between alternative actions, a person will choose that one for which, as perceived by him at the time, the value, V, of the result, multiplied by the probability, p, of getting the result, is the greater.[65]

Here we find Homans wrestling with the problems implicit in the other propositions. He needs to get some principle of choice built into the theory without making an assumption about the nature of man or about value. If he were to make such an assumption, he would have gone some way toward specification of mental or personal properties which might then constrain the range over which values could run, or he might alternatively restrict the concept of value too greatly and make the value proposition, the success proposition, the stimulus proposition, and so forth, lose their generality.

But in coping with this problem in terms of probability and value, he encounters his old troubles with measurement and vagueness. If we are to "multiply" together two quantities to make a prediction about which choice a person might make, each quantity must be a real one, e.g., we must have a measure of each, and of course, they must be separately observed entities. We have shown that no such measures yet exist to gauge the quantities Homans has in mind. In addition, from the logical standpoint, the multiplication together of two "quantities" which are not measured on comparable scales yields an indeterminant result. Hence the "mathematical" form in which this idea is put is an unfortunate choice, although to some extent the choice is dictated by the form taken by earlier propositions of the theory.

Aside from the logical difficulties, Homans has made it clear that he assumes a kind of "rationality"—but what kind? The phrase "as perceived by him at the time" makes imperative some kind of "observation" of another man's perceptions, which is difficult if not impossible. Hence, while the proposition might aid as a conceptual steering mechanism for a theoretician, it is of doubtful use as a high level statement for a deductive theory—a theory that Homans has been at considerable pains to elaborate.

CHAPTER 6

Homans' model of man and the problem of social organization—I

The previous chapter of this book has described the main sketches of man found in Homans' theory of social behavior. Homans contradicts these impressions in the last chapter of his book.[66] These contradictions are of a fundamental kind, not only because they are left unexplained in terms of his propositions, but because they suggest a departure from his attempt to liberate economic man. Rather than reaffirming that man may have any values whatever, in his last chapter Homans suggests (but fails to describe) a concrete nature of man on which the whole of society is built. A bit of this thinking will be related here to round out the picture painted of man. This chapter will then close with emphasis on the institutional and normative behavior which is to be the focus of the next.

Homans suggests, through an example, that "cultures" can not

pick up any old sorts of behavior and hope without more ado to carry them on generation after generation. What they pick up must be compatible with some fundamental repertory of human nature, though the compatibility may, of course, be complex.[67]

Further, his notion is that as people find it in their nature (not in the norms of an already existing culture) to do certain things, they *then* "begin to make a norm of it".[68] Homans sees the fundamental grounding of all institutions in some satisfaction of native human needs. He argues, somewhat peculiarly, that once the norm is built up from these basic satisfactions, about which there had been no norm previously, "then the other members of their group [who would *not* have otherwise followed the norm] may find themselves [following it] because other rewards and punishments have come to sanction the behavior".[69] It is not easy to see from his examples why Homans thinks that the satisfaction of a basic human need or the exercise of a basic human trait would ever require such secondary reinforcing; or why every member of the human race would not respond individually and without social sanction to the fundamental humanity on which the norm was based. This is not an exaggerated versions of Homans' point of view. He states,

No doubt the origin of many institutions is of this sort. The behavior once reinforced for some people in one way [the fundamental aspects of human nature he is discussing] which I call primary, is maintained in a larger number of people by other sorts of reinforcement, in particular by such general reinforcers as social approval. Since the behavior does not come naturally to these others, they must be told how they are to behave—hence the verbal description of behavior, the norm.[70]

An even more important argument shows that Homans does not think of this fundamental human nature as a primitive thing lost through the evolutionary development of man or buried in cultural masking of basic human nature. He argues that social approval and verbal descriptions of behavior can never operate alone. The continued force and relevance of the primary reward is imperative. In seeming contradiction to the interpersonal terms in which the propositions of the theory are couched, Homans says, "Social approval can come in to reinforce obedience to a rule only so long as some members of the group continue to find obedience rewarding for reasons other than the approval it gets them".[71] Homans might argue that the profit gained by following one's primary reward system is always more than that gained from exchanges of approval with other men. He gives no explanation of why some men respond to certain aspects of life while others have to be told how to act. He has even suggested in other contexts that human nature is fundamentally alike among all men. These views seem to contradict each other. Since the nature of man is so important to Homans' account of social order and the nature of institutions, this is no minor point.

Again by way of illustration of his thesis, Homans suggests that reaction to authority in the way suggested in his propositions (i.e., that subjugation to authority is demeaning, and thus to be avoided), is a human universal of the kind under discussion.

I do not think anyone can explain why so many societies in which legal authority over family is vested in the father are also societies in which a boy develops a close relationship with his mother's brother, unless he assumes that men, *as men*, react to authority in some such way as we have described in this book.[72]

Thus "human nature is the only true cultural universal".[73]

This point could be illustrated with further quotations but it seems superfluous to do so, since the root of the problem is never reached. Homans is in the position of developing a theory of human behavior as exchange in which he conceives of man as being "motivated by the pay-off", as he puts it. This view begs the question of what the pay-off will be. In the bulk of his theory and its illustration, Homans seems to hold to the principle set down in the beginning pages of the book—the pay-off may be anything, so long as the actor conceives it to be pay-off. This gives each individual the freedom to search the world for those things that pay, and to go about gaining those things for themselves according to the rationalistic, or maximization norm that was suggested.[74] This formulation is the basis of the propositions and their use in the theory. These propositions seemed to have some common sense validity. It is true that the interactions of persons, especially face-to-face interactions, can be conceived in terms of exchanges of one kind of "good" for another. But the question of order in social life is still left without an explanation. The propositions that form the main part of the theory address the question of the ordered relations among men. But it is again faced obliquely in Homans' last chapter. Under the beginning assumption of randomness of ends and means, it did not appear that order (that is, the explanation of regularized means being employed to gain a number of non-random ends) could be explained. Although order *that did exist* could be *conceptualized* according to Homans' propositions, he seems not to have shown the basis of order. It became necessary, perhaps not even consciously, to begin to narrow down the assumption of complete openness of values and randomness of ends of action. This narrowing is accomplished in the last chapter of the first edition of *Social Behavior* by the suggestion that there are basic and all-embracing human characteristics that delimit and specify rewarding and rewarded behavior. These form the basis of social institutions, and it is on these that all men depend for the stability upon which they base their lives. It is on these that norms ultimately depend. Thus it is clear that Homans' man is more than a rationalistic valuing creature who works out the means of getting those things that he wants by calculating relative value, basing his calculations on his particular past for his estimation of present possibilities. He is a creature that has fundamental characteristics in common with all his fellows.[75]

It seems that Homans has not accounted for order in his propositions. He has conceptualized order according to certain terms which he wishes to use. His account of *why* order obtains is not to be found in the propositions alone. It is not even always based on them. Rather, his account of order seems to rest more with his belief that men have a repertory of behaviors which they perform in situations involving basic human needs or propensities. Order is thus based on primary rewards which are universally relevant to human life because men are what they are. His propositions are placed in the paradoxical situation of accounting for the forces that give rise to ordered interaction among individuals when these "primary" rewards of human life break down.

Homans has written a theory to account for the workings of interpersonal dynamics that seem to come into play in keeping order only when men fail to respond correctly to their own nature. Certainly the "primary" rewards of living may be conceptualized in terms of profit and reward, but this seems to render the discussion of such things as influence and authority irrelevant.

Exactly what fundamental uniformities might characterize humanity is left unexplored. It seems justifiable to leave these unexplored since they are more properly the province of the zoologist, biologist, or geneticist. However, an account of the fundamental characteristics of humanity would make Homans' work more than a conceptualization of the ways in which social behavior might be built up. Since this matter of human nature was brought up in an attempt to solve the problem of the origin of institutions in Homans' theory, it is appropriate to ask whether or not man actually has the needs and desires that Homans' theoretical bent would lead us to suspect; and, if he does, where they come from. Are Homans' propositions about exchange behavior on the right track? Does this exchange depend upon a socially and culturally formed man or upon biology? Should Homans have considered a fundamental societal context where the requirements of society as a whole form the basis of institutions and patterned human action?

CHAPTER 7

Homans' model of man and the problem of social organization—II

The previous chapter brought us to another point of contact between Homans' view of man and his account of institutions and normative structure. In the present chapter, it will be necessary to backtrack somewhat to reconstruct Homans' arguments about social organization. These will take us through the purely interpersonal accounts of norms of behavior in informal groups in terms of exchange. Later, we will again face the question of institutions. From this vantage point, we can compare and contrast Homans' view of man in informal groups with his view of man in a wider societal setting with regard to his notions of the origins of norms. This will then be related to Homans' view of the nature of man. From this point, it will be possible to conclude with an estimation of Homans' theory in terms of the basic aspects of it which were considered in this book: its scientific character, its power to explain deductively, its view of man, its account of social order through norms, and lastly, its consistency in taking account of all the facets of social life to which it purports to address itself.

Homans' theory best explains normative behavior in face-to-face groups. It was devised to explain such groups, and regardless of its inherent weaknesses in other respects, the theory appears to perform well at this level at least. As in the major summary propositions of the theory, the main terms in the explanation of normative behavior are "profit", "reward", and "interaction". Often, Homans lapses into the terminology of *The Human Group* and uses the terms "sentiments" and "activities", which appear to have meanings articulated with the others. "Sentiments" are the feelings people have, the evaluative components of attitudes, that correspond closely to the term "value" in *Social Behavior*. Positive sentiments are attributed to certain behaviors if they are repeated and tend to increase in frequency, as with positive values. "Activities" are very difficult to distinguish from sentiments as the following example will show:

We have argued that when the condition of distributive justice is realized, each party is apt to emit, over and above the immediate exchange itself, sentiments of liking or social approval rewarding the other.[76]

Since the only observables in any situation are the behaviors of the actors, it is difficult indeed to separate conceptually those things that are "over and above" the immediate exchange from those things which are exchanged. This problem does not become crucial as long as we understand that the terms of the explanation are ambiguous. It is still possible to discuss with Homans the logic of the exchange relationship in vague terms, and to review his account of normative behavior, so long as we keep in mind the failings of the concepts used to explain.

People do those things which they value, and shun those things they do not value. This simple assertion contains the whole of the explanation of normative behavior in the simplest case. Once a person or group of persons has found it rewarding to behave in a certain way, (that is, they have found that the profit accruing to them is maximized when they behave in certain situations in certain ways), they tend to settle on that form of behavior in that situation. That form of behavior tends to become a norm to new persons entering the group and to those already in it. Since it has been found by the existing members of the group that certain behaviors are most profitable, they will specify these behaviors to the new members. At this stage in determining group membership, there is a choice. The group will tend to accept members who, for whatever reasons, conform to its norms, and shun those who do not. Also, persons will probably not seriously seek membership in groups whose norms are not to their liking. This common sense relationship between the recruiting to group membership and the norms of groups is explained simply and categorically by the assertion that values play the central role. Persons will do those things, join those groups, they find profitable, i.e., those which give the most reward for the least cost.

When the members of a group have been recruited and some stability has been agreed upon, the processes of influence and status suggestion will ensure that the traditions of the group to which the most prestigeous and high-ranking members subscribe will be the rules that will be followed. This is explained by the fact that there are the rules that are found rewarding by such distinguished persons.

"Social approval", as opposed to other kinds of rewards, must be distinguished at this juncture. Homans is vague concerning the reasons why some people find certain actions rewarding to begin with. Thus, as suggested in the closing paragraphs of the previous section of this book, it may be necessary to go beyond social approval itself to explain why things reward people initially. In an example, Homans says,

> We are not bound to explain why a workingman finds it valuable that he and his fellows doing the same job should peg production at a particular figure.[78]

The assumption is that such activity satisfies some desire, no matter if the thing satisfied is an inborn instinct or the product of conditioning or training. For reasons that are left obscure, people decide that certain activities are more rewarding than others. They decide this way not for social approval.

Homans reasons that there may be persons in the group, however, who have no strong desire, either intrinsic or not, to behave in any particular way with respect to any particular situation. These persons are the ones on whom social approval weighs the heaviest. Since they have no reason to behave in conformity with a group norm (profit from deviance would presumably be equal to profit from conformity), social approval tips the scale in favor of the normative standard. This is so because the approval of others in the group (assuming it is positively valued) will add to the rewards gained from conformity and increase its profit for the ambivalent members. Thus all members, except those who hold concrete values of a different kind from those of the group, will probably find group membership and participation profitable.

Social support is also a factor in determining conformity. If a person is doing something in isolation, perhaps at odds with the norms of a group relevant to his performance, he may find that the activity gains in reward if others can be found, or persuaded, to do the activity also.

This state of group rewards leads Homans to the conclusion that a kind of equilibrium is reached in group normative activities. That is, after a time there tends to be stability in informal groups regarding norms. This is so because, as the membership sifts out those who can not tolerate the norms of the group, or as the group persuades those within it to follow its norms, there tends to be stability gained regarding the actual activities of the group members. At this point, all or most members can be seen to follow the norms, and during the time when this is so, an equilibrium has been reached. It is only in this sense that a group can be said to have norms, since the equilibrium reached in this way is temporary, and not a property of the group itself, at the group level. Rather, it is simply the agreement of all members individually to act in a certain way. As we have seen, this agreement is reached *via* influence processes, factors involving esteem of each member for every other one, satisfaction of group members with the action of the other group members, and so forth. It is not necessary to describe each of these kinds of influences on group norms because they all follow the basic paradigm— people do those things that gain them the most profit in each situation. Given the alternatives to action of a group member, a person will select the activity that maximizes his personal reward and minimizes his cost in accord with his private set of values.

Thus we have seen, in briefest compass, the workings of the determinants of conformity and norm formation in small groups. Homans' argument is in accord with his basic paradigm, that people do those things that they find rewarding. It does not matter whether the reward is related to the doing of the activity itself or to the approval one receives from others for doing it. The simple point to be followed is always that people do those things that reward them and maximize their profits.

As people build up their activities over time from elementary social behavior, there emerge ways of doing certain things that endure longer than the life span of the participants and tend to take on a character of their own. Behavior of this kind is institutional.[79] It is expected of persons performing certain kinds of activities that they will perform them in certain ways. The institution is a different level of abstraction from that of the elementary social behavior that has been under discussion to this point, but Homans argues it may be analyzed according to the same general propositions about human behavior. There are several aspects of this kind of behavior that separate it from elementary social behavior. One is the complexity of the reward system and the complexity of the relations between the rewarding processes and the activity rewarded. In instutional behavior, generalized reinforcers such as money take on relatively greater importance than they had in the face-to-face group. These kinds of rewards Homans calls "secondary",[80] since they often come to the actor indirectly, rather than directly from the person with whom the actor interacts. Activity such as working for a living is rewarded after long delay (perhaps at the end of each month) by an impersonal, secondary reward. This does not negate the possiblity of a person getting primary rewards in his job. But it does include the possibility that the person will tolerate punishing relationships and activities during the course of the job in favor of the impersonal secondary reward that comes at the end of the month.

Another characteristic of the institutional system which complicates institutional analysis with Homans' method is the complexity of the exchanges. As labor is divided among several specialists, systems of trading are set up that do not directly reward the individuals involved in them. The exchange between the person who rewards (who may ultimately be the boss, or the financier) and the worker is so distant that the persons involved can not be said to have personal exchange (although they may, but need not, know each other's identity).

It is at the level of institutionalized behavior that Homans' formulations seem to break down. In the next section, we will examine some of the problems, suggesting as we did above that in Homans' theory, the motivation to act in certain ways may have less to do with the exchange of valuables than with the nature of man. The section will constitute the description of the ways in which Homans' view of the nature of man influences his theory of social behavior and the problem of normative action.

CHAPTER 8

Relations of the model of man to sociological explanation in Homans' theory

The overriding objective of this part is to show how Homans' view of man influences his theory of social behavior. We have noticed that the theory, as a scientific effort, is lacking in certain respects. Also, we have noted that the explanation takes a peculiar form, rather than being strictly deductive. It was suggested that the fallacy of affirming the premise plays a part in Homans' thinking. All this has shown that the theory is vulnerable in several ways. These will be taken up in the summary and conclusions of this paper, where it will be necessary to examine closely the consequences of each of these problems.

This part of the essay is concerned to summarize the relationships between Homans' model of man and his account of social behavior—ordered social action among men. The point of this section will be to show that the assumptions Homans draws about man directly affect the resultant account of sociological reality, as we might expect them to. Further, it will be shown that the assumptions Homans makes at various times put the major statements and assumptions of the theory in doubt, and call into question the efficacy of a psychologically-based theory of social behavior in accounting for the regularities found at the institutional and societal levels.

First to be considered is the small group or "elementary" behavior level and the account of normative behavior. It is at this level that Homans' theory seems to be most consistent and clear. Since the nature of man is rationalistic (not necessarily "rational" in the sense that an outside observer would agree to its rationality), he is confronted with choices which he weighs according to his value system. These choices regarding social action are the elements from which social norms are made. When persons agree upon a system of action, a norm has been reached. But it is most important to notice that the logical progression is from the desires of individuals, to the norm. If persons did not have choice and exercise it according to private criteria, there could be no norms. Norms in small groups are, then, the agreements people make between themselves to act in certain ways.

Under the assumptions of rationalistic choice and desire to maximize gain and minimize cost, persons make these agreements because the ways of acting they decide upon fill their requirements. Homans' assumption that man is a maximizing creature (or one who tends toward maximization) conditions the conception of norms that can be a product of the theory. Since each individual is essentially an atom, ultimately acting independently for private gain, there can be no "given" normative system. We saw that Homans argues theoretically that man was free to hold any values whatsoever. Since a presumed randomness of ends and infinity of kinds of values must be supposed for any body of people acting together in a group, the only concept of norm that can emerge is one based on agreement between persons at any particular moment.

This kind of logic leads Homans to his view of equilibrium. There is nothing in social behavior that warrants an idealist conception of equilibrium as a superpersonal entity, process, or property of society, apart from the participants. Rather, equilibrium is nothing more than the temporary settling upon certain common patterns of acting among members of a group with respect to some activity.

We see that the idea of "norm" is altered to take on a different meaning from that which it usually carries. The idea of "norm" that is rooted in cultural anthropology is more relevant to the societal than the personal level. The norms of a society are things that are "followed" in the sense that the participants in that culture learn the norms that will direct their lives. The norms, in this tradition, like other elements of the culture, are logically prior to human action. The norm is "there" apart from the individual. Once the individual learns the norms, he can function adequately in the social context.

Different from this conception of norm is Homans' use of the term. In the sense just given above, Homans does not use the concept "norm" at all. As we have seen, he means by it simply the congruency of personal actions with respect to a given situation. This conception of norm is different from that of the cultural anthropologists and realists' sociological formulations because in it, the individual is logically prior. Individual desires and values come first, not those of "society". Since the individual is the conceptual starting point for Homans, it is theoretically imperative that the individual have powers of choice and private criteria for choosing. Account must be taken in any social theory of the ways in which choices are made and patterns of action are organized. When the "culture" is viewed as making choices and setting criteria for individual action as in classical cultural anthropology, these attributes are not so important to the concept of man. The men that emerge from such formulations are "products of the culture", doing those things that are ordained in it.

In Homans' scheme, normative structure is viewed exclusively as the product of human interaction and therefore the individual must be viewed as having ability and criteria to use in choosing. Cultural and normative aspects of life derive from what men do for private gain and for individualistically conceived ends. Men are thought of as logically prior. Thus, with culture and normative behavior logically posterior, the point from which deduction begins, the individual, must contain the choosing and evaluative mechanisms that have been assigned traditionally to "culture" in anthropological literature.

Homans has argued that the men in his scheme may have any values whatever; but he also assumes that for normal persons, approval and other more tangible responses have a determinate effect on behavior. That is, while he asserts that men may have any values, his scheme could not make sense or predict unless it assumed (as actually is the case in the statements of the major propositions) that positive relationships obtain between certain classes of activities and certain classes of values. That is, men could not value "approval" in various ways, as Homans seems to suggest, since this would violate the idea that approval, when given to a man, will increase the frequency of the approved behavior. There is a problem here both with the conception of man in Homans' theory and with the status of the key concepts. While maintaining that man can have any values whatever, in fact, man must be relatively uniform in his valuation on such things as approval, for the relationships suggested by the propositions to be sensible. Since they all seem to indicate positive relationships between approval or reward, and the activity associated with the rewarded or approved activity, the assumption left unstated is that all men, by nature apparently, value approval positively. Proposition No. 1 covers this when it is assumed that "reward" and "approval" mean the same thing. Properly, the unstated assumption is that approval is a positive reward.

The theory is stated more generally than in terms of approval, however. The case of "approval" in Homans' theory is an example of the vacuous nature of the key concept—value. Since the propositions of the theory are stated in terms of "value" rather than in terms of something that could conceivably by ascertained independently of the associated behavior, it is possible to load the concept "value" with any substantive meaning one wishes. This is in line with the general nature of the theory, and the desire to liberate man to the point of letting his values take any form. But it does not bypass the need for making assumptions about the nature of man. If the term "value" is to be a working term in the theory, it must be accorded an assumed substantive referent of some kind. Once this is done, the assumptions under which the particular aspect of valuing take on meaning become part of the assumed nature of man—of the particular man in question, at least. Thus, writing a general set of propositions which does not specify the meanings of the key explanatory terms may appear to get around the making of assumptions about the nature of man and the nature of the value system each man holds. In fact, to make the theory a working tool, it must take on a set of specific assumptions about man.

These assumptions are about the nature of *man*, in Homans' theory, for a very special reason. Since it is the man who is logically prior in Homans' thinking, it is the man who must have a "nature" from which one can deduce the consequences for social action. This is why the assumptions about man are so important in Homans' theory; they form the beginning points for the deductive logic that characterizes the theoretical style.

It has been shown that, while Homans is reluctant to give a set of assumptions about man directly, he constructs concepts for use in his theory that presume a knowledge of the nature of man (his values, what he finds rewarding, and so on). The mechanisms by which he connects these concepts in his theory suggest some universal attributes of man, attributes that are relied upon implicitly to give the theory meaning. One of these is what was called the "norm" of rationalistic or efficient choice in human affairs. This was described as a norm because it seemed to be the thing that characterized the major assumptions in Homans' theory. Persons maximize profit by minimizing cost and maximizing reward. For this formulation to be useful, we must assume that persons will be interested in gaining the things they regard as valuable in the most efficient manner. It does not matter if a part of the reward is the process of gaining the reward (for example, inefficiently building one's own home rather than buying one). Since the norm of efficiency is always relative to what the individual values rather than to some outside criteria, it is always possible to conceive activity as rationalistic and efficient. This is so partly by design and partly because the concept of value is deficient. Since any man can have any value, by Homans' assertion, there can not be an outside standard of rationality or efficiency. Since, as was shown in this book, the concept of value is defined by the actual behaviors persons are observed to perform, the theoretical result is always that behavior is asserted to follow the rationalistic or efficiency norm. Thus efficiency is unlike equilibrium in Homans' thinking. It is not observed; it is assumed.

Homans directs us to men's histories to ascertain their values. In this he is following the form of psychological theories that rely upon known history of experimental animals to satisfy the requirements of meaning for theoretical concepts. We saw that the concept of "drive" could make little sense, (at least it could be used only very imperfectly), unless the history of the animal were known. That is, hunger could not be postulated as the drive which made the mouse run the maze unless we "knew" that the mouse was hungry. The only way this could be "known", since we could not ask the mouse, was by inferring his hunger state from his record of eating. Similarly, Homans argues that the histories of men are the keys to those things that they will find rewarding and valuable. This leads him to the concept of reward, borrowed from experimental psychology, and into the statement of proposition No. 1. It will be worth while to examine the concept of the past of man in the light of Homans' view of the origins of institutions. Since men's histories are experiences with institutional behaviors, it will be necessary to review Homans' theoretical account of the origin of institutions. This will lead us to the question of whether or not man's past determines his values. The circularity of the theory will become evident.

Above, we examined Homans' view of the origins of institutions and his speculations about the extent to which social approval and influence could set "norms" which would last for a considerable time. His conclusion was that these mechanisms which work on the interpersonal level were inadequate to explain the long-standing patterns of overall institutional behaviors. His suggestion, offered as speculative, was that there could be some deep-seated nature of man, or some set of drives or instincts in man as a species which could account for the continuing nature of some of the institutional arrangements that seem to obtain in human societies. It is interesting that Homans should suggest this, since it seems that it is in direct contradiction to the whole range of assumptions he finds it necessary to make about man in explaining the elementary forms of behavior, i.e., human values can be anything whatever; there are no intrinsic limits on what is rewarding, and so on.

Homans directs us to men's histories to search for their values. Values are important in his theory because they are the key theoretical explanatory terms. Men do those things that are most closely pursuant to their values. Therefore we should be interested in where men's values come from. Homans is careful to avoid discussion of this problem throughout most of his book. He is content to take a man's values as given in explaining his behavior. It was seen that a man's values were also inferred from the behavior being explained. In fact, we recognize the need for an outside measure of a man's values, separate from his behavior being explained, to remove circularity from the theory.

It seems that we can not base a theory of interpersonal behavior on the assumption that man can have any values whatever, and also look to man's past histories for his values. The contradiction here is that in looking to the past, we are forced to look to uniformities of social environment which condition values and restrict them, or to biological determination of values or trait, that also negate assuming that man can have any values whatsoever. If it is necessary to look to such origins of value, it seems that this must also be the place to start in explaining social regularity—normative order. It seems that because men are in many ways "the same" with respect to culture and biology, it is reasonable to conclude that their behaviors *because of this sameness* will be reasonably alike with respect to the goals they set and the means they choose to achieve them.

The general propositions Homans offers then take a secondary position. They can not account for the origins of normative behavior. The *why* of normative activity has been robbed from Homans' propositions by his own assumption that a man's values are rooted in his past which is similar to the pasts of those with whom he interacts. It is reasonable to assert that men learn to act in certain ways in growing into society, that their values may be any whatever. But before men can form norms about action and arrive at social order, as we have shown, the values among them must be very much alike. Since this is the case, within any society, we can not assume a randomness of private desire and ends and free choice among men, but rather narrow uniformity. This uniformity could account for the regularities found among men just as well as Homans' set of propositions borrowed from economics and psychology. This being so, the propositions reduce from explanations to simply unique descriptions of a more basic reality. Homans does not follow up the implications for his theory of the assumption of randomness of ends among men when he writes:

Since by the very fact of their humanity the social experience of most men has been to some extent the same, we assume that to some extent they hold similar values.

More nearly alike than that of all mankind is the social experience of members of a particular society . . . . Still more similar are the values held by members of a subculture.[81]

It is curious that Homans goes on in the next paragraph to conclude that it is social approval, and not commonality of experience and values, that determines normative behavior.

When we get down to particular groups of people, a special kind of reward, the reward obtained by conformity to a norm, becomes important.[82]

It seems appropriate to question why social approval should play such a great part in determining human action in face-to-face groups when culture and social determinism played such a great part in determining the values upon which men draw when fashioning their actions. Homans is using the commonality of experiences in social life to explain the values of men. But he seems to reject and accept social determinism at the same time. It is inconsistent and confusing to rely upon social determinism for the specific meanings of the key concept (value) and reject it when explaining the activities of men and their norms. If we are to reject social determinism in the case of norms, as Homans does in suggesting that norms are the congruency of men's privately calculated activities, then it seems that we have to allow, as Homans wishes at some points, the essentially atomistic and private nature of values. It seems that these two kinds of formulations can not go together in a deductive theory without encountering logical and substantial difficulties. It is this problem that is at the root of Homans' circularity in statement of the propositions. He wishes to avoid social determinism by allowing men to hold any values whatsoever; but he is unable to explain values apart from man's history, where it is necessary to violate this free-value assumption by suggesting social determinism. He wishes to allow man any values whatsoever, and is forced therefore to infer values from behavior directly. Such inference, with no outside empirical referent, makes it impossible to falsify the proposition about value, and reduces the propositions to circularities.

In short, we see that Homans has made two divergent assumptions about man which he employs at various points in his theory to explain social regularities. In the explanation of norms as the agreements made between men to act in certain ways because those ways are found valuable and profitable, values take on an explanatory character. They are the factors that explain to us why some men associate with each other, while others do not.

In explaining values, Homans must go to behavior. He must infer values from the behavior explained, and he must go to history, which is nothing more than the same kinds of behaviors as present ones, except that they are in the past. He suggests also that there may be some inherent qualities in man that ultimately rest with biology and condition in a general way the things man will do and value.

We see that Homans regards norms as the outcomes of men calculating their profits in social activities according to their own private criteria of value. For this assumption to be successful theoretically, it must be used in conjunction with the assumption of individuals as units, having individual value systems. For individuals to have choice there must be a range of choices available. This leads us to the assumption of a diversity of ends among members of a society, and among potential group members. Contrary to these assumptions, Homans finds it necessary to account for the values which explain men's normative action by reference to the commonality of experience and the uniformity that characterizes the social situation of men. This tends to contradict the valuerandomness assumption. Men learn their values by acting in society in concert with others. In this, Homans tacitly assumes that norms and values are "there" to be learned, and thus that they are prior. It does not seem that a general theory of human behavior can assume that norms and values are at once given by culture and common experience, and also that they are the result of men's private calculations according to rationalistic criteria which need *not* coincide with the criteria of other men.

CHAPTER 9

Summary and conclusion to part I

Several aspects of the theory of social behavior have been considered. It is appropriate to summarize the points and to conclude with an estimation of the theory and some general comments on theory in sociology.

Homans' theory is designed to be of the deductive type. That is, it is in the form of a system of statements of very great generality said to include the main parts of an explanation of human interaction. It is designed to be a theory of social behavior, rather than a theory of individual behavior, because it focuses on how human beings behave toward each other in collective action situations.

The system of statements that form a theory of the type Homans was attempting to write must have certain characteristics, most of which are dictated by the rules of logic. The system must be internally consistent. If the statements contradict each other, and no means are provided for deciding which statements are to be relevant at specific times, several deductions about the same event can be derived from the theory. This would violate the requirement that a deductive theory provide determinate predictions *via* deductive inference from its propositions.

The statements of a general deductive theory must take a special form, which is based on the syllogism. They must link two or more concepts of a determinate nature together in a determinate way. A statement must link classes of variables in such a way as to assert a general relationship between the classes so linked. It is then necessary to establish whether or not particular aspects of reality are of the classes linked together. When it is established that particular realities are covered by the generalities asserted by the proposition, then it is a simple matter to assert that the relationship between the generalities, or classes, stated in the general proposition also exists between the particular realities.

In order that all this be possible, the concepts involved in the theoretical proposition must be empirical in the sense that there must be acceptable operationalizations available for them. This is not to say that all theoretical concepts must be operationalizable or operations. It does assert, however, that if the statements are to fit the logic of deductive theory, they must be so.

Freud's works may be "theory", but this does not mean that we can operationalize ids and egos successfully. But Freud does not attempt a rendition of his theory in strict deductive form, although he may use processes of deduction in applying certain aspects of it.

Homans does attempt to write a deductive theory, one which summarizes an infinity of different behaviors in a small number of general propositions, with certain simplifying assumptions. Since Homans offers his as a deductive theory, it is necessary that the concepts of the theory meet the criterion of operationalizability noted above. To do this, the concepts linked in the statements must have agreed-upon empirical referents, other than the explicanda. That is, we can not define the concepts that appear in a proposition in terms of each other, since to do so would lead us to the truth of the statement by identity, and not by empirical test.

In Homans' theory, it seems that empirical test, other than inferences *suggested* by the theory, is impossible. This is an important distinction. Deductive theory is designed to yield hypotheses about real situations from which distinctive predictions or explanations arise. This is different from saying that the theory is designed to offer new or suggestive conceptualization possibilities concerning the data being analyzed.

The fundamental concepts in Homans' theory of social behavior seem to fail to meet the qualifications necessary for a determinate deductive theory. A major reason for this is inadequate definitions. It was shown that the definition of the key concept, value, was indistinguishable in empirical terms from the behaviors to which the term was relevant as explanation. This made the propositions using the term "value" (and other key concepts) true by definition and impossible to falsify, or test empirically. It seemed that everything in behavioral terms could be "explained" by value; everything behavioral could be conceived as the response to some value. This problem was aggravated in Homans' theory because it was asserted throughout most of the theory that the term "value" could take on any meaning whatever, according to the pecularities of the individuals and the behaviors being explained. This was a necessity from a formal point of view, since the theory was to be a general one, explaining diverse behaviors. It was also necessary from a theoretical point of view, since Homans' wish is to form a theory that could accommodate values of diverse kinds, and thus a theory of social behavior in general, rather than one which included only a small segment of the kinds of behavior available under its purview.

We have seen that Homans' theoretical style is strictly deductive and formalistic, since he wishes to give a theory that could be stated in a few general propositions covering a multitude of behaviors. It is also heavily nominalistic, in that Homans tends to deny the realities of exterior and prior aspects of social life. Thus his concept of norms is for the most part only of the temporary congruence of behaviors among persons whose similar behaviors satisfy each person's personal motives. These two viewpoints (deductive and nominal) make the concept of man in Homans' theory of paramount importance to the account of social reality derivable from the theory. Because Homans had to address the problem of social order, he had to solve the problem of how choices are made among hypothetically possible behaviors for large numbers of people acting together. Since his style is nominalistic, he had to begin with the individual. Homans therefore began with the individual as a theoretical entity and described him in general terms, arriving at general statements for his theory. He had to place a sketch of the individual at the head of his deductive system, so that from the general statements he could deduce an account of social order and allied issues, while keeping the individual prominent and retaining his deductive style. It was necessary to understand Homans' theoretical style in order to understand the importance of the statements in his theory. Thus the first part of the paper focused on Homans as a deductive theorist. It was also necessary to appreciate Homans' attempt to base his theory on the individual, rather than on some aspects of society, culture, or social life. This accounts for the emphasis on Homans' model of man. When the picture of the individual in Homans' theory is introduced into his theory at the level of the general propositions, it is then possible to see how he solved the problems of order and choice in social life; deduction from the individualistic propositions yielded a unique picture of how social order obtained and how change in social life occurred.

We saw that it was not altogether possible to count Homans' theory a success. His propositions did not meet the criterion for scientific statements suggested for them. The definitions of the main terms are vague, and often circular with the concepts being explained. Since this state of affairs is not acceptable in deductive theory, it may be concluded that Homans' is not a scientific theory, although it may appear scientific in format.

Homans' view of man is not consistent, either. This raised the question of how divergent assumptions about the nature of man could exist in the same theoretical structure, especially one of the deductive type in which the high level assumptions play such a key role. It was seen that in order to allow man an infinite number of possible values, and to make the theory a general one, it was necessary to assume that values could be anything. But allowing this, circularity became inescapable. There could be no outside criteria of values, and therefore there could be no way of telling whether or not men were indeed acting according to calculations of their own interest based on values. Values were undefined to allow man any values and thus liberate him from a range of limiting assumptions. When this was done, the only place to turn for definition of the concept "value" was to the behavior being explained —that which was assumed to be valued. This made the propositions using these terms circular.

The problem of defining the term "value" was solved by asserting that a man's history would be the place to look to ascertain his values. Even if this were so in the empirical sense, it is hard to see how this solves the theoretical problem raised by the concept of value in Homans' theory. Going to the past is nothing more than another way of committing the same circularity, defining values according to behaviors. Furthermore, it raises the problem of social determinism for the theoretical individual and for the nominalistic bent in Homans' explanation. Since we are directed to history in search of value, must we not postulate something in the past with which men had experience that gave them their values? Must this not have been a culture or normative system that was external and prior to the individual? And did not this invalidate the nominalism of the theory, and place the predominance of the individual's values in doubt of being the bases from which derived the social order? It seems that going to a history of ordered human action to find the values of men places severe limits on the range of values possible for men. This contradicts the assumption that men could have values of any kind. Since this is so, it limits the implicit assumption of an infinity of values among men, producing instead the assumption of a narrow range of values among them. Since this new assumption is really in operation, it seems that this should be the basis of an explanation of social order, in immediate contradiction to the explanation given by Homans.

The consequences of this theoretical difficulty are most evident in Homans' account of how social institutions are formed and maintained. Homans' himself asserts that institutions appear to be based on something other than the exchange of personal rewards. They seem to be related to certain long-standing aspects of human life that remain constant for all humanity. He suggests that there is a fundamental nature of man that accounts for the apparent stability and persistence of institutions. He argues that as the institutionalized arrangements men have devised for solving problems fail, there will be change which will bring men to solve these problems better.

It can be seen that Homans is here explicitly contradicting his assertion that his theory allows the theoretical man to have any values whatever. In fact, he is suggesting that ultimately, men have a set of values to which they refer when calculating action very much resembling those of every other man. The question of where this theoretical value standard is based can be answered from one of two theoretical points of view. Either it is rooted ultimately in biology and physical necessity, or it is a function of the social order, as it exists over and above the men in it. In either case, the answer that is given contradicts the assertions Homans makes in developing his theory—that the men involved can have any values whatever, and that their private gain through interaction with each other accounts for "normative" social interaction. In short, the theoretical problem Homans faces here is whether or not his theory is indeed based on the processes to which he directs so much attention in his postulates. Perhaps the theory really rests on inherent regularities in systems of social action, or biological necessity. The answer that must be drawn from the discussions of the genesis of values is that Homans' theory is not capable of accounting for social order without first *assuming* it in the form of assumptions that limit the value ranges among men.

We have seen that Homans' deductive style is inadequate to account for social order because the nature of the assumptions places the relevance of the theory in doubt and because the concepts necessary for a general theory of the deductive type seem not to be presently available. This led us to the conclusion that Homans' explanation is not really a theory in the sense that he wishes us to understand that term. It will be appropriate now to comment upon what his effort actually constitutes.

Theory, as Homans wishes to use it, is a set of general statements from which specific hypotheses and explanations may be derived deductively. There are other types of thinking that have gone under the name of "theory". It seems that Homans' effort most resembles the style that actually offers a detailed description of events by using suggestive and penetrating concepts. Zetterberg has called this sort of theory "dimensionist".[83] Rather than formalistic and deterministic, it tends to be programmatic and suggestive. As this style of theory is improved, the theoretical concepts in it become more direct and specific. They take on theoretical definitions. These concepts are linked by processes and entities that form a theoretical system something like pure mathematics, in that the terms and signs of the theory may have no empirical meaning. However, the analogy to pure mathematics is misleading because pure mathematics is not founded on the explanation of any reality, whereas a conceptual theory is.

As one develops a set of concepts, relations, and processes, he becomes increasingly able to understand that which he sees in terms of this theoretical system. In the strict sense, no hypotheses or predictions are derivable from this kind of theory. Rather, unique ways of looking at the world are developed through the use of the conceptual theory that lead one to make guesses and inferences about events. These need not be formally logical since there may be no rules of deduction applicable to the situation; the conceptual scheme may contain contradictions and fallacies that would invalidate any attempt to deduce logically from it. However, the use of such a scheme seems worthwhile in that it is suggestive of ways of acting and thinking that may lead to further and more precise conceptualizations of reality. Danger exists in this kind of theory in that it can not be invalidated directly by experience through the logic of hypothesis testing.

It seems that Homans' theory approximates a conceptual scheme more closely than a deductive theory. His desire to view human interaction in terms such as pay-off, reward and punishment, profit, cost, and justice is certainly not new, but it is the one serious and well-developed attempt in recent sociological theory. Taking the viewpoint of the individual, regardless of how that individual was formed and developed, is admissible in a conceptual scheme, as long as the scheme is not placed in the position of accounting for the individual. Viewed in this way, Homans' propositions are a set of general statements that intuitively make sense to twentieth century Western man. Perhaps we do conceptualize our actions in terms of profit, reward, and payoff. To do so is not to deductively theorize about them, however. It seems that Homans' scheme is useful in that it offers a unique perspective from which to view human action, and a suggestive one that makes us aware of alternative possibilities of conceptualization than those available in other theoretical efforts. At this stage of empirical analysis of human action, this is probably all that is possible.

Notes

1.   Exchange theory is based on the following works by G. C. Homans: *The Human Group* (New York: Harcourt, Brace and World, 1950); "Social Behavior as Exchange", *American Journal of Sociology*, **LXIII**, No. 6 (May, 1958), 597–606; *Social Behavior: Its Elementary Forms* (New York: Harcourt, Brace and World, 1961) and (2nd ed. by Harcourt, Brace, Jovanovich, Inc., 1974); "A Theory of Social Interaction", *Transactions of the Fifth World Congress of Sociology* (Louvain: International Sociological Association, 1964), 113–31. *Social Behavior* is the most comprehensive statement of the theory written by Homans, and it is from the first edition that most of the material used here was drawn. All references are to 1st ed. unless otherwise noted. Other works are less relevant to the topic at hand, but in the same line of thinking are Homans' articles, "Bringing Men Back In", *American Sociological Review*, XXIX, No. 6 (December, 1964), 809–18; and "Contemporary Theory in Sociology", *Handbook of Modern Sociology*, ed. R. E. L. Faris (Chicago: Rand McNally, 1964), 951–77.

2.   Homans' own book on explanation makes his position quite clear. G. C. Homans, *The Nature of Social Science* (New York: Harcourt, Brace and World, 1967).

3.   G. C. Homans, *The Nature of Social Science; Social Behavior*, pp. 9–12.

4.   Ernest Nagel, *The Structure of Science* (New York: Harcourt, Brace and World, 1961), 21–22.

5.   Rudolf Carnap, *Philosophical Foundations of Physics* (New York: Basic Books, 1966), pp. 11, 51–61.

6.   Homans, Social Behavior, pp. 8–12.

7.   *Ibid.*, p. 10.

8.   R. B. Braithwaite, *Scientific Explanation* (New York: Harper, 1953), Ch. I.

9.   Homans, *Social Behavior*, pp. 3–7.

10.   *Ibid.*, p. 8. He reiterates this point in the 1974 edition.

11.   K. R. Popper, *The Logic of Scientific Discovery* (New York: Harper, 1959), pp. 27–31.

12.   Homans, *Social Behavior*, p. 11.

13.   Nagel, *The Structure of Science*, p. 77. The scientific "law, characteristic of modern physical science, asserts a relation of functional dependence (in the mathematical sense of 'function') between two or more variable magnitudes associated with stated properties or processes".

14.   Carnap, *Philosophical Foundations*, pp. 45–47.

15.   See *Ibid.*, for an example of this explained.

16.   *Ibid.*

17.   A. R. Louch makes this point in discussing Homans' work. *Explanation and Human Action* (Berkeley: University of California Press, 1966), p. 14.

18. For a discussion of this, see R. M. MacIver, *Social Causation* (New York: Harper, 1964), Part One.

19. Homans, *Social Behavior*, p. 55.

20. *Ibid.*, p. 53.

21. *Ibid.*

22. *Ibid.*, p. 10.

23. Popper, *The Logic of Scientific Discovery*, pp. 27–34.

24. Homans, *Social Behavior*, p. 51.

25. Popper, *The Logic of Scientific Discovery*, pp. 34–42.

26. Homans, *Social Behavior*, 2nd ed., pp. 22–23.

27. *Ibid.*, p. 18.

28. Homans, *Social Behavior*, p. 54.

29. *Ibid.*, pp. 36, 55–56; Homans, *The Nature of Social Science*, p. 11.

30. Homans, *The Nature of Social Science*, p. 10.

31. Louch makes this point clear in *Explanation and Human Action*, pp. 13–15.

32. Homans, *Social Behavior*, 2nd ed., p. 16.

33. *Ibid.*, p. 20.

34. Homans, *Social Behavior*, p. 55.

35. *Ibid.*

36. *Ibid.*

37. Homans, *Social Behavior*, 2nd ed., p. 25

38. Homans, *Social Behavior*, p. 55.

39. Homans, *Social Behavior*, 2nd ed., p. 29.

40. Homans, *Social Behavior*, p. 54.

41. *Ibid.* p. 55.

42. The use of assumptions in this was called the "Flip-Flop Mechanism". Peter Park, "Some Methodological Problems of Homans' Theory of Social Behavior", presented at the annual meeting of the Canadian Sociological and Anthropological Association, June 6, 1968, Calgary, Alberta, Canada.

43. Carnap points this out for physical theory in *Philosophical Foundations*, pp. 45–47.

44. Homans, *Social Behavior*, p. 75.

45. *Ibid.*, pp. 57–61.

46. *Ibid.*, pp. 61–64.

47. *Ibid.*, pp. 72–75.

48. *Ibid.*, p. 75

49. Homans, *Social Behavior*, 2nd ed., pp. 37–39.

50. *Ibid.*, pp. 40–43.

51. J. S. Mill, *Philosophy of the Scientific Method* (New York: Hafner Publishing Company, 1950), Ernest Nagel (ed.). Book V, 307–56.

52. Peter Winch, *The Idea of a Social Science* (New York: Humanities Press, 1958), p. 72.

53. Homans, the Nature of Social Science, p. 44. Homans is here answering a charge that the social studies have no general propositions.

54. Homans, *Social Behavior*, p. 53.

55. *Ibid.*, p. 55.

56. Homans, *The Nature of Social Science*, p. 44.

57. Homans, *Social Behavior*, p. 6.

58. *Ibid.*, p. 13.

59. *Ibid.*, p. 42.

60. *Ibid.*, p. 41.

61. Homans says, "Indeed, we are out to rehabilitate 'economic man'. The trouble with him was not that he was economic . . . but that he was antisocial and materialistic. . . . What was wrong with him were his values; he was only allowed a limited range of values; but the new economic man is not so limited. He may have any values whatever, from altruism to hedonism . . . . Indeed, if he has learned to find reward in *not* husbanding his resources, if he values *not* taking any thought for the morrow, and acts accordingly, his behavior is still economic. In fact, the new economic man is plain man". *Social Behavior*, pp. 79–80.

62. profit = reward minus cost; or cost = reward minus profit.

63. Homans, *Social Behavior*, p. 75.

64. He is inconsistent on this point, since he seems to account for elementary social behavior in terms of social praise, approval, and influence, but he suggests that these determinants of behavior are relatively weak in his discussion of institutional arrangements and behaviors. See Ch. 6.

65. Homans, *Social Behavior*, 2nd ed., p. 43.

66. Actually, as Homans moves further from the face-to-face group toward greater inclusiveness and complexity, he finds it less useful to refer to his propositions.

67. Homans, *Social Behavior*, p. 381.

68. *Ibid.*,

69. *Ibid.*

70. *Ibid.*

71.   *Ibid.*, p. 382.

72.   *Ibid.*, pp. 383–84.

73.   *Ibid.*, p. 384.

74.   The reference to a maximization *norm* is to the norm shown to be implicit before Homans' theory can begin to apply. Thus the theory can not claim to begin with men as they are and build from that point. A norm of behavior, be it human nature or not, is necessary to form the basis of our understanding of the propositions linking values and activities.

75.   Or so it seems; Homans' discussion of men that do not conform to the basic human ways of being is unclear.

76.   *Ibid.*, pp. 109–16. This sort of thing is continued at more length in the treatment of esteem in Ch. 8 of *Social Behavior*, pp. 145–63.

77.   Homans has a chapter on influence that makes essentially these points in *Social Behavior*, pp. 83–111.

78.   *Ibid.*, p. 115.

79.   See *Ibid.*, Ch. 18, pp. 378–98.

80.   *Ibid.*, p. 380.

81.   *Ibid.*, pp. 45–46.

82.   *Ibid.*, p. 46.

83.   Hans L. Zetterberg, *Review of Modern Sociological Theory in Continuity and Change* edited by H. Becker and A. Boskoff, *American Sociological Review*, **XXIII** (February, 1958), 95.

Part II
Parsonian Functionalism

CHAPTER 10

Introduction to part II

It is common to notice that Parsons' theory "changes" from one of the texts he has written to another. These changes are sometimes understood to mean that the theory is inconsistent, or that it is so infinitely adaptable in its various applications that it constitutes only a scheme of categories, or a system of concepts. Parsons himself argues that his is not a system of "theory", since in his meaning of the term, a theory of social action is not possible at the present time. His scheme is, rather, a

theory of systems. It attempts to present the best attainable in the present state of knowledge with respect to the theoretical analysis of a carefully defined class of empirical systems.[1]

Further, Parsons argues that his approach is the only one possible, since it is necessary to have a clearly defined and understood set of related categories, a system, into which aspects of social life may be divided for analysis. He argues that such a set of categories is prerequisite to the development of a "system of theory".

Therefore, it is clearly understandable that his system may "change" in response to the demands placed upon it. Since he considers it a partial and tentative arrangement, it may add elements or drop them as it becomes necessary. However, it is maintained in this essay that the fundamental bases of Parsons' system and the questions he seeks to answer have remained the same from their inception, and that the changes observable from application to application of the system are understandable in terms of the points of view being taken by Parsons at any one time. His system of thought seems to be implied in its entirety when any one aspect of it is being discussed. Therefore, it is possible for Parsons to write a whole volume, *The Social System*,[2] in which he concentrates on one level of his analysis and on one category of elements in it. Parsons reminds his readers from time to time that the rest of the theoretical elements of the system are implied and stand in the background of the analysis at all times. The degree to which this is so will be examined in this book in Chapters 13, 14, and 15.

The ways in which Parsons emphasizes one segment of the total system at any one time seems to be the main problem in understanding how his system is really one at all times. The study of the concept of man in Parsons' thinking is one point at which the differences in emphasis seem to become differences in kind—perhaps implying incompatibilities among the assumptions upon which the theory is based. In any case, it will be shown that the concepts of man developed by Parsons and his collaborators tend to be more or less systematically spelled out depending on the levels of generality and analysis being focused upon. Also, we will see that the scheme tends to support one or another of two basic views of man, depending again upon the emphasis.

It is important to make it quite clear that we are dealing with problems of relative emphasis and the ways in which these shade off into differences in the basic character of theoretical thinking. It has already been said that there is a sense in which the whole of Parsons' thinking is implied by any part of it; it is very hard to locate statements in Parsons' works that are completely contradictory. It is not so hard, however, to begin to feel that Parsons is really talking about something different in one volume than he was talking about in another. In this part, a theoretical problem is examined which seems appropriate to the study of the concept of man in Parsons' writings, and which is a major theoretical concern within theory itself. This is the problem of locating the theoretical agent(s) of choice in the system that includes structural elements as well as human actors.

The objective of this study is to show that when Parsons emphasizes voluntarism, the actor's own determination of his performances, there is a more or less specific model of man implied. Alternatively, it is demonstrated that when Parsons emphasizes the analysis of structural aspects of social life, especially from the social system point of view, a second model of man emerges which is deterministic in its main outline, rather than voluntaristic. We will see that, depending on the model of man in view, the concept of role and the degree of specificity of cultural prescriptions change accordingly.

In laying the background for an understanding of Parsons, it is probably best to begin by reconstructing some of his thinking concerning the trends in Western social thought. This reconstruction emphasizes the problems that various thinkers solved best, and the ones they failed to solve, in Parsons' opinion. It also points up the aspects of their thinking that Parsons chose to take into his own scheme. It is necessary to show how he combines these elements into a conceptual whole—a system. The importance of the concept "system" can not be overestimated in this exploration of Parsonian theory.

CHAPTER 11

The bases on which Parsons' theory rests

This chapter takes up some of the history of sociological thought related to Parsons' work. The main concern is to focus on some theoretical problems which historically have been addressed by a comprehensive sociological theory—or by the first steps toward one. Clearly, if theory is to be written, certain preliminary questions concerning where one ought to start and what one ought to look at must be answered. Parsons has taken a thorough approach to this problem, and a scholarly one. He has examined the works of some major contributors to sociological and economic theory with a view to taking major insights from them, while avoiding their failures. The result of this "empirical"[3] investigation of theories has been the outline of Parsons' "action frame of reference".[4] Part of this scheme will be the main concern of the criticism and analysis in this paper. The frame of reference is related to the model of man in Parsons' theoretical writings both in terms of motivated, voluntaristic action, and in terms of action's structural determinants.

To begin, Parsons reasons that a theory of social action is concerned mainly with the actions of human beings in social situations. Thus we ought to look at theories which focus on this aspect of social action.

The starting point, both historically and logically, is the conception of intrinsic rationality of action. This involves the fundamental elements of "ends", "means" and "conditions" of rational action and the norm of the intrinsic means–ends relationship.[5]

We see that Parsons finds it profitable to concentrate on rationality and utilitarianism, although he considers them wanting in several respects which will be outlined below. Basically, the main feature of this kind of thinking is the means–ends scheme which places emphasis on action by persons or actors in relation to their particular goals in particular situations. It is the problems of where goals come from and what constitutes a "situation" that make Parsons reject other features of this branch of social thought in favor of that of Durkheim and Pareto.[6]

Utilitarian theory concentrates on the means–ends relationship almost exclusively. The ends themselves are often left unexamined, or, as in the case of Hobbes, are left to the common sense notion that the "rationality" of men will dictate certain fundamental ends that they will share by virtue of their being men. Thus the collective decision of men to place a sovereign at the head of government (in the broadest sense of this term) derives from the common interests of men to reduce conflict and danger from each other. This seems like a sound assumption to make, but it has no place in utilitarianism as a coherent system of thought. The means–ends scheme simply indicates that men will adopt rationally contrived means toward the achievement of their own private ends. The problem Hobbes solves by appealing to the seemingly normal and common desire of all men for security and protection is that of accounting for the ends of action by looking *outside* the means–ends scheme itself. This takes the form of the appeal to the ultimate rationally conceived end—survival.[7]

Implicit in this means–ends scheme at all times is the concept of voluntarism. That is, while the ends of action among men are left unaccounted for within the scheme itself, the voluntaristic nature of action is emphasized. Certainly, if ends are left unaccounted for, they may be assumed to be random in a collectivity. Since they are so, it is up to the individual man to select his ends, and rationally contrive their means of pursuit.

In this simple scheme, however, voluntaristic or individually contrived and executed action seems to exist in inverse proportion to the ordering or structuring of the ends of action. In other words, as order concerning the ends of action in a collectivity is introduced hypothetically into this simple scheme, determinism seems to be introduced as well. If action were viewed as the rational adaptation of means to a given set of ends, the norm of rationality would preclude variations in behavior forms, the ends now being given, and the means to them being governed by a principle—rationality itself. Behavior would theoretically be uniform among the members of a collectivity in this situation. The result of this circumstance would be that, given a set of ends, behavior would be determined by them and the rational standard of conduct. This would mean, of course, that the voluntaristic or individually contrived aspects of the scheme had been wiped out. Since behavior toward ends took the form of rational action, and since the ends were given, the behaviors could not be other than uniform.

This is a major reason for Parsons' rejection of simple means–ends thinking; however, the utilitarian *form* of analysis is not rejected. It is profitable to conceive of action as being oriented toward ends and voluntaristically conceived. The problem of the ends of action made it necessary for Parsons to examine other works of social and economic theory.

Hedonism or pleasure-seeking as the end of all action seemed a reasonable alternative, but proved useless after all, since it cut out the analysis of ends altogether.[8] If one postulates pleasure as the end of all action, it may be possible to argue that men do not usually act in ways which bring them pain, but the question of what brings pleasure to men has been avoided. When this question is confronted, its answer takes on the same indeterminate theoretical status as the assumption of random ends of action in utilitarian thought. Since it is not possible to say what brings pleasure to men in a certain collectivity, it is useless to speak in terms of pleasure-seeking when generating a theory of ordered social behavior.

However, Parsons does not reject the whole idea of hedonism out of hand. Certainly, if action is to be in any sense voluntaristic, some fundamental psychological principle such as pleasure, need, or gratification has to be incorporated into the scheme in order to account for the motivation of behavior. Motivational categories are central to such explanations. Clearly, the problem of ends of action and their pursuit within the context of voluntarism constitutes the main concern of a theory of social order. To discover how the problem of ends could be solved, Parsons advanced his study into more modern economic and political thought and away from utilitarian theory.

We have seen that Parsons views utilitarian theory as "inherently unstable"[9] and needing metaphysical assumptions, as in the case of Hobbes, to account for the relations of the ends of actions in a collectivity of men. In his treatment of Marshall's economic thinking, Parsons finds the first steps toward an account of the relationships of the ends of action, even though Parsons regards Marshall's efforts only a suggestion of a solution to the problem.[10]

Marshall refuses to accept categorically the utilitarian assumption of the independence of wants. He divides wants into "artificial", to which he finds he can apply the assumption of the independence of wants, and "wants adjusted to activities", to which he can not.[11] Obviously, the second category is the more interesting to the development of Parsons' thinking, since the idea of adjustment of wants to activities implies some determinate relationship between the system of ends of action and the activities of life. Parsons chooses to consider both the "wants adjusted to activities", and the activities to which the wants were adjusted as "primarily ... manifestations of a single relatively well-integrated system of value-attitudes".[12]

Certainly the introduction of a system of integrated value-attitudes was what Parsons was looking for in Marshall. It seems to be the first step in moving away from the assumption of the randomness of ends. It poses problems for Parsons' thinking as well as for this study, however. If wants are indeed somehow adjusted to activities, the question naturally arises concerning *how* activities and wants are related. The postulation of an integrated system of value-attitudes that somehow ties wants and activities together makes logical sense, since it can easily be supposed that wants and activities would tend to coincide under the influence of a common set of attitudes among men. But the question of where and how the value attitudes were generated still remains. This was a persistent problem for Parsons, which led him to the study of Pareto and Durkheim particularly.[13]

The question of the source of value-attitudes also guides this study of Parsons' theory, since the answer seemingly could take one of three forms. Men could exhibit the postulated integrated value system relating wants and activities because fundamentally, they were constituted the same. This would place the nature of man himself at the center of Parsons' study as well as of this one, since the answer to the question of exactly how man was constituted would also provide the answer to the question of the relationships of wants and activities in human collectivities. Men could develop wants which coincided with activities, alternatively, because the common experiences of men in collectivities made certain actions necessary for their survival, or the survival of their system of relations with each other. This would cause wants and activities to coincide in the sense that activities would tend to determine wants. This leads to a formulation of the relation of wants and activities similar to the theory of natural selection. Men would tend to have wants which coincided with their activities because the survival value of that particular system of relationships was especially great. The third logical possibility of the relations of wants and activities, tied together by a common system of value-attitudes, concerns the idea that wants and activities really "determine each other" in some kind of systematic interchange between the two. This would lead to the notion that the common system of value-attitudes was linked to both wants and activities because men tended to *want* to do what they also *needed* to do in social life.

In Parsons' writings there are clear indications that he actually takes all three of these routes. In Chapter 13 of this part, the "voluntaristic" emphasis in his theory will be discussed, showing that he documents a specific picture of the nature of man based on the actions of men in situations. In Chapter 14, it will be seen that, from time to time, the voluntaristic aspects of man's behavior have been neglected in favor of a more deterministic account. This corresponds to the second alternative above. In 15, the two divergent approaches are brought together, with special attention to the models of man derived from the voluntaristic and the deterministic emphases from Chapters 13 and 14.

Parsons argues that each alternative alone is insufficient in solving the problem of ends. In *The Social System*, he gives three reasons why the convergence of wants among collectivities can not be attributed to common personality or constitutional make-up alone.

Since all the different roles in which an individual is involved are interdependent in his motivational system, the combination of motivational elements which produces the uniform behavior will be different for different personalities.[14]

Similarly,

Role-involvements do not exhaust the orientation or interest system of any personality.[15]

Finally, Parsons argues that

there is every reason to believe that it is strictly impossible for the distribution of constitutional differences in the population of a complex social system to correspond directly with the distribution of roles.[16]

This rejection of constitutional or psychological determinism points up the relevance of this study for Parsonian theory and for sociology. Since the composition of man is rejected as the sole determinant of social organization, the questions of exactly what is the composition of man and what is his relationship to social organization become important. We can not build systems of social action while neglecting to take account of individuals, for while actors in the Parsonian sense need not be persons, for the most part they are. The focus of the Parsonian system on the role, rather than person, does not reduce the difficulty of dealing with men. We saw above that Parsons himself explicitly recognizes this in his rejection of radical psychological determinism. The person is in a dynamic relationship to his own set of roles, and the roles themselves "do not exhaust the orientation or interest system of any personality".

The second alternative to the question raised by Marshall, that of social of cultural determinism to account for the ends of action, places the problem of the nature of man in a different theoretical perspective. It was suggested that the "wants adjusted to activities" could be interpreted as social or cultural determinism. In this case, the question would become: what mechanisms in man himself make it possible for the varieties of culture and social structure to mold him; and, how are these brought into play in the context of social interaction?

The third alternative, that the interaction context has an impact on both wants and activities, will be discussed in due course. This alternative tends to devalue, but not deny, the impact of the individual actor on his action—this is the element of voluntarism that Parsons insists is always present. On the other hand, both the common culture and the structure of the interaction system in which the individual contacts others have an impact on the personality of the actor himself and determine to some degree the actions he will take. Parsons holds that his scheme steers a course between the Scylla of psychological determinism and the Charybdis of cultural and structural determinism by employing elements of both while not relying on either.

In Pareto's work, Parsons finds an indication of how activities and wants are theoretically related.[17] For Pareto, the "residues" are manifestations of sentiments, and it is sentiment that is the determining force in social equilibrium.[18] The question Pareto asked, and the one Parsons follows up in his analysis, is that of the relationship between the residues, the derivations (expressions calculated to account for the residues), and action that is non-logical in its essential character.[19]

Pareto divides action into the logical and non-logical. He defines logical action positively by relating it to the means–ends scheme and holding that logical action is that which is agreed to be such by an outside observer with extended powers of vision and analysis. The criterion by which the outside observer judges action logical is the norm of rationality, which forms the basis of utilitarian theory and Pareto's economics. His question concerning non-logical action (the residual category which includes illogical action) is: in what respects does non-logical action differ from logical action?[20]

We have seen that logical action was the linking of empirical ends with logically related means. This was "scientific" action. The problem for analysis, however, is the "unscientific", on which Parsons focuses. It seems that unscientific action can be accounted for in two ways. One is in terms of ignorance and error. In this type of account, the non-logical action of interest can be said to be erroneous or "wrong" action, given the end nominally in view.[21] Alternatively, action may involve elements that fall altogether outside the provinces of scientific design of behavior and logical analysis. This action is indeed non-logical, but it seems that it is only that; it is *not* illogical, but only non-logical. That is, the action may involve elements or entities that are unverifiable. In this sense, the problem of non-logical action is not resolvable in terms of ignorance or error. The action is not "wrong" action, but it remains non-logical in the sense that Pareto defines logical action. In logical action, Pareto stays close to the utilitarian means–ends scheme. He does not account for the relations of ends to each other. As Parsons interprets Pareto, the category of non-logical action which is not illogical action (not "wrong" action according to utilitarian principles) is of most interest, since it suggests a normative component that tends to account for actions in this category.[22]

The ends of action may be classified into subjective and objective categories. Obviously, the subjective class may not be dealt with according to logical principles by an outside observer. These subjective acts are those that are outside the criterion of logicality, and thus may be either "right" or "wrong". At least they have the potential of being "right", while remaining essentially non-logical under Pareto's definition. Actions of this type may have derivations associated with them that are either statements of "why" certain actions ought to be undertaken, or statements of appropriateness of certain actions and the ends toward which these actions are directed. Parsons concludes that the derivations which tend to state appropriateness of actions are based on an important class of residues which

take the general form of "a sentiment that such and such is a desirable state of affairs". Such statements are residues . . . because they embody ends of action which can not be justified . . . not because they are appropriate means to other ends, but because they are deemed desirable as ends in themselves. Such residues may be called normative residues.[23]

Parsons holds that the consequences of the discovery of this class of residues in Pareto's work contradicts the utilitarian position concerning the randomness of ends. The residues are not random data for a theory of action, but

on the contrary, [they] constitute a definite element of systems of action, in an understandable state of interdependence with the others . . . . So far as ends enter the category of residues as independent elements, they are not random ends, but stand in definable positive relations both to other ends in the same system, and to the other elements of action.[24]

Furthermore, there is no reason why the ends of logical acts, with which Pareto is less concerned, might not fall into this category. They might be manifestations of sentiments *as well as* the ends of logical acts.

For even though the means–ends relationship be completely logical there may be, and according to Pareto there are, certain ends which are not capable of justification in terms of scientific theory, the justifications of which at least contain residues, if not derivations.[25]

The possibility that the ends of logical action might also involve components of sentiment plays an important part in the formation of Parsonian theory, and also raises a major question for the study of Parsons' work. Parsons is suggesting that in Pareto's work he has found evidence for asserting that persons may act in a single way for more than one reason, and while the actions based on those reasons tend to coincide, the reasons remain analytically separate. Persons may be committed to ends because there is logical or physical necessity in their being so, as well as because they see the ends of action as "right", or justified somehow. These two categories of reasons for an act tend to be congruent in the person who is acting, since his views of appropriate action and of logical, necessary action tend to coincide. This insight is the basis on which Parsons can argue that structurally determined or socially sanctioned actions are also "voluntary" actions on the actor's part. The actor may see himself as having chosen deliberately those actions which, in fact, were not matters of choice.

This proposition raises questions related to the subject of this study. Specifically, in a system of action alternatives, where should the agents of choice be located? In what sense is it reasonable to speak of voluntarism in actors, when the actions for which they may "volunteer" may be strictly limited? What assumptions about the nature of man must be made to locate choice with the individual, or with the system, or to somehow inter-twine the two?

It was pointed out above that Parsons' theoretical writing is an attempt to employ elements of structural or social determinism, while not violating individualistic or voluntaristic aspects of human behavior. In the treatment of Durkheim, Parsons takes issue with the view that Durkheim's account of the relations between man and society is completely "sociologistic", or simply another version of a one-factor theory of causation.[26]

Durkheim in many respects tended to set a "sociologistic" factor theory over against the individualistic factor theories current in his day. But along with this heading there is a more important strand in his thought which generally increased in strength in the course of his career. This is a genuinely structural-functional treatment of the social system. . . .[27]

From Durkheim, especially from *The Division of Labor*,[28] Parsons takes some major features of his more structural emphasis, as well as more crit-icisms of the utilitarian position regarding means, ends and their relations.

Durkheim directs attention to the moral, ethical and normative aspects of life. According to Parsons, *The Division of Labor* was written to show that these were the central concern of persons no matter whether they lived in a society characterized by mechanical solidarity in which the common senti-ments and systems of acting are more apparent, or in organic solidarity, in which it appears that the mutuality of exchange and dependence might in itself account for the apparent order.[29] The utilitarian view of organic solidarity would have been as Adam Smith had it in *The Wealth of Nations*—basically that mutual dependence and trade linked persons together so completely, and the system of linkages eventually became so ramified, that it fused with the total system of mutual human involvement. That is, the tendencies observed in market relations between persons eventually applied to all aspects of life.

This division of labor, from which so many advantages are derived, is not originally the effect of any human wisdom, which foresees and intends that general opulence to which it gives occasion. It is the necessary though very slow and gradual, consequence of a certain propensity to truck, barter, and exchange one thing for another.[30]

Rejecting this scheme, Durkheim observed that the generalization of utilitarian theory fails to exhaust, even for purely economic transactions, the elements which are actually found in market relations and which must exist prior to them if the market situation is to remain at all.

What is omitted is the fact that these transactions are actually entered into in accordance with a body of binding rules which are not part of the *ad hoc* agreement of the parties.[31]

What has been called the "institution of contract" has not been entered into by any set of contracting parties explicitly, but is assumed by them at the time they enter the contract. It must have existed prior to and independently of the participants in any exchange. Further, these are not only legal rules of transactions. While social interchange of any kind might be conceptualized as exchange between persons, these exchanges take place in the context of a system of customary rules, conventions and systems of informal obligations informally enforced.

An important implication of this line of thought for Parsons' work is that this critique of utilitarian theory emphasized the continuing nature of the system of rules over time. The elements of utilitarian theory contain no basis for order, without the introduction of factors outside the utilitarian system. But even if such factors are admitted, utilitarianism provides no continuing context in which similar transactions among men could occur at another time. The duration of market relations among men is normally short. Under strict utilitarian assumptions, there is no reason for men to hit upon particularly adequate arrangements of contractual relations again, even if they managed to do so once. This raises the important theoretical problem of how to account for the continuation of a system of rules over time. Parsons has found it necessary to make this maintenance of basic patterns one of his prime concerns.

The rules relied upon in utilitarianism as they supposedly emerge from the transactions among people are purely regulative in character. They rely for their force on the assumption that the reason for being committed to them at all is the mutual desire for gain of the contracting parties. The rules have no binding character, no moral force, of themselves. They are merely part of the apparatus of conducting transactions among persons.

However, the fact that Durkheim placed major emphasis on the moral relevance of the rules appearing to be external to contractual relations points up two important aspects of these rules. They are not simply part of the hardware of doing business. The rules have taken on a moral aspect that merely agreed-upon regulations would not have. Also, since this is so, it is the commitment of individuals to these rules that gives them their impact on human conduct. Thus, Durkheim can not be interpreted purely as a cultural determinist who hypothesized the simplistic control over individuals of some "group mind", or social determinism agent.[32] Commitment to the rules and institutions of a society was what gave these their force in regulating conduct. It was the essentially moral character of people, leading them to make correct choices in terms of rules and to be committed to the outcomes of the choices they made, that characterized social life.

At this point we see one of the "convergences"[33] Parsons focuses upon in his treatment of Durkheim, Pareto, Marshall and Weber. Concerning

Pareto, we saw that Parsons concludes there are points of contact between logical action and non-logical action, in that action which is essentially logical can also be a manifestation of sentiment concerning the action itself. Parsons felt that Pareto was pointing to ways in which ends of action take on elements of sentiment, as well as utility for the system of action itself. It was argued that this was recognition on Parsons' part that an act could be desired as well as "correct" in terms of necessities. Similarly, in Durkheim, we see that necessary rules, those actually making social life possible, are also the object of commitment on the part of the persons who live within the framework of these rules. It is the commitment of these persons that gives the system of rules its measure of control over human conduct. This double emphasis (of necessity and commitment) is a main theme in the theory of social action developed by Parsons.

In Durkheim, Parsons also found material for his later concern with systems of symbols and their relations to systems of human action and personality. Inherent in the constellation of rules for conduct, there comes to be a value system. This system not only directs the ends of specific acts, but it governs all the actions of individuals. The organization in this system of values comes to be reflected in the organized activities of persons. This system of values is manifested as conditions under which certain kinds of acts are appropriate. Thus the system both defines the immediate ends of action and embodies a set of rules covering the complex of specific actions. From Durkheim's concern for order and its explanation, it follows that the system of rules must be tied ultimately to the concerns of persons. It is not enough that action follow rules; for those rules to be operative, they must be shared and related to the general concerns of persons. This is shown in Durkheim's treatment of *anomie*,[34] the case in which the individual is deprived of a systematic, stable arrangement of socially given norms, and in which the moral quality of conduct is reduced.

Thus, Parsons finds support for his notion that action is always essentially normative. Not only is it normative, but the norms to which action is related form a systematic whole. This whole is reflected at three levels of generality that have come to concern Parsons in his later writings. These are the personality level, indicated in Durkheim's work by the emphasis on individual commitment to norms; the social system level, in which actual behavioral manifestations of the commitment to norms are found; and the cultural level, consisting of the collection of symbols which have meaning in terms of the norms and performances based on them.

Parsons thus isolated three important phases of theoretical thinking that were to remain part of his work thereafter. These are the three levels of abstraction that he calls the personality system, the social system, and the cultural system. In main outline, they have the characteristics he found in

Durkheim's treatment of these abstractions. They are intimately related to each other via the congruence of the motivations to act, the act itself, and the regulative system current in culture that governed the act. Parsons had seen Marshall's rejection of the assumption of the randomness of ends in utilitarian economic theory and his substitution of the notion that ends become "adjusted to life". In Pareto, Parsons found that this insight was again confirmed, since even in Pareto's classification of acts into logical and non-logical, there is indication that actions are normatively oriented, and that these actions are tied to life experiences. Logical actions (those that logically relate ends and means) also become objects of sentiment. Persons tend to become committed to activities that are essential to their welfare, or at least to the maintenance of the system of social relations that comes to be common in a group. At least some such actions could also be called "logical", since they are carried out according to rules agreed to be "correct" with respect to efficiently relating means and ends. There seem to be obvious implications here for the sociology of knowledge.

In Durkheim, Parsons finds reason to advance his position further. Durkheim showed that even in the most contractual relationships, there is an external and prior system of normative elements regulating how the contracts are to be carried out. This normative system has the support of those it regulates, if it is to have force at all. There is an obvious parallel here with Pareto in that some logical actions also have the support of "sentiments". Finally, Durkheim argued that the normative elements manifested in social relationships form a system, a whole which is articulated with life experiences of persons governed by the norms, and which becomes generalized both to regulate specific acts and to provide a general framework of rules within which persons find meaning.

We will see that these main ideas, combined with some taken from Weber, constitute the basis on which Parsons builds his system of action. They are never really abandoned. Apparently, no matter how Parsons states his arguments, or which part of his system he is focusing on, he means to imply these elements of his system.

Parsons is concerned with Weber's work on capitalism particularly as it relates to the place of values in sociological theory. Weber's interest in capitalism consists in showing how it could be theoretically accounted for in the history of Western civilization, especially since he holds that certain aspects of that history parallel that of other parts of the world at various times.[35] Specifically, his interest is in rational capitalism, or the rational organization of free labor into a productive unit. This kind of organization is one aspect of the concept of "bureaucracy", which involves the organization of persons pursuing specific ends while serving the larger ends of the organization as a unit, which might be quite impersonally conceived. In this kind of organization, the office is thought of as a calling in which the tasks impose obligations on the incumbents. Thus a bureaucracy, which has the same general features as the rational organization of modern capitalism, has a compulsory yet voluntaristic element. Once the person is involved in the system his action is oriented toward goals which carry individual rewards and sanctions for their performance. These goals are organized on a higher level in terms of the total goals of the system within which each person's special interests are arranged. These higher goals, moreover, are usually beyond the control of the incumbents of specific offices in the bureaucratic structure. This is especially the case when the whole organization of Western capitalism is viewed as essentially a type of bureaucracy. Weber accounts for the goals of the system as a whole by examining the "ultimate goals and value attitudes" that are "anchored in and in part dependent on a definite metaphysical system of ideas."[36] This accounts for his attention to religious ideas in relation to the influence they have on capitalism. This eventually brings Weber to conclude that there is a close functional relationship among activities of man as they are oriented to specific goals in systems, and ultimate goals toward which those systems are in turn directed, and the dominant metaphysical system or meaning arrangements men hold. This argument constitutes a major theme in *The Protestant Ethic and the Spirit of Capitalism,* as well as a theme on which Parsons finds it useful to enlarge.

The theoretical beginning point for Weber, and for Parsons, is the standard of intrinsic rationality, or efficiency. The ultimate value element comes into Weber's work with the system of attitudes associated with religion. These attitudes are taken as data by Weber and called "religious interests".[37] Religious interests become associated with the ways in which men make a living through a manifestation of these interests in attitudes toward work. Thus Weber seems to be seeing a systematic interrelation among ideas of an "ultimate" nature, specific prescriptions for conduct which are closely associated with these but distinct from them, and the actual activities in which men engage. This could all be set in a context of voluntarism, since each man is concerned only with his set of specific interests. He might not be aware of (probably is not aware of) the greater systematic arrangement of these three aspects of social life. Thus man could go about his business, for-mulating his actions according to given specifics of the situations in which he acted, in accordance with his particular conception of values, while in the main being under the general influence of the systems of ultimate values current in society as well as the patterns of action of other men.

CHAPTER 12

Outline of Parsons' theory

The previous chapter attempted to show by consideration of Parsons' theoretical-historical essays in *The Structure of Social Action* that certain issues in the history of social thought are of importance to Parsons' own theorizing. These issues have been developed as the major relevant insights of the four thinkers Parsons treats, and the main breakdowns in the utilitarian conception of the relationships of means to ends and ends to each other. In the present chapter, the main conclusions of the substantive work just reviewed will be related to certain fundamental issues in the general theory of action as it is found in the later Parsons. This will establish that, while Parsons does indeed "change" in some respects, his thought should be understood as being all of a piece. The main problem with Parsons' work in this regard will be whether or not all the elements of it are capable of fitting into the same theoretical scheme.

Parsons argues that his work in *The Structure of Social Action* was to discover and document convergences in the writings of members of divergent "schools" of social thought. Several of these convergences were pointed out in the previous chapter. The immense problem Parsons has set for himself is to unite these convergent elements into a single theory of social action, while avoiding the pitfalls and blind alleys of the "schools" from which the theoretical elements are taken. This chapter will demonstrate that, indeed, Parsons does employ the theoretical insights documented in *The Structure of Social Action* in his theory, as well as some others that he finds congenial.

We will now turn to a preliminary sketch of Parsons' theory. After this, the following two chapters will treat Parsons' voluntaristic emphasis, from which a distinct model of man emerges, and his deterministic emphasis, in which a different and less specific model of man is implied. This will have the effect of dividing Parsons' theory and examining one half of it at a time. The chapter following these examinations will again unite the theory with special regard to the models of man.

One of Parsons' main concerns has been to spell out his "action frame of reference" as completely as possible.[38] When he begins with individual actions and the problem of how to conceptualize them, he usually starts with the actor in a situation. He holds this actor-situation combination to be the main "precipitate" of utilitarian theory.[39] That is, the fundamental aspects of social action for Parsons are (1) the actor, involved in (2) a situation, which includes (3) goals toward which the actor would like to move.[40] The technological aspect of how the actor moves toward his goals is included in the concept of the means–ends scheme. We saw that no matter how the strict utilitarian scheme is formulated, it always involves a problem of the ends of action. This is the weakness of utilitarianism for Parsons. Since the ends of action are not specified, it is impossible to speak about order in social action coming out of a simple linking up of means to ends; the ends must be regulated somehow. This does not violate the fact that conceptualizing action in terms of means and ends is useful. It remains the starting point for Parsons' action frame of reference.

This conceptual starting point implies certain logically-related questions which Parsons recognizes. If action is to be conceived in terms of means and ends, the social regulation of the ends themselves might ultimately lead to complete social control over the ends. Since the means to ends are governed by the notion of intrinsic rationality, this leads to the conclusion that the regulation of means would be a consequence of the specific regulation of ends. Action in roles would therefore be uniform. This is the extreme "socio-logistic" position that Parsons wishes to avoid. Avoiding this problem is critical to the success of the theory of action, since action, while having its ends somehow regulated, is also conceived to be voluntaristic.[41]

The solution to this problem involves a shift away from the simple conceptualization of action as somehow "programmed" into actors, and therefore determined, and toward account of the "organization of the actor's orientations to a situation".[42] The emphasis here is on the *actor's* system of organization of action, and away from the organization of ends of action *for* actors. The distinction is crucial. Ordered social actions are not conceived as especially rigid types of acts or arrangements of action into which an actor must "fit". Rather, the order observed in social life is conceived as a result of the interaction of actors who are oriented similarly to goals and situations. As such actors meet each other, their activities are not "determined", in the sense that they are preplanned or pre-ordained; actors are not robots. However, the organizations of the actors' orientations to situations ensures that, when all is working well, the actors themselves will wish to act in ways that might be predicted if an observer were familiar with the actors' personal systems of orientation. These acts certainly are predicted by those with whom the actors come in contact.

Thus, the utilitarian scheme of goals and means remains. Actors are the authors of their own actions. The problem of establishing the orientations of actors is essentially one of establishing the criteria by which they are liable to evaluate given objects in their field of action. This is the aspect of social action toward which Marshall, Pareto, Durkheim and Weber were pointing. Action becomes normatively oriented *via* cultural, symbolic representations that are both external to and internalized by the actor. The internal–external distinction is important. Abstracted as the cultural system, the set of symbols constituting the generalized values among men in collectivities can be said to exist outside the persons that carry them. They can be passed among persons, and they remain when individual contributors to them are no longer present. But to be important to behavior, the representations (the "culture") have to be "internal" to the actors. To have all the properties that make it seem "external" to the participants in it, it *must* be internal to them, since it is not reasonable to speak of ideas, symbols, and the like having an existence in an ontological sense.

The facts that action is normative in Parsons' theory and that it shows the impact of culture raise the problem of the nature of man as a cultural being. Obviously, there is a sense in which individual attitudes and systems of value *are* the culture; there is also a sense in which each person does not participate in the whole of the culture. Parsons tries to keep the distinction between these two senses clear by saying that the cultural system is "articulated with", or "interpenetrates" the personality of the actor.[43]

All of this is to be kept separate from Parsons' social system, which is neither the culture, nor the personality of the individual actor, but a separate "system of action".[44] That is, the social system consists of the actual components of the actions that are transmitted and received among interacting persons or collectivities. To be *social* action, it must be the non-random action of two or more actors involved in the same culture; this action is motivated in each actor according to the orientations to action that are shared between them.[45] The antecedents of this kind of theoretical action are probably seen best in Parsons' discussion of Weber's *Protestant Ethic and the Spirit of Capitalism*. Weber points out that it is the particular elements of orientation having their origins in Protestantism that fit in with the demands of capitalism. These issue in the specific system of values that is termed the "Protestant ethic". Individuals having the "ethic" are likely to design their activities, (that is, to make choices among alternatives to action), to fit the ethic in that specific kinds of economic behavior ("capitalistic" activity) will be the result. This example shows how Parsons argues it is possible to have a highly generalized cultural standard "internalized" in individuals, while not at the same time assuming that the culture specifically "determines" action for individuals.

An aspect of social life emphasized by Durkheim, and discovered in Pareto, was that persons show commitment to the normative structure they follow. This commitment is important to Parsons' system of analyzing social action, since it provides a vehicle for maintaining the voluntaristic element of action, while restricting it to certain acts aimed toward certain ends. It also raises the problem of the socialization of motivation. Parsons argues that the role (the interlinking of rights and duties associated with a status) is the basic unit of social systems.[46] A role does not exhaust the personal repertory of individual actors in the theoretical situation in which the role is involved, but it does place demands on persons from the point of view of the social system, a system of roles itself. If roles are to be enacted in a way that fits the needs of the social system as a whole, persons have to be motivated to act according to role prescriptions. Since the role is at the social system level of abstraction, in a theoretical sense, it is the meeting point of voluntaristic action and culturally prescribed demands. Persons must be induced to volunteer their actions in accordance with the demands placed by the role and articulated to the individual *via* the cultural system. These demands are worked out through a system of reciprocal expectations and duties of the role that are inherent in the structure of the role system itself. Thus, a role always implies a complimentarity of actions among two or more persons. Since cultural determinism is to be avoided, yet necessities of the system above the individual level are to be attended to, the system of roles must be engaged both to satisfy the individuals that volunteering for the role is "right" for them, and to maintain the functional role *vis-à-vis* the social system itself.[47]

The problem of how to achieve this double aspect of role behavior is solved by the socialization of motivation and by the structure of the role system itself. In a general sense, the individual takes on the standards and ideals of his group in the process of socialization.[48] That is, these become part of his personality. He is socialized so that situations in which alternatives are involved will be little or no problem for him. He will know how to act, since he will have learned criteria for making choices concerning the behaviors required of him. The summary statement of this is that the mechanism of socialization has ensured that, given alternatives, the individual will be motivated to act in accordance with cultural standards.

It is not necessary here to take up the process of socialization specifically, as long as it is understood how it is conceived by Parsons. Essentially, socialization harnesses the diffuse needs and organic desires of the individual and directs them into socially approved channels. Gradually, the individual comes to be gratified in social relationships by rewards others are capable of giving him. He is also able to reward persons in socially expected and approved ways. Once this kind of socialization has been completed, each individual role player has a part of the total conformity-maintaining mechanism under his control, since each has the capacity to reward the other.

It can be seen that, since roles involve a set of expectations and rights, each role's rights become its opposite number's duties.[49] Sanctions[50] may be brought into play be each actor because, due to the process of socialization, persons have the capability of rewarding or punishing each other. Role behavior becomes contingent upon the rewards and sanctions that pass between Actor and others. Persons will want to do those things that amount to the duties of their roles, because the persons to whom those duties are rights will hold the power of negative sanction (punishment), as well as the power to reward correct performance.[51]

This is only half the story, however. We saw that internally, individual role players come to an understanding of the roles they play and the ideals of the culture they carry. From the position developed just above, it may seem that role behavior is imposed on the role player through a system of punishments and rewards. While this is true, the individual also appreciates the roles for their own sake. That is, he wants to perform according to role prescriptions. Role playing according to the system's demands is itself internally gratifying.[52] There is a convergence, then, of the role player's desires for action with the desires of other role players. Thus, conformity as a direct means of fulfilling internal desires tends to coincide with the conditions under which the role player will be rewarded by others.

This discussion demonstrates the fine line Parsons draws between the demands of voluntarism on the one hand and cultural and social determinism on the other. Without one side or the other of this double gratification scheme (internal–external) he has worked out, his system would deteriorate into either one based on external force or one based on internal individual desires. In either case, this would throw him back into the "utilitarian dilemma".[53] Force alone would stand outside the action system *vis-à-vis* any actor, making this very similar to Hobbes' solution to the problem of order. The other side of the double gratification system alone would put Parsons squarely in the psychological determinism department, which might deny the existence and need of culture and social system abstractions altogether. It has been pointed out that the subleties of the Parsonian scheme involve matters of emphasis, rather than clear differences in statements or contradictions. This is particularly the case here. When the question is one of choice in the system involving actors and their interactions, the emphasis on one or the other side of the double gratification scheme will make all the difference.

Certainly so long as it may be supposed that actors choose the same actions voluntaristically as would be chosen for them externally, no difficulty arises. But if these two choices diverge, the question becomes one of defining whether internal or external agents for determining action are likely to win out. This internal–external duality runs through much of Parsonian theory. It is pointed up especially in his consideration of deviance as essentially voluntaristic action, and social control as imposed constraint, or in his categories of types of deviance and their paired categories of successful social control.[54]

In reviewing *The Structure of Social Action*, we saw that Parsons pays special attention to aspects of theories that supply theoretical reasons for roles being what they are in society. That is, it is one thing to say that the social system can not be arranged so that the ends of action within it are random, another to notice that ends of action tend to become identified with certain sectors of social life. It is quite another still to give an account of why actions tend to get institutionalized in the particular patterns they do. The account of how this happens thus forms a very crucial part of Parsons' theory. Up to this point, it has been suggested that Parsons can account theoretically for the role behavior of individuals, for the impact of culture on personality and on behavior itself. If we have followed Parsons this far, we have tentatively agreed that socialization can be relied upon to prepare persons for role playing by committing them to certain kinds of needs that will be gratified internally when role behavior is performed and will be attended to externally through the rewards received from other actors for correct role behavior. It would be unreasonable to stop before accounting for the roles themselves and why certain ones tend to be those which become sanctioned as well as gratifying. As with the social system itself, it will be impossible to rely on individual determination to account for the structure of roles. Similarly, it is argued that "culture" can not contain prescriptions for any roles whatever. Roles must be tied to the needs of the person as well as to the system's need to maintain itself.[55]

In accounting for the kinds of roles that Parsons sees as basic in social systems, we will be laying the groundwork for his notion of functional prerequisites of systems. The following four paragraphs outline the thinking underlying the idea of the four functional problems that are to be dealt with in due course. These four problems are adaptation, goal attainment, integration and tension management-latency.[56]

To account for roles, Parsons goes first to the basic motivational elements in role behavior. Roles are played because gratifications accrue to the individual role player. Gratifications are both external and internal to the individual. Beginning with the external, Parsons postulates that the means of gratification are inherently scarce. This postulate comes from the "scarce resources" foundation of economic theory.[57] This means that rewards in the system must be controlled, since if they were not, and rewards remained scarce, great confusion and conflict would be introduced into the system *via* unrestrained competition. Thus the system itself is seen as requiring that rewards be distributed according to some culturally established arrangement. This means that a crucial category of norms in the system will be concerned with the regulation of rewards and their distribution in the system. Roles coming specifically under this system of norms are directly associated with this functional problem.

The obverse of designating a role as helping to control the allocation of rewards in the system is designation of it as being integrative. According to Parsons, roles which pertain to the allocation of rewards have functions for the system both in terms of allocation itself, and in terms of integration, since roles concerning allocation of resources also serve to knit the system together. Without the allocative function of certain roles there would be chaos. With the allocative function, there is integration through the reduction of disruption in the system from undue competition. The role players are abiding by a system of rules which pertain to the very foundations of integrated role behavior itself—the allocation of gratifications. Thus there is a two-pronged reason why social systems have to rely upon norms (and therefore roles) that are concerned with the allocation of resources. The personality systems of actors require such norms in order to design their actions according to institutionalized expectations of rewards. Also, the system requires the same set of norms (and therefore roles), since without it, the system as a relatively stable and harmonious whole could not be maintained. Thus, there is an internal and an external reason, from the point of view of the actor, why there should be a system of norms and roles focused around the allocative-integrative aspects of social life. The allocative and the integrative dimensions therefore define together two categories of roles. These two are associated with two of the "functional problems" or functional prerequisites of social systems. If these two functional problems are not solved (as well as others to be developed below), social systems, according to Parsons' theory, could not exist. These problems are named "integration" and "goal attainment".

Also from the scarce resources postulate, it follows that no matter how well the allocative-integrative roles are performed, it is practically impossible to conceive of a system in which no strain or disruption occurs, either because of frustrated desires internal to actors, or because of failures in the system's role performances to allocate rewards appropriately. This is simply a way of saying that, given scarce resources and the need for control of the allocation of these resources, strains will occur, both for the system and for the individual. Thus, to alleviate the adverse consequences that follow from the fact that resources are limited, there needs to be a system of roles and norms focused on the problem of tension and its reduction. This role area, then, is named the "latency" or the "tension management" function. This is the necessary function both of organizing the means of reduction of tensions in the system, and maintaining value patterns over time. This will be taken up in detail in Chapter 14.

Finally, derived from the fact that to act, persons must have the energy for action, and from the fact that if there are no persons, there is no action in the social system, a very important sector of the role system is focused on the production of "means". That is, all the other role areas mentioned up to this point have been contingent upon the production of resources for the social system and for the individual. Without this, no action exists. Parsons associates this fact with the need of social systems to adapt instrumentally to their environment. The "adaptation" prerequisite thus derives directly from the fact that social systems are not conceived as passive, but are active in the sense that their ends of action require "means". The adapting social system uses energy placed at its disposal by actors playing particularly adaptive roles, from the point of view of the system.

In view of the discussion here, it seems appropriate to answer some of Parsons' critics who argue that he assumes stability and harmony in his theory.[58] He is not assuming the complete congruence of social action, role prescriptions and culturally determined ideals. The system places great emphasis on the mechanisms that deal with the disruptive results of allocating scarce resources among recipients in the system. Thus, at any one time, the working system may appear to be characterized by consensus, although Parsons does not assume consensus as a starting point.

We have seen that it is Parsons' problem to account for social order without relying on any kind of pure "determinism"—psychological, social, cultural, or biological. This does not mean, however, that he does not place heavy emphasis on each of these. On the contrary, these four aspects of life form the main concerns for Parsons, but they are concerns insofar as they may be related together systematically, not one by one. It has been pointed out that, to avoid any of the determinisms, Parsons set out to develop a scheme into which they all fit (in that they are all accounted for), but in which none has a total determining impact on behavior, at either the system or the individual level. Since each of the four aspects of determinism were seen as playing some part in the total resultant social life, they could each be seen as placing certain demands on it. These four aspects of life in terms of their demands placed upon persons and social systems and in relation to their contributions to life constitute Parsons' notion of the system problems that have to be met for life in society to go on. He argues that when a collectivity has successfully met these problems, a society has been formed and can maintain itself.[59] The integration of these kinds of determinism, and the meeting of the demands they place on social life, constitute the main outline of Parsons' notion of "system", which refers to the ways in which each of these, usually referred to as subsystems, contributes to and demands certain things from the system which involves all of them.

In *The Structure of Social Action*, Parsons documents his view that social life places demands that are understandable in terms of the biological environment, the personality, the society, and the culture. These main categories have been formalized and related to the main problems of establishing society just discussed in the following way. Since ends of action could not remain random in a collectivity, a role and norm system was implied which regulated the sector of social life concerned with the allocation of rewards available in the system. This led to concern with the integration of elements of the society in conformity with the way in which rewards were distributed. It followed that, since resources were scarce, and since priorities had to be set in terms of the appropriate ends of action, strains would be placed on the system in relation to the severity of the allocations problem. Therefore, a persistent problem for the system would be the alleviation of tensions thus created and the maintenance of the patterns of allocation and integration made necessary by the scarceness of resources in relation to wants. These problems are related back to the specific levels of analysis mentioned in relation to the subsystems of the total system—biological, personality, social and cultural.

The four main system problems just described were formalized into the following four "functional categories",[60] (1) the concern with the maintenance of the highest "governing" or controlling patterns of the system ("pattern maintenance"), (2) the internal integration of the system ("integration"), (3) the orientation to the attainment of goals in the system ("goal attainment"), and (4) adaptation to the system's environment ("adaptation").

The first category, pattern maintenance, is organized around the cultural system, since it is uniquely culture which deals only in the symbolic statements of the patterns as they are at any one time. Second, it is the social system which "contains" the actual role enactments. The interlinking nature of these roles concerns itself with the mutuality of expectations and duties, as was seen above. The social system is therefore mainly functional for the total system in terms of its "integration" of it. Third, the personality system is the abstraction which for Parsons is closest to the idea of the person. Since action for actors (usually persons) is ultimately conceived as voluntaristic, it is the person who is involved with orienting himself to the situation and acting in it. That is, goals in relation to situations are always being set by persons. It is appropriate that the "goal-attainment" problem should be organized around the personality system, since it is this system that works out the means of attaining each goal. Finally, the problem of "adaptation" to the environment is the problem of the organism to survive. While societal survival is not altogether a non-social problem, it ultimately rests on materialistic problems most associated with the maintenance of the organism itself. These relationships are illustrated in Figure 1.

Parsons has argued that functions are focused around the four areas illustrated in Figure 1. Therefore, within the voluntaristic context of actors

Functional problems of systems	Subsystems of the action system (the "interaction environments")	Material base
Pattern maintenance	Cultural system	
Integration	Social system	
Goal attainment	Personality	
Adaptation		Behavioral organism

Figure 1 The relationships between the functional problems of systems of action, the subsystems of an action system, and the material base of social life.

acting in a situation, certain guides have to be set for the development of actions which will enhance the functions of each of the areas. That is, we have already mentioned that the social, cultural and personality systems interpenetrate in that none alone is responsible for actions. The ways in which this penetration is accomplished from the cultural system, into the personality system, *via* the social system, have been formalized into the "pattern variable" scheme.[61] The pattern variables, or sets of "dilemmas" or alternatives, constitute a description of the fundamental choices that have to be made before action in a situation is possible. The interpretation of the pattern variables is particularly crucial for the problem of where to locate choice in the system, a problem which is to be examined in the following chapters where the model(s) of man in Parsons' theory are examined.

We noticed that it was imperative for Parsons to keep the interlocking nature of role enactments dependent on both an external (to the actor) contingency and an internal one. The removal of either would have necessitated psychological determinism or an extreme sociologistic position relative to the selection of actions for actors. The "dilemmas" of action must be seen both as dilemmas for the "system", in that the system requires certain actions be performed in certain ways, and "dilemmas" for the actor; insofar as action is voluntaristic, choices concerning how to act are personal to actors.

The pattern variables (alternatives describing required choices for action) have been at the center of considerable controversy about Parsons' theory.[62] From the origins of this scheme in the early 1940's,[63] it has grown and shrunk, changed the name for certain of the variables, and undergone severe criticism. Since the pattern variables have had this history, it will be useful to examine several of Parsons' treatments of them as texts from which to develop them in this book. The notion of what the pattern variables are will be discussed and they will be linked with the problem of choice in voluntaristic systems, a basic concern of this book.[64]

It has been emphasized that because of the nature of social action, choices have to be made concerning acts. These choices fall into analytical categories, according to Parsons. Choices in each one of the categories have to be made before any action is possible. The choices necessary fall into one of two general types. They are either choices about how the objects in the social world are to be categorized by the actor, or choices about what attitude the actor himself will take toward objects. The first set of choices Parsons calls the "modality set";[65] it deals with how the objects themselves will be viewed. The second set of choices, the "orientation set",[66] concerns the attitudes of the actor himself to the objects as they are. These choices are based on Parsons' model of the social act. Before action can occur and have meaning to the actor, the objects of action must be observed and categorized according to the nature of the object itself, the actor must assume a certain attitude toward the object, and he must decide whether or not to act in the ways available to him in the situation.

These same choices are required at the social system level as well. The roles that "ought" to be played from the viewpoint of the functional necessities of social systems have certain requirements that can be formalized into the same pattern variables.[67] Parsons brings these two sets of choices and requirements together, as we have seen. The actor becomes willing to volunteer action which fits in with the demands made by the social system itself. Thus internally motivated action on the part of the actor tends to coincide with externally required action (from the actor's point of view.) Thus as Bales points out in his discussions of small groups as systems,[68] some persons fall into specific roles which appear to be very functional for the system as a whole. The "expressive leader" is an example of this kind of "volunteered" role behavior which is also, in the sense employed here, demanded by the social system for its survival.

In the "orientation" set of choices concerning how the actor will view the objects, the pattern variables are, "specificity-diffuseness" and "affectivity-affective neutrality". Beginning with the "orientation set", Parsons argues that the minimum orientations an actor needs for action are:

1) *whether to take an "affective" or "neutral" attitude toward the object.*[69] A basic element of family relations is affectivity, whereas a basic element in the relationship of professional to client is neutrality. The theoretical meaning here lies in how long the actor ought to delay gratifications in order to realize benefits. In families, gratifications are usually emphasized in the short run (affectivity), whereas professional relationships usually provide the "pay-off" after long delay.

2) *whether to take a "specific" or "diffuse" attitude toward the object.*[70] This dichotomy indicates the individual's dilemma of whether to consider the object in relation to specific aspects of it, or in relation to its totality of attributes. We would expect the normal actor to take specific attitudes toward business associates and diffuse one toward his family members.

Before introducing the "modality set" of pattern variables, which deals with objects' categorizations, it will be useful to see how the "orientation set" is associated with the social system level of generalization and the system problems.[71] It has been pointed out that Parsons considers the pattern variables to be associated with the basic problems of actors in making choices for action. They thus have an individual level meaning. They are also associated with the four system problems discussed above in the following way. When an affectively neutral attitude is combined with one of "specificity" toward an object, the combination is appropriate for attitudes of "interest in instrumental utilization".[72] In plain language, this means that the objects are being viewed by the actor as appropriate for his *use* in relation to a goal which he wants to achieve. This is associated with the production of "means" for the system of roles as a whole, and therefore an appropriate set of attitudes toward the object for the "adaptation function". If the attitude remains specifically trained on one or a few attributes of the object, but the decision for immediate gratification is made ("affectivity"), then the set of the two pattern variables in this combination is correct for the "goal attainment function", the second of the four functional problems. This is so because it is in the "attainment" of a goal that gratifications are realized. Thus "affectivity" is the correct attitude toward an object considered as a "specific" goal.

If "diffuseness" is selected as characteristic of the actor's attitude toward the object, as well as "affectivity", the function of "integration" is served best, since the object is being oriented to in terms of gratification, and in relation to its totality of attributes—it is thus "integrated" into the system containing actor and object. If "diffuseness" and "neutrality" are selected by actor, his attitudes toward the object are appropriate to the "pattern maintenance" function, since the individual's diffuse view of the whole object is combined with a long term commitment to interaction with it, thereby maintaining an interaction pattern over time.

The way in which the first two pattern variables, those concerned with how (specificity-diffuseness) and for how long (affectivity-affective neutrality) to hold attitudes, are manipulated by the actor has considerable relevance to the social system's maintenance as a functioning whole. The way the actor sees his role in terms of the pattern variables appropriate to attitudes partially determines the social system problem that will be most associated with the actor's performance. Thus, there is again the double emphasis on the actor as volunteer of action and the actor as functionary in service of the system's needs. The problem of which level makes the choice for action, and how the choice could become a problem within this theory, is again observed.

Concerning the "modality set" of pattern variables ("performance-quality" and "universalism-particularism"), the problem is not one of the actor's attitudes toward the object, but of defining the object itself.[73] Taking "performance-quality" first, the dilemma is whether to evaluate the social object according to its own attributes or for its attainments. Thus an attitude characterized by "quality" concerns the object's "being", while "performance" evaluates the object in relation to its competences or attainments. In the dilemma of "universalism-particularism", the problem for the actor is whether or not to evaluate the object objectively. As Parsons put it, this dichotomy concerns

the criteria for the eligibility of services in a functional role. The criteria for eligibility of the services of a physician was to be sick, which is defined as an objectively determinable condition which "might happen to anyone" (universalism). On the other hand, the obligations of kinship applied only to persons standing in a particular pre-existing relationship to the actor.[74]

As with the "orientation set" of pattern variables, these two types of dilemmas concerning how to evaluate objects in the actor's perview also articulate with the four system problems.[75] If objects are evaluated universalistically for their performance, they are objects of "utility", and therefore fit to be utilized by the actor. This utilization of objects for their value is appropriate for the "adaptation" function. If objects are evaluated particularistically for their performance, they are "objects of cathexis" and fulfill "consumatory needs" for the actor. In this case they fit into the "goal attainment" function, since certain attributes of objects are associated with actor's goals ("cathected") in related to "what the objects can do". If objects are evaluated according to their "quality" and "particularistically", they are "objects of identification" for the actor. Actor is viewing certain objects in relation to their "being", not necessarily in relation to what they do or are capable of doing for Actor. Roles defined this way fill needs of "integration" of the social system. Finally, if objects are evaluated "universalistically" in terms of "quality", they are not objects of identification, since identification can occur only with a particular object, but they are objects of "generalized respect", and the associated role pertains to the functional problem of "pattern maintenance".

In discussing the pattern variables, it has become clear that they come to form the meeting ground of the individual actor and the demands of the system. In one way, they formalize the choices actors must make to evaluate and relate to objects before meaningful action can occur. Certainly, without joining Parsons' critics concerning whether the pattern variables he advocates are the only ones or the right ones, it does seem reasonable to agree with him in principle that they do define important aspects of the way in which a voluntaristic actor must go about cognizing and evaluating his world. When the emphasis is placed on the actor performing these functions for himself, the system Parsons shows us seems very voluntaristic indeed.

The pattern variables are also associated with the functional problems of the social system, as has been shown. When they are seen from the point of view of the social system, they seem to be criteria for defining roles to be filled by actors who in general do what the system "tells" them to do.

We have seen Parsons argue that the nature of social interaction accounts for both of these possibilities at once. The actor comes to see his desires for action as identical with the demands placed on him by the system. But what of the assumptions about the nature of man under these conditions? Can Parsons show us a set of assumptions on which such a happy union of man and social order can be based theoretically? It is true that the system makes demands for *roles*, not persons. However, this does not eliminate the problem. In reciprocal fashion, the person places demands on the system that are not abstractable in ways similar to the way role is used in social system terms. If the system requires only roles, the actors filling those roles (when actors are persons) are *total* persons. Thus the interchange between the system and the individual actor is not at the same level of abstraction. Therefore, it is relevant to ask, what assumptions about the theoretical person are made by the theory as a whole from the system point of view? Similarly, from the voluntaristic point of view, what are the kinds of systems that the theoretical person can fit into? Parsons argues that system demands and volunteering tend to coincide in identical action. It has never been determined whether the assumptions about man on which this solution is based are compatible. The assumptions concerned can conveniently be organized similarly to the way in which the pattern variables are formulated—in terms of choices.

In regard to any given act, where is it reasonable to believe that choice actually lies? It might be admissible to speak in general terms about requirements of the system, without seeming to violate the voluntaristic element of action. Similarly, it seems possible to formulate general schemes about voluntaristic action without running afoul of social necessity. But when it comes to the problem of the unitary act, that is, the actual dilemmas involved in the formulation of a single act in terms of alternatives available to the actor and in terms of the requirements of the system itself, it seems natural to ask, "Which chooses"? Should the actor be seen as the agent of choice, emphasizing the voluntaristic; or should "the system" be seen as the ultimate agent of choice, emphasizing the case in which the actor is more the agent for the system than the volunteer of action? This question is a logical one as well as a substantive one. It is logical in that the answer "both choose the same" is only admissible under conditions of complete conformity; in this case it is purely a logical question, since there could be no data which would separate the two interpretations. If deviance exists in the system, the question becomes substantive, since it is answerable in terms of motivation, and hence, voluntarism or determinism.

When emphasis is on the voluntaristic, a well developed and fairly specific model of the human actor will be evident as the basis from which the argument is made. When the emphasis is on determinism, the assumptions under which determinism obtains will compose a different picture of the model of man. Perhaps the models are comparable or compatible; however, it does not seem that both sets of assumptions can remain operative simultaneously in the theory. If they do, divergent schemes for explanation of behavior exist within the same system of theory. This situation permits the application of whichever scheme seems to "fit" best, while only lip service is paid to the other.

CHAPTER 13

Voluntaristic social organization in Parsons' theory and the voluntaristic model of man

It has been suggested that Parsons appears to have two models of man implicit in his general theorizing, one of which comes into play according to the context of action or the level of analysis. These models do not appear to be so different that it would be legitimate to call them contradicting or incompatible. Nevertheless, it does seem that the two shade off from differences in emphasis to differences in kind. In this chapter, the model emphasizing voluntarism will be spelled out in detail as it is built up around the idea of the social act. Since the previous chapter of this paper gave a general description of Parsons' theoretical scheme, it will now be possible to become specific about the connections of the theoretical actor to his system in terms of voluntarism. The process of theoretically connecting the actor to the scheme of action will uncover the model of man assumed by Parsons in heavily voluntaristic action. We will see that when voluntarism is emphasized, normative order is given less attention. To begin, it will be well to follow Parsons very closely, so that his meanings can be interpreted later with the confidence that we have understood him.

Action is defined as behavior

oriented to the attainment of ends or goals or other anticipated states of affairs. It takes place in situations. . . . [involving] expenditure of energy or effort[76]

and is motivated and normatively regulated. Each action is the action of an actor. We will be concerned in this part only with the analytical picture of the motivated actor in the cases when this is a human being.[77] The fact that collectivities may be treated as actors does not reverse the fact that persons are treated as actors, too.

Action takes place in situations in which the actor is but one element. The other elements of situations, from the actor's point of view, are *objects*.[78] These may be other actors, or physical or cultural objects. The objects of the situation become cathected (wanted or not wanted)[79] and they therefore take on significances for the actor. This is the sense in which the utilitarian means–ends scheme is at the basis of Parsonian thinking. In utilitarianism, the actor relates to his objects as they are relevant to him as ends, or useful means to the achievement of greater ends. All objects in the situation are cathected; otherwise, they are irrelevant and thus not *in* the situation of action as it is defined by the actor.

All action is motivated. The ultimate source of energy in the action scheme is under the influence of the cathexes established toward the objects in the situation. A system of "orientations" is developed toward the objects in the situation based on choices formalized in the pattern variable scheme. The orientations are in turn established in systems of action that are abstractable at different levels. Two of these, social systems and personalities, are

conceived as modes of organization of motivated action (social systems are systems of motivated action organized about relations of actors to each other; personalities are systems of motivated action organized about living organisms.) Cultural systems, on the other hand, are systems of symbolic patterns.[80]

A social system involves the process of interaction of two or more actors in a situation in which action is interdependent and in some sense a function of collective goal orientations or common values and a consensus of cognitive expectations. A personality system is a system of action that comprises the interconnections of action of a single individual organized around needs integrated in a non-random fashion.

A cultural system

is a system which has the following characteristics: the system is constituted neither by the organization of interactions nor by the organization of the actions of a single actor (as such), but rather, by the organization of the values, norms, and symbols which *guide the choices made by actors and which limit the types of interaction which may occur among actors.*[81]

Based only on Parsons' view of situations, actors, and action, it is possible to begin building the model. Parsons is concerned with the organization of elements as much as the elements themselves. The human actor is conceived as an organization of elements of the action system appropriate to the personality level. Man is not conceived as the depository of a random variety of drives, wants or propensities. Rather, he is the determinate organization system which unifies these things into a working whole. The emphasis on motivated action points up Parsons' ultimate dependence on individual psychology. The energy for action comes ultimately from the body itself, but the social individual is the one who has successfully oriented this energy toward action organized around a system of needs.[82] It is already possible to see the role that needs will play in the model of man in social and cultural contexts. Needs are to be regulated, and it is the fact that a basic system of needs exists that makes socially appropriate action possible. Such action is a result of the harnessing of these needs in action volunteered toward socially appropriate goals.

It is important to point out that in this model, Parsons is emphasizing the voluntaristic aspects of action. Thus we see his picture of the cultural system as the "guide" to choices *made by actors*. It would seem that he would answer the question of which system chooses action in a given situation by saying that choice is always with the individual actor. Thus he says that in the cultural system are organized the "cultural elements which guide choices of concrete actors".[83] This picture of culture is one of a highly general system of values, beliefs, and symbols that give nothing specific to the actor in terms of directives. The emphasis lies on the categorization of objects and attitudes toward them and the resultant evaluations that lead to voluntary acts.

Basically the thinking seems to go in the following way. Since the fundamental elements of action systems have been identified and theoretically accounted for in terms of functional necessities and system problems, the same fundamental categories of analysis ought to apply at whatever system level is being discussed. Since the personality is considered a system of organized action elements, it faces the same system problems as any action system (adaptation, goal attainment, integration, and pattern maintenance). These categories of functional necessity are associated with basic needs of the personality as a system. We see in this Parsons' ever-present emphasis on the relation of man to the social order. His solution to the problem of how the two relate does not make one a mirror image of the other in the voluntaristic model.[84]

The system problems were identified as adaptation, goal attainment, integration and pattern maintenance. Just as a social system must solve problems in each of these areas to remain stable and functioning, so the personality of the individual must also solve the problems in these areas. The four system problems are not necessarily specific substantive ones; they are, rather, areas for theoretical concern for every system of action. As we saw above in the discussion of the pattern variables, in order for action to take place, the actor has to make choices concerning the objects in the situation. The kinds of choices lead to the division of the pattern variables into two classes—modalities of the objects themselves, and orientations or attitudes of the actor to the objects. These are related to the basic problems of the actor: (1) conceptualize the object; answer the question, "What is the object"? and (2) cathect the object; answer the question, "What does the object mean"? From these two derives the third aspect of action which incorporates the outcomes of these two—evaluation of the object as an element with which to interact in the system. Associated with the object category, or the concern with the question of what the object is, were the pattern variables, "universalism-particularism" and "quality-performance". These same pattern variables define the dimensions of what Parsons has called "performance values" in the personality, and are associated with basic need dispositions of the individual as a social actor.[85] (See Figure 2.) We see, then, that the fundamental problems of how to treat objects are associated with fundamental needs of personalities. These two sets of considerations are related via the pattern variable scheme. *Universalistic evaluations of objects based on performance* yield a concern with achievement. *Universalism* and *quality* point toward ascription. *Particularistic* evaluations of objects based on *performance* are associated with appreciations, whereas *particularistic* evaluations combined with evaluation based on *quality* yield concern for moral integration. These four cross-classifications of the object modality pattern variables define the four areas of "performance values" as they relate to personalities. Parsons' next step is to associate achievement with "adaptation", appreciation with "pattern maintenance", moral integration with "integration" and ascription with "pattern maintenance".

	Universalism	Particularism
Performance	"Achievement"	"Appreciations"
Quality	"Ascription"	"Moral integration"

Figure 2 Classification of "performance values" of the human personality derived from a cross classification of the "object modality" pattern variables

Concerning the attitudinal side of the pattern variables, four similar categories, classifications of the attitudinal values, can be generated in the following way. *Specificity* and *affective* attitudes yield an attitudinal value on "response", *specificity* and *neutral* attitudes yield value on "approval". *Diffuse* and *neutral* attitudes relate especially to "esteem", and *diffuse* and *affective* attitudes to "acceptance" as an attitudinal value. (See Figure 3.)

The values developed from the object side of the pattern variables and those developed from the attitudinal side are associated in the following

	Affective neutrality	Affectivity
Specificity	"Approval"	"Response"
Diffuseness	"Esteem"	"Acceptance"

Figure 3 Classifications of "attitudinal values" of the human personality derived from a cross classification of the "orientation set" of pattern variables.

way. We have just seen that values discovered in the object set of the pattern variables become "performance values". They are associated with the actors' relationships to the objects as they are, i.e., based upon his cognitions of them. Those discovered in the attitudinal set define the "sanction values" associated with the actor's attitudes toward the objects.[86] Thus *achievement* as a performance value is associated with *approval* as the appropriate sanction value. *Appreciation* as a performance is associated with *response* as a proper sanction. *Ascription* as a performance seems curious, but it is indeed an objective part of life, and Parsons associates it with *esteem* as the proper sanction, which seems reasonable. *Moral integration* as a performance is associated with *acceptance*. These four pairs of variables define what Parsons called the "need-dispositions". They are based on the needs of the personality as a system to survive *via* cognizing, cathecting, evaluating and voluntaristically acting in a situation. (See Figure 4.) This is the sense in which the needs of the personality are reasonable and logical for Parsons. The argument has been that systems have basic needs which must be fulfilled if the system is to survive. Since personalities are conceived as systems, they have needs that must be fulfilled if they are to be functioning systems, capable of social action as persons. The needs of personality systems must be associated with the fundamental problems involved in the categorization of objects and cathexis. This is accomplished by making use of the pattern variable scheme in the voluntaristic context. Therefore Parsons seems on good ground logically, if the assumptions under which he treats the concept of system itself are accepted.

"Performance value	"Attitudinal value	Related need-disposition
"Achievement"	"Approval"	"Adequacy"
"Ascription"	"Esteem"	"Conformity"
"Moral integration"	"Acceptance"	"Security"
"Appreciation"	"Response"	"Nurturance"

Figure 4 Derivation of the need-dispositions of the human personality from Parsons' "performance values" and "attitudinal values".[87]

The performance values and the sanction values are combined in Parsons' notion of the "need-dispositions", as shown in Figure 4.[88] These need-dispositions are: *adequacy* (achievement–approval), *nurturance* (appreciation–response), *conformity* (ascription–esteem), and *security* (acceptance–moral integration.) These four need–dispositions give rise to a set of generalized goals for personalities. (See Figure 5.)[89] "Success goals" are based on

Need-disposition	Generalized goals	Personality's functional problem
"Adequacy"	"Success goals	Adaptation
"Nurturance"	"Hedonistic goals"	Goal attainment
"Conformity"	"Accomplishment goals"	Pattern maintenance
"Security"	"Satisfaction goals"	Integration

Figure 5 Classification of generalized goals of the human personality and their relationships to the personality's functional problems as an action system.

the need–disposition of adequacy. This is most closely associated with the personality system need of adaptation. As a subsystem of the total personality, success goals can be thought of as systems themselves, involving all the needs of systems in general. These are all associated with the personality's need to be directed outwardly toward the world to which it adapts. Similarly the "nurturance" need-disposition gives rise to what Parsons terms the hedonistic class of goals. These are essentially the giving and receiving of pleasure. This is associated with the goal attainment subsystem of the personality system, since the sanction for the giving of pleasure is in every case the receiving of pleasure. The "conformity" need-disposition is generalized by Parsons to give rise to "accomplishment goals". We saw that this need disposition was identified by the linking of the performance value of ascription and the sanction value of esteem. Thus the "accomplishment goals" articulate with the tension management-pattern maintenance requirement of personality systems. Finally, the "security" need-disposition, which is associated with the need of personality systems to be integrated, gives rise to Parsons' "satisfaction goals". These are: intrinsically satisfying performance, supportive activity, and acceptance of status. All have intrinsically satisfying qualities and express them.

Since the complexities of Parsons' terminology and the economy of presentation here may have done violence to the development of the idea of "need-dispositions" and the idea of the personality as an action system, it might be well to recapitulate and generalize the discussion at this point. For Parsons, the personality system is the system "comprising the interconnections of the actions of individual actors". The actor's actions are organized by a structure of "need-dispositions".[90] Just as the actions of a plurality of actors can not be randomly assorted but must have a determinate organization of compatibility or integration, so the actions of the single actor have a determinate organization of compatibility or integration with one another. Thus it seems that, in Parsons' voluntaristic model, the picture of the personality system is almost identical to the picture of man. It is not completely identical, since the personality system is the product of socialization; this assumes certain propensities and abilities that are not discussed in the context of needs and need-dispositions. These are mainly derived from Parsons' understanding of Freud's theory of the person as an energy system.[91] Leaving these aside, it is possible to see fairly clearly Parsons' picture of the individual personality in the voluntaristic model.

Individuals who have been correctly socialized can be conceived as having personality systems. As such, they exhibit the same general features as other action systems. These features are based on the notion of functional requirements, which are implicit in the definition of system itself. A system is that which fulfills the requirements of a system. These requirements have been accounted for as follows. Since the system is self-directed, it must have goals; a part of the system is concerned with the goals of the whole. It must be concerned with its own adaptation to the environment in which it operates. If the system is to be goal oriented and active in adaptation, it must have mechanisms for insuring that the system operates as a whole and maintains itself over time as a unit. These requirements lead to the last two functional requirements of systems, integration and pattern maintenance.

To continue the recapitulation: individual persons, to operate in a world of objects, have to evaluate the objects in their world. To do this they must answer for themselves two questions about objects and the relations of the objects to themselves. These questions are: "What is the object"? and "What does the object mean"? These two questions divide the concerns of the person into the objective categorization of the object (cognition), and the attitudinal categorization of it (cathexis). In order to have a basis on which to answer the two fundamental questions, the person must have a set of attitudinal values and a set of object values which are based directly upon the needs of the person as an action system. It is from this distinction as well that the double nature of the interpersonal bond emerges. Other is treated as an object, and as such he is categorized both as an object and for his meaning to Actor. Directly from this emerges the fact that persons perform together in role relationships for two reasons—they objectively know that certain rewards are contingent on certain performances, and internally they have favourable attitudes toward acting in certain ways.

Based on the attitudinal and object categorizations that must take place for action to occur, and the functional requirements of systems of action in general, Parsons is able to derive the need-dispositions of human actors (persons.) These are the needs of adequacy, nurturance, conformity, and security.

Parsons' next step is to establish that the general system needs and the personality need-dispositions of human actors are articulated together in the following way: (1) adaptation and adequacy need-disposition, (2) goal attainment and nurturance need-disposition, (3) integration and security need-disposition, and (4) pattern maintenance and conformity need-disposition. These four groupings define four major areas of goals which persons are said to have, and which derive directly from the four system problems and the categorization of objects and of attitudes toward them. These goals are: "success goals" (adaptation), "hedonistic goals" (goal attainment), "satisfaction goals" (integration), and "accomplishment goals" (pattern maintenance.)

So far in this chapter, the substantive as well as the methodological outlines of Parsons' voluntaristic model of man have been set out. It is now possible to see that the assumptions on which Parsons set his voluntaristic model of man derive from three sources, the roots of which were developed in *The Structure of Social Action*. The three sources are the "precipitate" of utilitarian theory and its implications; the notion of system and system needs, so prominent in Parsonian thought; and the pattern variables as they formalize dilemmas in a voluntaristic system of action.

From utilitarian thought, Parsons has chosen to keep the idea of action as means to the gaining of ends. We have seen that utilitarianism poses the problem of how the actor establishes the way in which he is to treat social objects (or non-social ones), i.e., what are his goals? This led Parsons to a division of the basic problem into questions of how to treat an object in the social sphere and how to regard it attitudinally. These are basic to the formulation of action on the utilitarian model. For a man to act toward an object, to treat it as an end or as an intermediate end toward some greater end, he must first categorize the object in some known system of objects. That is, he must cognize it; he must know what it is. Knowing what it is, he must determine what it means to him. That is, he must come to some attitude toward it. These two activities lead to the evaluation of the object and finally to the action of the voluntaristic actor toward it.

Thus two major assumptions about the nature of man arise from Parsons' use of utilitarian thought. Man is a cognizer, having the ability to relate specific objects to categories according to the attributes of the objects. He is also basically emotional, since before he can act, he must establish a cathexis with the object of action. The use of the term "emotional" in this context is meant to connote an analytical difference between the acts of recognizing objects for what they are and developing attitudes toward the objects for what they mean to the actor. Based on these two mechanisms, the voluntaristic actor makes evaluations of what action ought to occur in the situation and acts accordingly.

With the above assumptions about the nature of voluntaristic action accounted for, it is possible to move to the nature of the person as a system

of action. These considerations imply the four functional necessities on which
Parsons' thinking about systems at any level is based. Since the personality
is to be conceived as a system, these four necessities give rise to four specific
kinds of problems that must be solved on the personality level. These are the
adaptation, goal attainment, integration and pattern maintenance problems.
In order that the personality operate as a unit, it must satisfy the requirements placed on it by the functional problems of systems in general. As we
saw above, these four problems are solved by Parsons' identification of the
four areas of need-dispositions and the associated goals. Thus the personality
which is functioning as a system in the Parsonian sense is fulfilling goals
satisfactorily in each of the four goal areas of the personality: success, hedonism, accomplishment, and satisfaction. These are goal areas based on the
need-dispositions of adequacy, nurturance, conformity and security. These
four aspects of personalities, which derive from Parsons' notion of systems in
general, constitute four more assumptions about the nature of man in
Parsons' voluntaristic scheme.

We saw that the four areas of goals for personalities were developed via
the use of the pattern variables, especially as they related back to the basic
division between viewing the object for what it means and for what it is.
Thus in the voluntaristic context, the pattern variables should be interpreted
as formalizations of the dilemmas *faced by actors* in situations. Actors, in this
model, have choice and the ability to exercise it.

Parsons has taken over the Freudian idea of internalization or intro-
jection as a fruitful concept which helps to account for the nature of the fit
between the voluntaristic man, the social system, and the culture it carries.
Above, we outlined some assumptions about man as Parsons sees him—a
socialized animal who is capable of playing voluntaristic roles in social life.
In this voluntaristic model, these goal areas and need-dispositions are the
end product of the process of internalization. In the context of voluntarism,
we see the picture of culture Parsons is presenting. True enough, the culture
is seen as limiting and setting standards for action of individuals. But in this
model there is no talk of the exact nature of role prescriptions for each
individual relative to situations in which he will be involved. Culture and
norms in this model are exceedingly general and abstract. While voluntaristic
action is limited by culture, culture and normative order are not oppressive.
Rather, the essence of the normative order is its constraint of action within
very broad limits. The voluntarism of individuals may thus be seen as being
bought in return for extreme generality and wide limits where culture and the
normative order are concerned.

Any one component of the personality Parsons has identified does not
determine action by itself. Here again we see the emphasis on voluntarism.
The elements of the personality constitute the motivational categories in

which action can be conceptualized, but each of the goal areas is involved in every action. The specific ways in which they are put together by each actor define the ways in which he will act. That is, the basic aspects of this motivational, voluntaristic man have to be mobilized and organized each time action occurs. The ways in which the actor organizes them determine the action that is the result. The organization of these is partly a matter of culture, but it is more a matter of choice for individuals.

Parsons' analogy of the "keyboard" is apt, for it points out how the culture and the personality can be tied together, yet be separate and not deducible from each other.

A given role orientation is a "tune" played on [the keyboard of the need-dispositions]. Many different tunes will strike the same notes but in different combinations, and some notes will be altogether omitted from some tunes. Some will be louder than others. The "pattern" of the tune is not deducible from the keyboard, but it is impossible to play a tune for which the requisite notes are not provided on the keyboard. The composer's standards of a "good tune" are the analogue of the social value patterns, while the keys and their arrangement are the analogue of the genealogical tree of the need-disposition system.[92]

The picture of voluntaristic action comes out clearly in the analogy of the keyboard in which the actor "composes" the tune. The "tune" is composed according to standards of "goodness", but the composer is *not* conceived as the performer of tunes who reads sheet music provided by the culture, striking each note according to the instructions given by the culture in the score. If this were the case, the involved nature of the personality would be irrelevant, since the person would be the functionary for the culture and not in need of a personality system of his own at all. It is interesting also that Parsons chooses in the analogy of the keyboard to speak of "role orientations", rather than roles. It seems that the voluntaristic model and the implied model of man, in all its complexity and highly developed aspects, does not permit Parsons himself to speak comfortably of specific roles. When reasoning from the individual actor toward the social system in levels of generality, the assumptions of the voluntaristic model limit the applicability of the idea of specific roles. Thus the specificity of the theory breaks off at the level of role orientations; there is little suggestion of specific roles and their relationships to specific actors in situations.

CHAPTER 14

Deterministic social organization in Parsons' theory and the deterministic model of man

In Chapter 12, it was shown that the pattern variable scheme is related both to the social system level of generalization and to the personality level. In this sense, the pattern variables can be seen as the linking concepts defining the ways in which the two levels of generalization are related. They can also be seen as the instruments with which the structures of personality and social system can be analyzed separately. In Chapter 13, the voluntaristic emphasis in Parsons' writings was considered. In these terms, the pattern variables formalize the choices that actors make in the course of social action in situations composed of the actors and related social and non-social objects. The emphasis is clearly on the actor as author of actions. The pattern variables are the scheme Parsons offers for understanding the kinds of dilemmas the actor faces each time action is called for.

In this chapter, the other emphasis in Parsons' work will be considered.[93] Specifically, the viewpoint will be that of the social system and its unique requirements for survival. Whereas in the previous chapter the personality was seen as a system giving rise to a model of man, this chapter will focus on the social system into which actors must be fit so that their actions somehow contribute to the on-going nature of the system of action as a whole. Where choice in the previous chapter was found to lay mainly with the actor, in this chapter choice will be found to lay mainly with the system of action among actors. This interpretation of the problem of choice will be shown to derive from a distinct use of the pattern variables. Whereas the pattern variables in relation to the personality served to tie the actor's requirements for cognition and cathexis (and thus evaluation) to the needs of the personality as a system, we will see now how the pattern variables are employed to tie the requirements of the interaction system to the roles that must be played if the social system is to remain. The latter use of the pattern variable scheme will be seen to entail a model of man based on his capacity as role player rather than his capacity as cognizer and cathecter. The extent to which these models of man are compatible will be discussed in due course.

The scheme presented so far in this Part has dealt with Parsons' concern for motivated action, focusing on the kinds and variations of problems that go into it. The resultant theory was very voluntaristically oriented in that it went a long way toward categorizing the problems of action and the types of solutions from which actors theoretically could be expected to choose. The emphasis was on motivational aspects of the system of action rather than on the structural aspects of it.

When these structural aspects are dealt with explicitly, we see the narrowing of Actor's alternatives for action. The limits of voluntarism become increasingly tight as the assumptions about systems in general are applied to the system of interaction, rather than to the personality as a system. We will see that as Parsons turns his attention to problems of interaction, i.e., to the social system level, he is able to afford less voluntarism for actors in situations. In the voluntaristic model, situations were characterized as placing problems before the actor for his solution. As the situations become linked with the interaction process as a system in "moving equilibrium",[94] situations come to be characterized as placing certain demands on the actors, in order that the system into which the situations are fit may survive. This change of emphasis from motivational to structural concerns calls for a different application of the pattern variable scheme. In the new use, the pattern variables appear as prescriptions for patterns of action rather than formalizations of dilemmas for actors.

To begin working through this aspect of Parsonian thought, it is necessary to go back to the idea of the four system problems and view them from the vantage point of the interaction system as a whole. These four are the problems of adaptation, goal attainment, integration and latent pattern maintenance. These constitute the theoretical subsystems of the total system, in that solutions must be found which satisfy the requirements of each of these main problems if the system is to remain.

These four problem areas can be seen as structural aspects of systems of roles. That is, roles must either have particular relevance to one or more of these four areas, or they must change over a period of time such that at any one time, they can be visualized as being in a state of satisfying the requirements of the system in any one area, or being in a state of transition toward satisfaction of one problem and away from relevance to another problem. This latter conception of the four system problems is used by Parsons in his consideration of social action as a process.[95] The four main problems of systems define the main concerns of systems of action in their totality, without respect to time. But when time is introduced, it is possible to conceive of action as a process which moves through each of four main phases. These phases are associated with the four system problems in that during any one phase, a role system can be theoretically thought to be maximizing its potential for solution in that phase, at the price of inattention to problems of the other three phases. This is a relative conception of phase movement, since no phase is conceived as taking up the whole potential of a system to mobilize its resources in the solution of a single problem. This conception of phase movement in relation to energy and its expenditure is related to Parsons' principle that any expenditure of energy or "resources" implies that the same energy can not be applied toward a goal different from the one toward which it was initially applied. This corresponds to the notion of the conservation of energy in physics and the idea of the distribution of scarce resources in economics. As we already have seen, the principle of scarce resources led Parsons to consideration of the normative regulation of the expenditure of energy in social systems. It has a similar issue in the discussion of phase movement.

Some further preliminary points ought to be made concerning the notion of phase movement and the four system problems as phases in a process described in structural terms.

Every system is conceived to be made up of two or more units or members which interact with each other.[96]

These units are roles, played by actors.[97] Insofar as actors "play" roles, this means that the attention will have to be focused on how the system mobilizes the units (roles) in the service of it survival. This in turn raises the question of voluntarism in a new context. In what way is voluntaristic action possible in the context of system demands?

The system being spoken of here is the system of interlocking roles and sanctions. Whereas in the previous chapter we treated the person as a system in the sense that the general scheme of the needs of systems was applied to the person, in this chapter we will be concerned with the ways in which the general notion of system applies to the next higher level of generality—the interlocking roles that constitute a system of roles, i.e., a social system.

The social system is conceived as being imbedded in an environment and having the ability to adapt to its environment and absorb parts of it into itself. The system may change: in fact, the essence of the notion of system *is* change, not stability. If the problems of systems may be conceptualized as remaining the same over time, the character of the system, its actual constitution, does not stay the same. However, change in social systems can occur only through the interaction of its member units—through the interaction of its constitutive roles, played ultimately by persons. This emphasis on the interaction system should clarify the meanings of the system problems, as they apply on this level of generalization. Adaptation refers to the adaptation of the *system* to its environment, which is achieved via the interaction of the system's member units. When Parsons speaks of adaptation on the social system level, he is referring to the interaction of member units viewed from the perspective of that interaction's contribution to solution of the *system's* problem of adaptation to *its* situation.

This level of system analysis raises a serious problem for Parsons, one which is basic to the concerns of this book. When one is dealing in system terms at one level of generality (i.e., the personality system or social system level), it is almost impossible to treat the units of that system, the constitutive members of it, as other than undifferentiated entities that are mere functionaries.

Thus we saw that in Parsons' treatment of the person as a system of action having an organized personality, the personality was broken down into its constitutive units. These were the need-dispositions. Once this was accomplished, it was possible for Parsons to theoretically put these units together to build the system (in this case, the personality) in terms of the units he had discovered in the application of the system needs to personality. Similarly, when Parsons turns to the treatment of social interaction as a system, he is able to be very analytical about properties of the system, but he is only able to derive the units of that system from the requirements it places on its incumbent units for *its* survival. Thus, when Parsons deals at the social system level, he is almost forced by the mode of analysis to abandon concern with the individual (the model of man) in favor of treating "roles" as the system-constituting units at the social system level.[98]

This raises the problem which is the focus of this paper—of the ways in which the assumptions and theoretical derivations about the nature of man can be fit in with the notion of action as occurring in social systems. This leads to the conception of role (and by implication, the role player) as a "particle" to be analyzed for the ways in which it acts toward the maintenance of the social system over time.

We saw in Chapter 12 that the pattern variables are associated with each of the four system problems in particular ways. For instance, it was shown that Parsons considers the universalistic side of "universalism-particularism" and the specific side of "specificity-neutrality" to be the most appropriate to the system need of adaptation. This kind of thinking is enlarged upon in this chapter. We will see that the object or modality set of pattern variables is combined with the orientation set to form a complement of specifications relative to the functional problem faced by social systems during any one phase. When the phases are treated simply as the four system problems, without regard to phase movement, it will be seen that each system problem implies a set of demands placed upon role players. Insofar as roles contribute to the maintenance of the social system (that is, to the solutions of the system problems), roles have an explicit set of demands for action built into them which may be expressed in the pattern variables. In this connection, we see that norms become prescriptions of how one ought to act in a given situation, rather than guides to making choices, as in the voluntaristic model. The upshot of viewing the pattern variables from the perspective of the social system problems is the conception of the pattern variables as a means for expressing the social systems' demands upon actors. They do this via the specification of which attributes of possible roles are compatible with the needs of the social system. This emphasis on the pattern variables as expressions of demands is markedly different from the conception of them as the formalizations of choices for actors.

We will now set forth separately the four phases through which systems may be conceived to move in terms of the pattern variables most appropriate to these phases. This will establish the fact that Parsons sees one side or the other of each pattern variable as most appropriate to the solution of specific kinds of social problems.

Taking adaptation first, we will discuss Parsons' view of the nature of efficient adaptive activity.[99] Successful adaptation must involve an accommodation of the system to the demands of "reality". In this sense, reality is somehow problematic to the system; the notion of adaptation implies demands placed on the system from the outside and flexibility on the part of the systems so that they can adapt. These demands of "reality" call for transformation of the system, but not to "reality" as it is. The nature of reality is changed, too, in the process of a system's adaptation to it.

The eventual mastery of the external situation [adaptation to it] through instrumental activity necessitates "realistic" judgments in terms of generalized predictions concerning the behavior of objects.[100]

This implies the importance of the cognitive orientation of actors. Among the variety of cognitive orientations, adaptation calls especially for universalistic orientation to objects. That is, the emphasis in adaptation is orientation to objects in terms of their relation to other objects and as members of classes with predictable behaviors. Furthermore, for adaptation to occur it is necessary that an attitude of specificity be taken to objects. That is, the objects have to be seen in relation to specific goal interests and dealt with in such specific contexts. Activity appropriate to adaptation involves the manipulation of aspects of the environment. This involves the viewing of the objects in terms of what they do, how they perform, and how their performances may be harnessed toward the main goal state of the system in the process of adaptation. In pattern variable terms, this is orientation to the objects in the situation in terms of their performance. Finally, in adaptation,

where the goal is not yet attained and where one must deal with objects in a "realistic" way, it is necessary to inhibit affective or emotional reactions to the objects in order to avoid being drawn off toward other goals, to avoid making inappropriate choices as to how the objects shall be treated, and to avoid premature relaxation of instrumental efforts. Hence the attitude tends to be marked by a certain inhibition or *neutrality*, with affect to some extent held constant.[101]

Parsons views certain patterns as being appropriate to the demands of a system in its adaptation phase. That is, if the system is to adapt when the time arises, the roles appropriate to adaptation *must* be performed according to certain patterns of attitude and orientation. In pattern variable terms these are orientations to objects in terms of *specificity* and *neutrality* and attitudes characterized by *universalism* and *performance*. It should be emphasized that these four choices among the pattern variables are "made" by the system *via* its need to adapt, and the choices "made" at the system level are transmitted to the individual role player in terms of demands emanating from the system to him.

Turning to the second functional problem of systems, that of goal attainment, we see that a similar analysis of this process as a phase of social systems leads to a similar determinate set of pattern variables.[102] Two of the choices made in the adaptation phase remain the same in the goal attainment phase. The appropriate interest in the object must still be specific, and it must still be viewed in terms of what it does toward gratification of a need. That is, it is still seen in terms of its performance. But the essence of goal attainment is gratification. Whereas in adaptation, the emphasis had to be on neutrality, the emphasis here shifts to affectivity, since it is in goal attainment that affective attitudes toward objects may be realized. Similarly,

the relation to the object no longer tends to be universalistic, concerned with realistic prediction of later effects or relations to other objects. It gives way to a relation of *particularism*.[103]

Where the object is a goal, it is possessed, enjoyed, consumed, in its particular relation to the actor.

A similar analysis of the pattern variables appropriate to adaptation is called for in the case of goal attainment. Parsons sees that certain orientations and modes of evaluation are required of the constituent role players if the system is to accomplish its goal attainment phase. These are attitudes of *affectivity* and *specificity* and orientations characterized by *particularism* and *performance*. For roles to be played in accordance with the needs of social systems in the goal attainment phase, they must be played in terms of these four options from the pattern variables. Here again, it appears that the choice of which side of the pattern variables to opt for in role performance is made by the system. Thus certain roles seen as especially relevant to the area of goal attainment have certain characteristics, or, taking the process view, as the system passes through a phase of goal attainment, prominent roles must take on these attributes.

The scheme by which Parsons analyzed the demands of the integration phase should be easily anticipated.[104] Integration of system members involves a "generalized and durable" affective attachment between them. Thus the attitude toward objects (social objects) is characterized by affectivity. Since integration of the system inherently involves the discrimination of which objects are part of the system and which are not, a particularistic mode of evaluation of them has to be in force so that the requisite discriminations may be made. Thus affectivity and particularism are appropriate to integration.

However, the specific interest in specific goals characteristic of the goal attainment phase gives way in the integrative phase to a diffuse interest, and the object tends to be regarded in terms of its diffuse or global quality, rather than its specific performance as related to a specific goal.[105]

It is Alter

in his diffuse quality as a system member rather than Alter as an incumbent of a specific status or performer of a specific role to whom Ego is attached.[106]

Hence the attitudes of Ego must be marked by diffuseness and his orientations to Alter are marked by quality orientation. Here again we see the pattern variables as the delineations of demands placed upon actors.

It is important to notice that Parsons couches his account in terms of actors and persons rather than in theoretical terms alone. Thus we see that the system demands that Ego see Alter in his "quality as a system member" in order that the system incorporating the two (and perhaps more) should be integrated. Indeed, by definition, for the system to remain, it must be integrated; thus it is imperative that Ego and Alter have the "correct" attitudes toward each other and see each other as objects in the "correct" way. In the integration phase, as indeed in all phases, the system of action places demands upon the actors that may not be choices from the actor's point of view. These choices have been "made" for the actor in that the system of action requires certain kinds of performances of him.

The latency or pattern maintenance phase is interpretable in the same way as the previous three phases although it seems to present special problems, since it is the phase in which little or no action takes place. Indeed, the essence of the latency phase is the maintenance of cultural and motivational patterns in actors such that, when the time arrives, the system can mobilize its role players to a new adaptation phase. Latency shares certain attributes with the integration phase that will be taken up first. As a result of the system's phase movement thus far, the existing objects are integrated into the system in terms of their quality. Similarly, the attitudes appropriate to objects that are "in" the system are diffuse ones, appropriate to match the many qualities of the objects. But the idea of latency involves the readiness of the system to meet new adaptive exigencies. Thus affect is to be stored and kept ready.

Seen from the point of view of its significance for the system, the primary feature of the latent phase is the latent reservoir of patterned but inhibited motivational potential in which it consists.[107]

This leads to the conception of the latency phase as one of guarded neutrality. It is also the phase of universalistic orientations to objects; that is, the object has been integrated in the previous phase where it was treated particularistically. In the latency phase the object has been established in its relations to other objects, and it is no longer seen as a goal object, or associated with a single goal; it is only one of a set of objects existing in the system as a whole.

We have seen that Parsons treats latency as both a beginning and a final phase in a phase movement cycle. He sees adaptation, integration and goal attainment phases coming essentially between periods of latency. But when these phases are passed through, they must be negotiated successfully if the system is to again reach a period of latency. This means that latency, with its readiness to enter a new integrative or adaptive phase, is a functional necessity for the system as a whole. As such, it demands orientation to objects in *neutrality* and *diffuseness* and *universalistic* evaluations of objects based on considerations of *quality*. These four choices on the pattern variable scheme are necessities, as seen from the social system point of view, and thus define aspects of role performance in this phase for the actor.

It may be useful to summarize the demands placed by the system on the actors in relation to the four system problems and the pattern variables. The adaptive phase (system problem) was seen as characterized by the needs of the system to have its constituent units maximize their role behavior in terms of "specificity" and "neutrality" concerning attitudes, and "universalism" and "performance" concerning orientations to objects. In the goal attainment phase, the requirements were in terms of "affectivity", "specificity", "particularism" and "performance". In integration, they were "diffuseness", "affectivity", "particularism" and "quality". In pattern maintenance-latency, they were "neutrality", "diffuseness", "quality" and "universalism".

The importance of this conception of the functional problems seen as phases of maximization of certain characteristics of roles (and thus role players) can now be seen. This conception stresses the impact of the system on the actor. For each type of system problem, there seems to be one appropriate orientation posture available to actors, and one mode of categorization of objects involved in solving the system problem at hand. This has the effect of delineating only four types of social acts, which are describable in terms of the pattern variables—one each for each of the system problems.[108] This is an enormous simplification of the scheme worked out under voluntarism, in which the actor chose his type of social action from the varieties of modes of orientation to objects and according to the varieties of attitudinal options open to him. This simplification has a direct bearing on the model of man implicit in the system level determinism.

The human being who fits in with the system level solutions to system level problems must have characteristics compatible with the demands that will be placed on him in his work as role player. One obvious and major requirement of man in this capacity is simply his "plasticity".[109] As system demands are placed on individual role players, they must come to accept the roles as they are described in the pattern variable scheme relative to the social system's needs. This means that they must have the ability to learn which kinds of performances are appropriate to each situation in terms of system demands, and the ability to perform in each of these capacities. As Parsons puts it, this is one of the "fundamental properties of human nature" that are assumed in the context of the social system. In Parsons' terms, this is the

"plasticity" of the human organism, its capacity to learn any one of a large number of alternative patterns of behavior instead of being bound by its genetic constitution to a very limited range of alternatives.[110]

In this passage, Parsons is laying the groundwork for the notion of role behavior as being quite diverse. Perhaps the explicit natures of specific roles call forth slightly varying performances, depending on the nature of the situation; but we have just seen that, in broad outline, the system places a very narrow range of demands on persons as role players. Rather than the organism perhaps being limited by its constitution, the constitution of the organism gives rise to a greater variety of behaviors in roles than are appropriate as seen from the system point of view.

The second feature of the nature of man implied in the system level analysis in which we are now engaged is man's sensitivity to the demands the system places upon him.[111] It is not clear from Parsons' own writings how the role player gets the "message" regarding each of the social system demands. Perhaps it is through the unconscious or unrecognized aspects of situations that the demands come to the actor. That is, he may "see" what is called for by the system without being aware that he is making an analysis of the situation and acting in the best interests of the system. It is not reasonable to argue that others in the situation place especially system-relevant demands on the actor, since they are presumably no more in a position to be authoritative about how to act than the actor himself.

This problem, which must be regarded as serious, appears to account for the naïve view of Parsons' work which holds that "internalization" of culture really means the "programming in" of all the role characteristics that Actor will use in all the situations he will meet in his life. Indeed, this might be one way of solving the problem. If it could be supposed that internalization of culture applied to every detail of each role, then the problem of the system demands and the actor's action could be solved. But this would constitute the extreme case of determinism that Parsons wishes to avoid, since in this case, the last bit of voluntarism would be pushed out of action in favor of a system determinism which covered every aspect of action. Actor's need-dispositions and abilities to choose would become irrelevant.

Concerning choice, it will be remembered that a major element in the model of man under voluntarism in Parsons was the ability to cognize, take an attitude and thereby evaluate objects in situations and design behavior according to choices made. In the model of man seen from the structural point of view of the social system, we see that options here are not open. It is out of the question to suppose that, in any large number of cases, men could be aware of the demands of the system, yet perform in ways that do not conform to those demands. By definition, if this were the case the system would not survive. Perhaps this is an empirical question as well as a definitional one; but from the theoretical perspective alone, we see that decisions for action are really "made" at the social system level and carried out by men playing roles. Therefore, from the point of view of the social system, the question of choice among action alternatives must be seen to lie *with the system itself* and not with the individual. This constitutes the major divergence from the model of man found in Parsons' voluntaristic emphasis.

The picture of man that emerges from the consideration of Parsons' structural model focused at the system level is thus one of man playing roles according to the specifications laid down by the system of action itself. This is not a hypothetical matter. It is clear that these specifications are carried out; if they were not, by definition the system could not remain. The individual has no choice concerning the type of social act in which he will engage in each of the roles he plays. The acts have been "typed" according to the needs of the system itself. Rather than having any significant opportunity to refuse action, the actor is seen as a functionary for the system, acting in ways that are determined by it. This leads to the view of the role and the norm governing the role as essentially artifacts of the needs of systems of action to survive, rather than of common life experiences of persons, or agreements made between persons concerning the exchanges they will regard as proper in complementary role behavior.

Finally, considering the conclusions of the previous chapter, it may be argued that in Parsons' theory, both voluntarism and determinism concerning role performances exist and have a reciprocal relationship to one another. Depending upon the emphasis one wishes to consider at any one time, the theory may appear extremely voluntaristic, having little specification of the kinds of roles that ought to be played; or it may be very explicit concerning roles and norms while allowing little voluntarism.

CHAPTER 15

The problem of the agent of choice—relating the two models of man

We have reviewed Parsons' fundamental starting points and requirements for his theory of action. From this, it was possible to see he tries to draw up a theory which builds on the work that has gone before while avoiding the problems that have plagued earlier theorists. The outlines of the theory as a whole were presented, with emphasis on problems of choice in the theory when seen as a combination of possible system foci. Following that, we took up one emphasis in Parsonian theory and examined what has here been called the voluntaristic model, in which the social act is built up theoretically from consideration of the needs of actors who cognize and cathect objects in situations in order to deal with them. This led to a description of the pattern variable scheme as the formalization of the choices confronting actors in their activities as cognizers and cathecters, and thus as authors of action in a highly voluntaristic sense. Finally, it was seen that there is a rather specific model of man derivable from this line of Parsonian thought. It consists in a picture of man with a determinable set of need-dispositions that derive directly from the notion of the personality as a system. Voluntary choice of actions by actors is a central feature.

Chapter 14 considered a divergent emphasis in Parsonian theory, that which is specifically concerned with the social system as a point of reference and with the actor as role player who performs certain activities. The activities he performs were seen to be directly related to the functional problems faced by systems of action, and these problems set specific limits on the voluntarism which was discussed in the previous chapter. Finally, it was shown that implicit in this less voluntaristic view of action was a model of man characterized especially by the ability to perform needed tasks as they arise, but with little dependence on the processes of cognition, cathexis and evaluation. Similarly, it appeared unnecessary to involve the need-dispositions of actors, since the basic scheme into which the action of actors fits is the system of social relations, not a unified system of goals derived from the needs of persons.

While it is remembered that Parsons says he is always concerned with the *dual* nature of motivation and role behavior, it is difficult to see how this is so in the deterministic emphasis. While he does not see actors as robots playing their appropriate roles, he places so little emphasis on voluntaristic behavior in the deterministic model that the internally contrived and gratifying aspects of social behavior appear so minimized that they become irrelevant. In this emphasis of his work, the pattern variables appear to be formalizations of demands placed on role players by the social system. As we will see in this chapter, the implicit problem of how to balance voluntarism and determinism has plagued Parsons throughout his work. It seems that he has not yet given a thorough and adequate answer to this question.

In this chapter, we will restate the main elements of the models of man that have been derived in the ways just described, and examine some of Parsons' answers to the problems raised. Specifically, while Parsons has never addressed himself to the models of man in this theory, he has found occasion to answer critics of his pattern variables, the scheme around which the analysis in this paper has been formed.

The pattern variables figure prominently in discussion of systems of action at every level of generality, but Parsons has considerable difficulty making them perform satisfactorily in knitting the levels of generality together. This is pointed up by the divergent assumptions about man at various levels of analysis.

We saw that the pattern variables work best when they are grouped in pairs. The two groupings, presumably no matter how many pattern variables in each, should match in number, so that the derivations from them can be made in terms of cross-classifications.[112] Also, the nature of the actor-situation relation is theoretically such that two categories have to be built up (object and attitude categories). It seems that the pattern variables, when employed to suggest further analytical categories in the theory of action, work best when linked to the object-attitude differentiation. Thus Parsons says at one point that with respect to number, "it must be either four or six pairs", and the choice is a "matter of definition".[113] In the most recent articles dealing with them, he limits them to four pairs.

However, for a long time after the pattern variable idea emerged, there was a fifth one, which was particularly hard to handle since it was unaligned with any other, i.e., unpaired; yet it seemed important to Parsons. This was the "self-orientation—collectivity-orientation" pattern variable.[114] The list of five pattern variables appeared prominently in most of the Parsonian literature up to *The Social System* and *Toward a General Theory of Action*. It constituted a set of dichotomies in "symmetrical asymmetry".[115] That is, the object pattern variables were paired, the orientation variables were paired, and the fifth, the "self-orientation—collectivity-orientation" variable, was conceived as somehow in the middle of the two and was unpaired.[116] This unpaired dichotomy has a direct relationship to the subject of this study; specifically, it addresses the problem of the location of choice in the system, since it concerns the "choice" of *how to choose* between demands placed by the system and personal desires for action.

To understand the thought that went into the formulation of this pattern variable and its later elimination, it is necessary to remember that the system idea, when used by Parsons, is always concerned with the relations of elements in the system to each other. In discussing the structure of the social system, the sub-systems were seen to be laced together via the interlocking nature of some of the pattern variables between each of the four basic functional categories. Similarly, on the level of personality, the need-dispositions were seen to derive from the relational nature of the personality's four functional problems.

Concerning the relationships of personalities to social and cultural systems, it is necessary to move to a still higher level of generality and include in the system the personality system, the social system and the cultural system as parts of a functional whole. This means that the choices now to be considered are concerned with the relations of personalities, social systems and cultural systems in their capacities as subsystems of a larger system. When considering the social system alone, pattern variables were the means of formalizing the dichotomous nature of action alternatives that fit in best with the needs of the subsystems of the social system. On the system level which includes the personality, cultural and social systems, similar dichotomies present themselves.

Uniquely, however, it is only the social system and the personality system which are comprised of systems of social action. These two systems plus the behavioral organism (considered as a system) and the cultural system comprise a systematic interrelationship of four elements at the highest level of generality. The behavioral organism is a system of biological and physical action, but not of social action; the culture is a system of symbols, not of action. Considered altogether, these four subsystems (cultural, social, personality, organism) comprise a total system at the highest level of generality at which Parsons deals.

At this level of generalization, and considering the fact that the two subsystems comprised of social action are the social and the personality subsystems, the problem arises of the action relations between the two. These relations have been the concern of this book. In Chapter 13, the personality was considered as it "looked out" to the social system. In Chapter 14, the social system was considered for the ways in which it "looked down" on the personality. In terms of models of man, these two sections described voluntarism at the personality subsystem level and determinism at the social subsystem level. The models of man in each case were found to be products of the kind of analysis being carried out, as well as the level of generality being maintained. The problem for Parsons was that of making the two systems "fit" together in acceptable ways, using the models of man in each and avoiding determinisms.

It is now necessary to focus on the issue of the fifth pattern variable. Given that Parsons conceived of the personality and the social system as the two concerned specifically with social action, it is natural that a solution to the problem of which "chooses" action might be solved voluntaristically, making the whole of the theory appear more voluntaristic than not. This could be accomplished by the inclusion of the fifth pattern variable, specifically concerned with the actor's dilemma of whether to become oriented to the needs of the collectivity (collectivity-orientation) or pay more attention to his own personal desires (self-orientation). In Parsons' terms, this

concerned the structure of the market relation in terms of the extent to which pursuit of "advantage" took precedence over the performance of "service".[117]

"Collectivity-orientation" formulated the

respects in which membership in a superordinate system is a directly governing consideration for action in or as a member of any given sub-system.[118]

On the other pole, "self-orientation" formulated the

area within which the norms of interest of the superordinate system are not directly governing, that is, where they may be treated only as "regulative" rather than "constitutive" of the relationship in question.[119]

This formulation of the fifth pattern variable was troublesome for at least two reasons. The obvious one is revealed by the wording of the definition of the pattern variable itself. The working of the "collectivity-orientation" side of the definition quoted above seems to imply voluntarism on the part of the actor. This is in terms of the collectivity as a "governing consideration" for actors. But the other half of the definition is in terms of system determination. It formulates "areas in which ... norms of interest of the superordinate system ... are not directly governing". This implies that there are definitely areas in which such norms *are* directly governing, and that in those areas, action *will be* contrived according to those norms. This seems to make the fifth pattern variable bridge the gap between the personality and social systems, but it states it with a foot in both, and not in terms of either. Because of this, it was never clear in Parsons' writings how this pattern variable was to be considered (voluntaristically or deterministically).

The other reason for the trouble with this pattern variable seems to be that, no matter how ambiguously it is defined, the question of choice is still present and unsolved. Interpreted voluntaristically, the fifth pattern variable can be thought to fit into the voluntaristic scheme; but it raises questions of how and when the actor will choose action according to the "norms of interest of the superordinate system". Similarly, if the pattern variables are interpreted deterministically, the fifth one can be thought of as a part of this interpretation, but the question arises of when the interests of the superordinate scheme are not in force, and of what happens to action when they are not.

For several reasons, Parsons appears to have found it advantageous to drop the fifth pattern variable. He has said that he came to consider it a "special case" of the other four, and therefore redundant.[120] This leaves the question of the relationships between the personality and the social subsystem of the total system somewhat unaccounted for. However, Parsons has taken what appears to be a more satisfactory approach on the problem of these relations, which at least begins to give the answer to the question of choice in the system. (It is not yet clear whether the solution will remain satisfactory—especially in relation to the model of man in Parsons' theory.) This solution is that of the cybernetic relations between the four subsystems of the total system.

At the same time that Parsons was reconsidering the pattern variables in response to criticism of them, he was formulating a conception of the relationships between the subsystems of the action system in terms of relative "hierarchical" importance regarding the setting of limits and the controlling of actions.[121] We saw that the fifth pattern variable, "self-orientation—collectivity-orientation", was conceived as formalizing the kinds of demands that could be placed on the actor, and the kinds of freedom the actor would have. This kind of thinking relative to the pattern variables must have given rise to more general thinking concerning the relations of the personality and the social system when considered in the context of the environing systems—the biological organism of the actor and the cultural system, composed of a system of norms. At one point, Parsons referred to the fifth pattern variable as the instrument which clarifies the relationships of the personality and the social system and the "hierarchical" nature of the relationship between the two. The idea of the hierarchy was not worked out until several years later. During this time, Parsons abandoned the fifth pattern variable, and concentrated more on detailing the hierarchical relationships of the four subsystems of the action system.[122]

We saw in Chapter 12 that the four general system problems were associated with four aspects of the social world. That is, only the social system, the actual system of roles played ultimately by persons, can be said to include social interaction, in the sense of two or more roles being complementary and acted out by two or more actors. The other aspects of social life constituted "environments" in which this interaction took place. That is, when the entities that are the actors, the personality system and the cultural system are considered in relation to the social system itself, the totality of these form a systematic relationship characterized by interchange among the four. This is the essence of the idea of system, for Parsons. In order for social interaction to take place according to normative orientation, there must be goals and there must be energy, or the means of reaching goals. Considering the greatest level of generality of the idea of system, these four problems fit into the four system prerequisites.

Considering the social system and its environments, the pattern maintenance function is associated with the cultural system. This system is constituted by the system of norms, and thus intimately associated with institutionalized patterns of behavior. The integration function is associated with the social system itself. It is uniquely the social system which is comprised of *inter*action. Thus the social system serves the integrative function of the total system by interlinking the various normative components and personality variants via social interaction. The personality system is associated with the goal attainment function since, especially in the voluntaristic emphasis, it is this system which formulates and articulates goals, and designs the actual behaviors toward their pursuit. Finally, we saw that Parsons' is an action system based on energy used for the achievement of goals. This reliance on the concept of an energized system places the "behavioral organism" in close relationship with the total system's need for adaptation. It is adaptation that is conceived as the process of producing the "means" which are directed toward the total system's goals.[123]

The hierarchical relationships mentioned above are in terms of *conditioning* and *control*. That is, the *conditioning* heirarchy runs from behavioral organism, through personality system and social system to the cultural system.[124] This means that at any one level of analysis, as Parsons arranges these systems, there exist the requisite conditions for the operation of the next level of analysis. For example, the social system is at the third stage in the conditioning hierarchy, with the personality system standing above it and above that, the behavioral organism. As Parsons reasons, the social system depends for its basic conditions of operation on the personality system, which depends in turn on the constitution of the organism. Here is a sense in which the social system is dependent on the personality system. This means that personalities, constituted differently among persons, will have an impact on the way roles are played and the character of the social system itself.

The other hierarchical arrangement of these four subsystems of the total system is that of cybernetic *control*. Whereas the conditioning hierarchy sets out the order in which necessary prerequisites to action must be worked out with respect to the whole, the *controlling* hierarchy designates the order in which control over the next stage in the hierarchy is exercised. This hierarchy begins at the level of the cultural system, goes through the social system and the personality and ends with the behavioral organism. This means that in relation to control, the social system stands below the culture (and thus under its control).

There is need for considerable development which Parsons has not yet provided concerning exactly what constitutes control and conditioning. It is to be noted that the hierarchy of control runs in the same direction as his model of socialization,[125] while his model of Ego's instrumental act runs in the same direction of that of conditioning.[126] This means simply that when considering the process of socialization of the child, Parsons considers the cultural system and the social system into which the child is to be integrated as above the level of the personality of the child. That is, the child is seen as taking on aspects of the culture *via* interaction with members of the social system. The child is considered as basically *tabula rasa*, with only the abilities to learn, notice and change. In order of conditioning factors, the child stands below the behavioral organism. That is, the assumptions about socialization are based on the assumption of these abilities as part of the biological equipment.

The model of the instrumental social act, once persons are socialized, however, runs the other direction. It is conceived as a progression of stages from latency, through adaptation, goal attainment, integration and back to latency. This is the order in which phase movement was described in Chapter 14. Parsons conceives of the instrumental act as beginning from a stage of latency. Problems of adaptation then may arise, moving the system as a whole into consideration of its goal state and how to achieve it. Goal attainment is therefore the next phase, in which the goal is achieved. The system is now changed somewhat, and requires reintegration, especially with respect to the goal it has just achieved. As the integration is achieved, the system moves back into a new period of latency.[127] Therefore, in this case, the personality (associated with the goal attainment problem) stands above the social system (associated with integration).

If these processes are generalized and taken out of their temporal context of child and adult role player, it seems that the cybernetic model of the relationships of the functions of the system and their associations with concrete aspects of life has great potential. Only lately has Parsons turned his attention specifically to the ways in which the social system and its environing systems cooperate. If he decides to follow out this line of theory, he may arrive at a more satisfactory solution to the problem of interweaving voluntarism among actors into a rather deterministic system. He has given suggestions of an answer to the question of "Who chooses?"

In the sense . . . of emphasizing the importance of the cybernetically highest elements in pattern-ing action systems, I am a cultural determinist, rather than a social determinist.[128]

We have seen from his arranging of the factors of conditioning and control that this is so. But he makes it clear that it is only in the sense of cybernetic hierarchies that he is any kind of determinist. In placing the adaptation function and the behavioral organism at the top of the conditioning hierarchy, but at the bottom of the controlling hierarchy, he seems to be attempting a specific alternative to the Marxian model, which in terms of control, gives priority to what Parsons would call adaptation. Parsons goes on,

I believe that, within the social system, the normative elements are more important for social change than the "material interests" of constitutive units.[129]

This we have seen in Parsons' arranging of the hierarchies of conditioning and cybernetic control.

Some comments are appropriate concerning the relationships of the models of man to each other in terms of the cybernetic hierarchies that Parsons has recently developed. As a conditioning factor, the voluntaristic model developed in Chapter 13 seems to fit into Parsons' scheme above the social system. Thus the need-dispositions, the consciousness, and the goal directedness of actors that comprise the outlines of that model are requisite to the operation of the social system. These elements of the nature of man may not be interpreted to set any specific behaviors as patterns, however. The hierarchy in which they stand above the social system is that of con-ditioning.

Alternatively, the social and cultural systems stand above the personality (and thus the person) in terms of control. However, we noticed that Parsons' deterministic emphasis afforded the less specific and delineated model of man. The outlines of this model were in terms of learning and plasticity only. This means that the culture, introduced through social interaction among persons, is relatively clearly stamped on the personality of the individual. The culture, however, must be within the nature of the voluntaristic individual, for it is this system which stands above the culture in terms of setting the conditions under which culture can operate as a system.

It appears that Parsons is on the track of a conceptual device which could be used to spell out the exact ways in which the nature of the individual as a system of action influence the culture he carries. Similarly, the ways in which the culture and the social structure influence the person may become clearer. This aspect of the Parsonian scheme has already had considerable attention. Clearly, the main job of relating the two natures of man in Parsonian theory lies in detailing of the conditioning factors in the hierarchy of conditioning. Unfortunately, Parsons has not yet attempted this in a systematic manner.

Appendix

Some further comments on Parsons' theory seem appropriate. To begin, it will be noted that Parsons', like Homans', is a deductive theory, although not hypothetico-deductive.[130] Some aspects of its deductive nature lead directly to a consideration of the major points of considerable vulnerability of the theory. Perhaps these points are those at which the most telling critisms have been made. This study has followed up one of these points. Secondly, a brief note is in order on circularity in Parsons' work. Finally, some comments on how Parsonian theory may be applied and on its usefulness in the study of social change are offered.

Clearly Parsons' theory, which has been called "programmatic", is deductive.[131] That is, from a few starting points, Parsons works out the consequent derivations. The idea of system is the central theme in Parsonian writing. The inherent needs of systems imply certain conclusions in terms of the things that will have to be accomplished if a system is to survive. From the starting point of system and system problems, Parsons extends the analysis to the ways in which the system might solve its problems and face the further issues that the solutions raise. We see that, if one began with systems at the highest level of generality, the subsystems making up this system could also be conceived as systems, implying yet lower levels of analysis, which imply the analysis of each sub-set of these systems in yet lower levels of analysis, *ad infinitum*. The logical regress involved in this process need not become a problem, as long as practical limits are set concerning where to stop. The enormous volume of Parsonian writing can be understood as the detailing of the aspects of systems, and their subsystems, as well as the ways in which they fit into yet greater systems.

Thus for all its apparent formidability, Parsons' theory seems to reduce to the notion of system (implying the four functional problems of systems) and a set of devices for relating the four system problems together in the course of any single analysis. In Parsons' work, the pattern variables perform the latter function.

When applied to any problem, these formal aspects of the analytical structure are seen to take on content appropriate to the analysis in progress. That is, Parsons' conceptual scheme takes on meanings according to the problem under examination. The meanings according to the examiner are not part of the formal deductive system, but only problematic in terms of whether they are the empirically "right" ones. Most criticisms of Parsons' work concern whether his starting points are correct, and whether the way he employs his system fits the "facts".

Considerable attention has been drawn to the concept of functional prerequisites (Parsons' functional problems).[132] As we saw, Parsons has settled on four as the correct number. Others have expanded and contracted the list. Parsons argues four is correct and any others that have been proposed can be understood as reducible to his four, while any less than four do not attend to the problems of survival implied by the existence of each. Clearly, if one is uncomfortable with Parsons' rendition of the system problems, there is little chance for accepting his whole scheme.

Criticism has been levelled at Parsons' treatment of the relational system designed to fit the system problems together (the pattern variables).[133] It is possible to agree with Parsons on the system problems, but disagree on the composition of the pattern variables, since the two are not directly derived from each other, although they are related and intertwined systematically. We have seen that the number of pattern variables has been a problem for Parsons, and that to some extent, the solution to the problem seems to have been suggested by the ease of cross-classification using multiples of two.

If one tentatively agrees with Parsons on the system and its associated problems, and is willing to go along with the pattern variables, criticism and analysis of the scheme can take one of two main forms from that point. Either analysis can be concerned with the ways in which Parsons conceptually works out the interrelations between the two sets of analytical tools, (system and pattern variables) or it can be directed toward the ways the system is "applied" to empirical problems. This study has chosen the former. The concern with the model(s) of man in Parsons' work is basically a concern with the ways in which the person fits into the social order. That is, the focus of this study has been on the kinds of relations Parsons sees between levels of his action system, specifically with regard to the relations of the personality and the social system.

Taking the other route in criticism of Parsons would entail an analysis of the ways in which Parsons loads his theoretical terms with concrete empirical referents. The fact that the writings of Parsons do not include any detailed set of criteria by which he accomplishes this loading must be considered a deficiency.[134] This deficiency leads to the criticism that Parsons is giving description of the "way he sees it" in terms of *his* set of categories, rather than a theory of the "way it is". In this connection, some problems relating to the definitional circularity of the theory may be mentioned.

The definition of a social system entails the ideas of interaction and meaningful action. But its essence seems to be the idea of the fulfillment of the system's requirements for survival. This means that the system is defined by the problems it solves. Since if a system fails to solve these problems, it does not exist, the definitions of the system's problems and of the system itself tend to be identical. That is, at the outset the scheme incorporates two kinds of definitions (of the system and of the system problems) that are really one. This leads to the conclusion that, no matter how much the analysis is in terms of the system's having *problems*, the fact must be that it is successfully solving these problems. Otherwise there would be no analysis, because there would be no system. It seems that this kind of definitional circularity is necessary in programmatic theory. Given the deductive nature of the scheme itself, it must begin with some concept which inherently implies others defined in terms of each other.

It is this definitional circularity over the system and its solution to problems, combined with Parsons' concern with and emphasis on the problem of order, that has led critics to conclude that the model is static and that it is incapable of dealing with problems of change.[135] They argue that since order is the main concern, and since the system is (by definition) solving its problems, there must be only minimal disruption. Thus, "authority" rather than "power" is a concern in Parsonian theory because "power", as such, never becomes problematic.

However, it seems that the scheme Parsons offers could be used to analyze change, or even conflict and revolution. The logic of the four system problems was in terms of the "scarce resources" postulate of economic theory and the problems of tension management and integration caused by the fact that all the means of the system could not be directed to all goals at once. If disorder had been the main concern, perhaps instead of *Economy and Society*, Parsons would have written a book on the disintegration of systems and the ways in which empirical systems have tended to fail to solve their problems (and thus passed out the existence). Indeed, his recent book, *Societies*, can be seen in this perspective. With respect to speed of change, however, Parsons has chosen to consider the slowest alternative. From the logic of the theory itself, there does not seem to be any reason rapid and decisive change could not be analyzed in essentially the same terms.

Notes

1. *The Social System* (New York: The Free Press, 1951), p. 573.

2. (New York: The Free Press, 1951).

3. Parsons argues in Chapter XVIII of *The Structure of Social Action* (New York: The Free Press, 1949) that he has treated the thought of Marshall, Pareto, Durkheim and Weber as *data*, just as any other piece of data might be treated, and therefore he has produced an empirical study.

4. This is the name given to what has become the "Parsonian" outlook. For more detail, consult especially Parsons and E. A. Shils, *Toward A General Theory of Action* (New York: Harper and Row, 1951), Parts I and II. Almost all of Parsons' writings start with some recapitulation of or reference to "the action frame of reference".

5. *The Structure of Social Action*, pp. 689–90.

6. *Ibid.*, Part II.

7. In this book it will be shown that the means–ends scheme remains a central feature of Parsonian thinking. For a cogent analysis of the means–ends scheme, and a positivist critique, see R. Bierstedt, "The Means–ends Schema in Sociological Theory", *American Sociological Review*, **III**, No. 5 (October, 1938), 665–71.

8. *The Structure of Social Action*, Chapter III.

9. *Ibid.*, p. 701.

10. *Ibid.*, p. 702.

11. *Ibid.*, p. 703.

12. *Ibid.*

13. *Ibid.*, Part II.

14. *The Social System*, p. 44.

15. *Ibid.*

16. *Ibid.*, p. 45.

17. *The Structure of Social Action*, Part II.

18. *The Structure of Social Action*, pp. 196–200.

19. *Ibid.*, pp. 250–64.

20. *Ibid.*, p. 201.

21. *Ibid.*, p. 202.

22. Concerns of this kind seem to have led Parsons to make motivational categories central to his theorizing. From the strict positivistic point of view, the inclusion of such categories makes Parsons' theory unverifiable, and therefore unscientific.

23.   *The Structure of Social Action*, p. 206.

24.   *Ibid.*

25.   *Ibid.*, p. 207.

26.   For an example of this view see P. A. Sorokin, *Contemporary Sociological Theories* (Harper and Row, 1928), Chapter VIII, "Sociologistic School".

27.   T. Parsons, "The Present Position and Prospects of Systematic Theory in Sociology", in T. Parsons, *Essays in Sociological Theory* (New York: The Free Press, 1964), p. 227.

28.   *The Division of Labor* (New York: The Free Press, 1964); Parsons' treatment of this book is found in *The Structure of Social Action*, Part II.

29.   *The Structure of Social Action*, p. 710.

30.   Adam Smith, *An Inquiry Into the Nature and Causes of The Wealth of Nations* (Homewood, Ill.: Richard D. Irwin, 1963), p. 11.

31.   *The Structure of Social Action*, p. 311.

32.   Parsons, "The Present Position and Prospects of Systematic Theory in Sociology", p. 227.

33.   Parsons concludes in *The Structure of Social Action* that his study of the history of social thought, and specifically the study of Marshall, Pareto, Durkheim and Weber, has led to the discovery of common ideas and problems that, when viewed for their relevance for sociological theory, constitute points at which the authors he analyzes were dealing with the same things, although in different terms. He calls these points "convergences".

34.   *The Structure of Social Action*, pp. 324–39.

35.   Max Weber, *The Protestant Ethic and the Spirit of Capitalism* (New York: Scribner's, 1958), Part I.

36.   *The Structure of Social Action*, p. 510.

37.   *Ibid.*, p. 717.

38.   For a short schematic view of this see, T. Parsons, "The Point of View of the Author", Max Black (ed.), *The Social Theories of Talcott Parsons* (Englewood Cliffs, New Jersey: Prentice-Hall, 1961), pp. 310–63, especially Section 2, pp. 323–48. The first part of *Toward A General Theory of Action* is also particularly clear in its presentation of the action frame of reference.

39.   *The Structure of Social Action*, p. 718.

40.   *Toward A General Theory of Action*, Introduction; *The Social System*, pp. 3–24.

41.   It is the point of this book to show that part of Parsons' theory emphasizes voluntarism while part of it minimizes or eliminates it. But when describing the general nature of the frame of reference and the scheme as a whole, it is convenient to think of action as being voluntaristic.

42.   *Toward A General Theory of Action*, p. 4.

43.   For a fairly clear account of Parsons' meaning of "interpenetrate", see his discussion of the personality as an environment to society in *Societies* (Englewood Cliffs, New Jersey: Prentice-Hall, 1966), pp. 11–15.

44. Systems of action are, basically, the applications of Parsons' systems theory to problems of the interactions of persons. The idea of system includes the notions of system problems and the satisfactory solution to those problems in the context of a general unity of the system parts with each other.

45. *Toward a General Theory of Action*, Introduction.

46. *The Social System*, p. 142, categorizes some types of roles.

47. *The Social System*, p. 38.

48. For more detail, see Parsons, *The Social System*, Chapter VI and Parsons and R. F. Bales, *Family, Socialization and Interaction Process* (New York: The Free Press, 1955).

49. This is basic Parsonian thinking. A clear statement of it is found in *The Social System*, Chapter II.

50. rewards or punishments.

51. This kind of mechanism is very similar to that postulated by Homans in his theory of social behavior. See the present study, Part I.

52. *The Social System*, p. 38.

53. See *The Structure of Social Action*, p. 344.

54. Talcott Parsons and R. F. Bales, "The Dimensions of Action Space", in Parsons, Bales, and E. A. Shils, *Working Papers in the Theory of Action* (New York: The Free Press, 1953), p. 74.

55. See *The Social System*, Chapter IV.

56. The detailing of these problems is paid special attention in Parsons and N. J. Smelser, *Economy and Society* (London: Routledge and Kegan Paul, 1956), Chapter II.

57. *Economy and Society*, Chapter I, outlines other points of contact between economic and sociological theory as well. The following four paragraphs constitute a summary of many of Parsons' writings on the derivation and justification of the four system problems. *Economy and Society*, Chapter I; *The Social System*, pp. 26–36; "The Point of View of the Author", table, p. 331; *Toward a General Theory of Action*, Chapter V, "Phase Movement in Relation to Motivation, Symbol Formation and Role Structure"; *Societies*, Chapter II.

58. The example of this view usually given is that of Ralf Dahrendorf, "Out of Utopia: Toward a Reorientation of Sociological Analysis", in N. J. Demerath and R. A. Peterson, *System, Change, and Conflict* (New York: The Free Press, 1957), pp. 465–80. Also see this volume for a variety of other criticisms of Parsons.

59. See *Societies*, Chapter II as well as *Toward a General Theory of Action*, Part II, Section 4, "The Social System".

60. See the diagram in *Societies*, p. 28. These relationships are illustrated in Figure 1 on page 158 of this book. Figure 1 is a simplification of the diagram in *Societies*.

61. Concern with the pattern variables is spread throughout Parsons' work. There seems to be no single source which sets out a definitive and conclusive statement of them. They are elaborated and explained in several of his major writings: *The Social System*, p. 67; "Pattern Variables Revisited: A Response to Robert Dublin", *Sociological Theory and Modern Society*, pp. 192–

220; "The Point of View of the Author", Max Black (ed.), *The Social Theories of Talcott Parsons*, pp. 311–63, (much of this is a restatement of the paper, "Pattern Variables Revisited"); *Toward A General Theory of Action*, Introduction and Part I; An especially succinct statement concerning the pattern variables appears in *Economy and Society*, pp. 33–38. A good secondary source on the pattern variables is William Mitchell, *Sociological Analysis and Politics* (Englewood Cliffs, New Jersey: Prentice-Hall, 1967), pp. 103–10, 31–32, 52, 71–73, and 165. The pattern variables figure into Parsons and Bales, *Family, Socialization and Interaction Process* and Parsons, *Social Structure and Personality* (New York: The Free Press, 1964), especially in relation to the personality of the actor.

62.   For example, see Dubin's article cited above, "Parsons' Actor: Continuities in Social Theory", and Max Black, "Some Questions About Parsons' Theories", Max Black (ed.), *The Social Theories of Talcott Parsons*, pp. 268–88.

63.   The pattern variable scheme was developed to help in the analysis of the characteristics of certain roles. An early statement of the problem later developed into the full complement of pattern variables is found in T. Parsons, "The Motivation of Economic Activities", T. Parsons, *Essays in Sociological Theory*, pp. 50–68. This was originally published in 1940. The idea for the scheme comes from Tönnies' concepts *gemeinschaft* and *gesellschaft*.

64.   The present set of four pattern variables is taken from a recent statement of them by Parsons. It should not be taken as final, since the scheme seems to be the most changeable of all Parsons' conclusions. Nevertheless, the pattern variable idea, and the bases from which they were developed, has remained constant in his thought.

65.   *Toward A General Theory of Action*, Part II.

66.   *Ibid. Toward A General Theory of Action* is the best source for explanation of the relationships between the pattern variables and the cognitive and cathectic processes in actors.

67.   This point will be enlarged upon in connection with the deterministic model of man in Chapter 14. For a source on the pattern variables as related to structural concerns, see *Working Papers in the Theory of Action*, Chapter V.

68.   R. F. Bales, *Interaction Process Analysis* (Cambridge, Mass.,: Addison Wesley, 1950).

69.   *Toward A General Theory of Action*, p. 78.

70.   *Ibid.*

71.   This discussion is based on the chart in "The Point of View of the Author", Black (ed.), *The Social Theories of Talcott Parsons*, p. 331.

72.   *Ibid.*

73.   *Ibid.*

74.   *Economy and Society*, p. 34.

75.   "The Point of View of the Author", Black (ed.), *The Social Theories of Talcott Parsons*, p. 331.

76.   *Toward A General Theory of Action*, pp. 56–57.

77.   It need not be, in the general sense, the actions of *persons*, since a collectivity can be abstracted in Parsonian terms as having the above characteristics and therefore it could be analytically treated as an actor.

78. *Toward A General Theory of Action*, pp. 56–57.

79. *Ibid.*, p. 54.

80. *Ibid.*, p. 55.

81. *Ibid.* Emphasis is mine.

82. Parsons enumerates several "mechanisms" whereby this comes about. It was not necessary to list and discuss them. For detail, see *Toward A General Theory of Action*, Part II, Section 2.

83. *Toward A General Theory of Action*, p. 55.

84. See Parsons' note on "individuality", *Toward A General Theory of Action*, pp. 155–56.

85. This discussion and Figure 2 are derived from Parsons and Bales, *Family, Socialization and Interaction Process*, Chapter III, especially the chart on pages 172–73.

86. The duality here is also related to the double nature of the motivation to play roles that is usually divided between external and internal inducements.

87. Figure 4 is based on the discussion in Parsons and Bales, *Family, Socialization and Interaction Process*, Chapter III.

88. See *Ibid.*, especially the chart, pages 172–73, for illustration.

89. Figure 5 is derived from the present discussion.

90. *Toward A General Theory of Action*, p. 55 and Part II.

91. For details of this aspect of Parsons' writings, see especially *Social Structure and Personality*, Part I and his article, "Psychoanalysis and the Social Structure", T. Parsons, *Essays in Sociological Theory*, pp. 336–47.

92. *Family, Socialization and Interaction Process*, p. 171.

93. The deterministic emphasis seems to be especially strong in *Working Papers in the Theory of Action* and *The Social System*, especially in the discussions of "Principle Types of Social Structure", pp. 180–200, and similar topics.

94. *Toward A General Theory of Action*, p. 107; The concept of moving equilibrium is used considerably in Parsons' discussions of social change. See *Societies* and "A Paradigm for the Analysis of Social Systems and Change", Demerath and Peterson, *System, Change, and Conflict*, pp. 189–212.

95. See especially *Working Papers in the Theory of Action*, Chapters III, V.

96. *Ibid.*, p. 174.

97. *Ibid.*, p. 87.

98. Parsons sensed this even before he had worked out the implications of the "types of social structure" idea. In *Toward A General Theory of Action* he noted a "paradox":

"One of the apparent paradoxes of the theory of action stems from . . . the lack of concern for internal structure [when dealing at a given level of analysis]. The paradox is that with all the emphasis on structure, the theory of action describes an actor who sometimes does not seem to have any internal structure at all. This paradox arises only on one level of conceptualization;

that level in which the actor is treated as the unit of interaction within a larger system of action. On the level dealing with the dynamic analysis of social interaction, however, the actor does indeed have very much of a structure". (p. 62).

It appears, then, that Parsons would agree with the thesis of this book, that the models of man in his theory tend to change to fit the kinds of analysis being undertaken.

99.   *Working Papers in the Theory of Action*, pp. 180–84. This reference puts it very clearly and succinctly.

100.   *Ibid.*, p. 183.

101.   *Ibid.*, pp. 183–84.

102.   *Ibid.*, pp. 84–85; *The Social System*, pp. 180–200.

103.   *Working Papers in the Theory of Action*, p. 184.

104.   *Ibid.*, p. 184.

105.   *Ibid.*, pp. 184–85.

106.   *Ibid.*

107.   *Ibid.*, p. 107.

108.   Dubin makes essentially this point in "Parsons' Actor: Continuities in Social Theory", p. 532.

109.   *The Social System*, p. 32.

110.   *Ibid.*

111.   *Ibid.*, p. 33.

112.   For a time, it seemed that Parsons was willing to recognize six pattern variables, but he never said what the sixth would be. Cf. "The Point of View of the Author", Black (ed.), *The Social Theories of Talcott Parsons*, p. 329.

113.   Parsons, "The Point of View of the Author", Black (ed.), *The Social Theories of Talcott Parsons*, p. 329.

114.   *Economy and Society*, pp. 33–38; *Toward A General Theory of Action*, Part I; *The Social System*, p. 67.

115.   T. Parsons, "Some Comments on the State of the General Theory of Action", M. L. Barron (ed.), *Contemporary Sociology* (Toronto: Dodd, Mead, 1964), p. 578.

116.   See the diagram, *The Social System*, p. 105.

117.   *Economy and Society*, p. 34.

118.   T. Parsons, "Some Comments on the State of the General Theory of Action", p. 582.

119.   *Ibid.*

120.   "The Point of View of the Author", Black (ed.), *The Social Theories of Talcott Parsons*, pp. 329–30.

121.   "Some Comments on the State of the General Theory of Action", p. 582.

122. Work leading in this direction is found in "The Pattern Variables Revisited"; "The Point of View of the Author"; and *Societies*.

123. See the chart in *Societies*, p. 28.

124. *Ibid.*; also Cf. "The Pattern Variables Revisited", especially the chart, p. 208. A similar chart is found in "The Point of View of the Author", p. 334.

125. Parsons and Bales, *Family, Socialization and Interaction Process*, p. 408.

126. *Ibid.*

127. *Working Papers in the Theory of Action*, Chapter V.

128. *Societies*, p. 113. He does not mean this to say that he has become "sociologistic", but rather that he considers the role of ideas extremely important in determining the shape of social interactions.

129. *Societies*, p. 113.

130. Perhaps a reasonable term for Parsons' deductive theory would be "typologico-deductive".

131. Cf. Richard Ogles, "Programmatic Theory and the Critics of Talcott Parsons", *The Pacific Sociological Review*, **IV**, No. 2 (Fall, 1961), 53–56. Zetterberg has called essentially the same thing "dimensionist" thinking. H. L. Zetterberg, Review of *Modern Sociological Theory in Continuity and Change*, by Becker and Baskoff, *American Sociological Review*, **XXIII**, No. 1, (February, 1958), 95–96.

132. Homans has criticized Parsons in this regard. Cf. G. C. Homans, "Contemporary Theory in Sociology", R. E. L. Faris (ed.), *Handbook of Modern Sociology* (Chicago: Rand-McNally, 1964), pp. 951–77. Also see D. F. Aberle *et al.*, "The Functional Prerequisites of a Society", *Ethics*, **60**, (January, 1950), 100–111. Barrington Moore has argued against the "scholasticism" of the Parsonian approach in "The New Scholasticism and the Study of Politics", B. Moore, Jr., *Political Power and Social Theory* (New York: Harper, 1958), pp. 89–110. For a different rendition of functional necessities, see M. J. Levy, Jr., *The Structure of Society* (Princeton: Princeton University Press, 1950).

133. Cf. Max Black, "Some Questions About Parsons' Theories", Black (ed.), *The Social Theories of Talcott Parsons*, pp. 268–88. Also see Dubin, "Parsons' Actor: Continuities in Social Theory", p. 521–36.

134. For an example of an attempt to apply the pattern variables empirically, see the research report in John C. McKinney, *Constructive Typology and Social Theory* (New York: Appleton-Century-Crofts, 1966), pp. 137–98.

135. Cf. A. K. Davis, "Social Theory and Social Problems", *Philosophy and Phenomenological Research*, **XVIII** (December, 1957), 190–208. Also Ralf Dahrendorf, "Out of Utopia".

Part III
Symbolic Interaction

CHAPTER 16

Introduction to part III

The study of symbolic interaction theory leads in several directions at once. One could detail the writings of Mead alone to begin such a study. This would lead into an examination of all the intricacies of Mead's work, which several persons have already attempted and partially accomplished. The fruits of this kind of analysis of symbolic interactionist literature are the clarification of exactly what one of the acknowledged founders of the approach had to say, and the indication of areas which need further attention. A second approach to the study of symbolic interaction theory would be to study the later books and papers that have acknowledged this tradition as their foundation, in order to ascertain the latest or most complete view of this approach in modern social science.

There are difficulties with both these approaches to the study of symbolic interaction, but they are not insuperable. Studying Mead alone has two main disadvantages. In the context of the present work, which attempts a broad overview of contemporary North American sociological theory from the standpoint of one theoretical problem, the study of Mead alone would seem out of place. Because Mead wrote more than forty years ago, his works have been expanded and extended by more recent writers whose contributions ought not to go unexamined. The study of Mead alone is a dubious approach to the study of symbolic interactionism also because his works to which most symbolic interactionists refer were not meant for publication. Rather, they are the compiled and edited lecture notes of several members of his classes in social psychology[1] and the history of ideas.[2] As much as these books are seminal and provocative, they do not constitute complete, consistent statements of Mead's main ideas.

The study of the later writings which take Mead's work as an important point of departure would contribute to the understanding of symbolic interactionism as a modern theory, but this approach has both practical and theoretical difficulties. Such a large volume of material would have to be covered that the task would be very unwieldy. This is demonstrated by the fact that until recently, there was available neither a unified statement of symbolic interactionist principles[3] nor a comprehensive reader.[4] There are several alternate varieties of symbolic interactionism that might be studied, none of which can claim to be the sole "true" heir of the work done by Mead in laying down the principles of the orientation.[5] Both of the recent works in symbolic interactionism mentioned above emphasize that they represent tentative and inconclusive statements, and that the field is by no means adequately summarized in them.

Nevertheless, because so many claim it as their theoretical orientation, the study of symbolic interactionism remains an integral part of the present work. A means has been found to accommodate it in a general consideration of the nature of man in relation to sociological explanation in modern sociological theory. This Part will use both of the approaches outlined above, making certain additions and deletions while concentrating on the core concepts in the approach—communication and language. Mead's work, so important in the foundations of symbolic interactionism, is given heavy emphasis; *Mind, Self and Society*, as well as other works of his, are used as major texts in this investigation. Several of the more reputable commentaries, criticisms and extensions of them are employed, as well.[6] It is necessary to deal with some modifications and extensions, as well as with Mead himself, in the study of symbolic interactionism. This is because Mead's work, while seminal, is sketchy and in some respects poorly edited.[7]

It will be argued that the model of man in symbolic interactionism could benefit from some studies of language that are being made mainly outside sociology.[8] The philosophical accounts of the various connotations of "symbol" and the impact these understandings may have on symbolic interaction theory have received little attention. In this Part, it will be argued that while Mead was essentially correct in focusing on language and communication as fundamental, the formulations of them which he achieved are inadequate in several respects. Moreover, when examined critically, the inadequacies indicate that the view of social organization at the sociological level commonly derived from symbolic interactionism is unacceptable in that it fails to take account of the full implications of basing a theory of social order on language. It will be seen that these inadequacies derive directly from the model of communication, which is the basis for the model of man.

The strategy for Part III in the study of the concepts of man in relation to sociological explanation in modern sociological theory will be as follows. The basic tenets of symbolic interactionist theory will be derived mainly from the works of Mead. This will take the form of setting out the accounts of the mind, the self, and social order. It will be seen that society is of prime concern to symbolic interactionists both as a phenomenon to be explained and as a starting point from which to analyze the individual. It will be stressed that language and symbolization play key roles in each of the areas of concern in symbolic interactionism. Without clarity concerning the place of "symbol"[9] in mind, self, and society, there can be no understanding of symbolic interactionism.

Since the focus of symbolic interactionism is the individual and his relationships with others, it will be found to contain a fairly explicit model of man. The concepts of "mind" and "self" speak directly to the problem of the nature of man. We will see that the problem of social organization ("society") is dealt with in terms of the individual, his abilities to use symbols, and his language.

Once symbolic interactionist theory is explained and the model of man identified and made clear, an analysis of the model will be attempted in terms of its major mechanism—signification, both to the self and to others. A criticism of the use of the term "symbol" will then be brought to bear on symbolic interactionist theory. We will see in this criticism that rather than social organization being the result of the fitting together of individual lines of action, at least one aspect of social structure is external to individuals and out of their reach in terms of negotiation and control. It will be emphasized that this aspect is concerned with language, the very heart of symbolic interactionist thinking. Since the full study of vocabulary, grammar, syntax, and so on, is too broad for application to symbolic interactionism in this essay, the comments and conclusions drawn here will have to remain tentative. However, the analysis of symbolic interactionism in these terms should provide some avenues for the convergence of the three types of sociological theory dealt with in this work.

CHAPTER 17

The model of man in symbolic interaction theory

It has been suggested that Mead's *Mind, Self and Society* has been edited in the wrong order,[10] and that the study of symbolic interactionism should begin with society, not mind. This contention comes from those who would use the theory to explain the nature of the individual and the way he develops through socialization. They argue that society has to be conceived as prior in time to any individual in it. This means that society ought to be characterized as a process of symbolic interaction into which each individual member is more or less gradually initiated.

For the present purpose, however, it appears that the original order of the presentations in *Mind, Self and Society* should be maintained. This order emphasizes the individual as a minded organism with a self. This emphasis is derived mainly from the central place of language and communication in the theory. These key ideas also form the bases on which an account of social organization is carried out in symbolic interactionism. To successfully communicate to others, it is necessary, in Mead's view, to communicate with one's self in just the way that one communicates with others—symbolically.[11] Thus the ideas of minded behavior, the self, and society all relate to the communicative act.

According to Mead, mind is not an essence, a substance found in the body, or a special sector of the nervous system. Rather, it is that aspect of the individual characterized by reflective behavior concerning his own actions.[12] Mead's notion concerning mind is that it emerges in the life-process through communication. In humans, communication takes place via significant gestures, or ones that have meaning.[13] Mead explains that this human communication is different from the communication occurring among animals. Animals may use signs. That is, they may cry out or gesture to each other in various ways through posture, snarls, and so on. But the animal gesture is a communicative act only in that the animals respond to gestures directly. This kind of communication in animals, Mead holds, is rightly called communication, but it has nothing to do with mind because it does not involve meaningful gestures and their interpretation.

Mead's view of meaningful communication is at once simple and complex. We have seen that an animal's gesture can be a body movement or cry. Basically the same thing holds in human communication, except that an interpretation is mentally inserted between the gesture and the response to it.[14] This interpretive activity is minded behavior. In humans, a vocal gesture may seem to cause a reaction in another person. But Mead asserts that the reaction is not to the gesture directly, but to the hearer's interpretation of the gesture. That is, the gesture has become a symbol for an act or event. The reaction noticed is to the act symbolized by the gesture and not to the gesture directly. Mead illustrates this with an example of a person coming upon a bear track in the woods.[15] It might be observed that the person, on seeing the track, became afraid. The fear, however, was not of the track but of the thing the track symbolized, i.e., the fact that a bear was near. Recognition that the track symbolized the nearness of a fearsome animal constituted minded behavior. That is, minded behavior is the mental extension of the meaning of the symbol to a possible eventuality—actually coming upon the bear.

Similarly, the symbol (track) is more than simply an impression in the ground indicating the presence of a bear. It is the symbol of a possible completed act or series of possible acts. Each of these possible acts are epitomized or telescoped into the symbol. It is these possible outcomes that constitute the meaning of the symbol.[16]

Minded behavior, in Mead's view, arises in problematic situations.[17] If one is confronted with a problem to which the answer is not immediately apparent, but yet a solution is necessary, minded behavior occurs in the following way. Several possible solutions might present themselves. The individual's problem solving takes the form of trying out each of these solutions mentally, (without any overt action at all), until one is found which seems to be appropriate. That is, the alternate solutions are symbolically extended to the situation, and the consequences of taking each alternative are worked out before any action is attempted. This process involves "thinking", or self signification through the use of symbols. Thus minded behavior occurring in problematic situations takes the form of a "conversation" with one's self concerning the alternatives in any problematic situation. Instead of the individual manipulating the situation directly in the solution of his problem (trial and error), he performs a mental trial and error process by using symbols for the elements of the situation and manipulating the symbols until the correct outcome is found.

This process implies a further property of minded behavior—namely, the selection of features of the environment to which one will attend.[18] Problems arise only in the relationship of the individual to the environment. Every individual, because he has a unique relationship to the environment, will attend to different aspects of it. Therefore, each individual's environment (each individual's symbolic representation of the environment) will be different. The process of minded behavior implies that the environment will never be the same for different persons, although similar environments will certainly appear similar to different persons.

It is clear, then, that Mead's understanding of mind is in terms of symbolic behavior. This behavior is the individual's signification to himself using symbols. The acts that result from minded behavior are those that have been formulated in the process of mental activity; that is, they have been tried out mentally. This mental trial is possible because the person has the ability to manipulate significant symbols which come to stand for aspects of the environment.

Up to this point, since no interhuman communication has come into the discussion, the term "significant symbol" has referred only to the symbols used in the individual's conversation with himself—in his minded behavior. At least logically, if not empirically, an individual could have a private language used only in communicating with himself. The symbols contained in that language (its "words") would have meaning only to the individual. That is, it is logically possible for a person to represent aspects of his environment by symbols having only private meaning. The "meaning" of these symbols would be related to the fact that the same vocal gesture always signified (stood for) the same environmental property for the individual who invented the symbols. Presumably, this private language would be adequate for minded behavior on the part of the person who invented it. But it would be useless for communication with others.

Language that is useful for communication with others is made up of "significant symbols" in another sense of the term "significant".[19] While it is logically possible for symbols to be privately significant to individuals in that they call up certain responses in them alone, Mead uses the term "significant" for symbols that have *shared* meaning. For Mead, meaning is social and is derived from the communicative usefulness of symbols rather than from individuals assigning meanings to symbols privately.

The relationship of [a] symbol to [a] set of responses in the individual as well as in the other . . . makes the vocal gesture what I call a significant symbol.[20]

In minded behavior concerning a problem, we saw that aspects of the problematic situation are singled out symbolically and the symbols manipulated until the correct combination is found for the solution of the problem. The symbols are then examined for their relation to properties of the environment. This relation indicates the correct behavior with regard to the actual environment; it is possible to extend action into the future by symbolically representing it. Thus the problem is solved mentally before it is solved physically.

In communicative behavior between persons, symbols play a similar central role. When symbolic meanings are shared, it is possible for one person to express himself to another such that the other can interpret the intentions of the speaker, as well as his present activity. Thus adjustive behavior is possible for the hearer. Since the speaker communicates to himself at the same time as he communicates to the other, he, too, has the possibility of interpreting his own communication and adjusting his behavior accordingly. The mutuality of the possibilities of adjustment and interpretation of the symbols used indicates the meaningful nature of the symbols. They are interpreted in the same way by the hearer as by the speaker; that is, the symbols have the same meaning to both. (This does not imply that similar adjustive activities will be observed after the symbols have been used.)

Conversation involves mental activity, since it has both inwardly and outwardly directed aspects. If a person speaks, he hears himself speak. Thus he signifies to himself the meaning he intended to convey to the other. The symbols have the same meaning to the speaker as to the hearer. In this sense, communication is both to the other and to the self. Communication is based on the proposition that the symbols turned both inwardly to the speaker and outwardly to the other have the same meaning—that is, they "signify" the same things.

In Mead's theory, the concept of "meaning" centers on the fact that communicating persons interpret given symbols in the same way.

Meaning [is] . . . the common response in one's self as well as in the other person, which becomes, in turn, a stimulus to one's self.[21]

Temporally, meaning is related to the future just as much as to the moment the vocal gesture is uttered. Since the symbol epitomizes an act, that is, since it telescopes the representation of a future state of affairs into itself, its meaning includes an image of that future state of affairs. This is the basis on which persons can interpret and react to each other's intentions as well as their overt behaviors. Vocal gestures are interpreted by participants in conversation mentally, in terms of the future situation epitomized by the gestures. Thus conversation is more than trading symbols which stand for aspects of the environment or the self. It is the trading of those symbols as they relate to each participant's operations and intended operations on the environment (which could include other participants in the conversation). This allows persons to adjust their activities to impending states of affairs, which in turn may result in the alteration of each person's intended activities. This unending adjustive mechanism in which persons are constantly redesigning their activities in the light of the activities of others or their inter-pretations of the intentions of others is central to the social interaction process.[22]

It will be wise to point out that the foregoing discussion of meaning and conversation through vocal gestures has applied only to *conscious* meaning and *conscious* use of significant symbols. Meaningful gestures can be made unconsciously, as when a gesture such as a facial expression denotes the state of mind of the person making the gesture. It is, however, only when the gesture becomes identified as a symbol and when the symbol signifies a meaning to the self that *conscious* meaning is present. This differentiation corresponds to the separation of natural signs such as animals use from symbols. Obviously, then, symbols are completely arbitrary in that they could be *any* gesture, so long as the participants in the communication in which they are used agree upon their meaning.

The mind arises in the social life-process. Children do not invent their own languages, but take on the ones in use around them by learning the meanings of the gestures used by the adults of their culture. This learning of minded behavior is equivalent to developing "intelligence".[23] "Intelligence" in common usage, refers to some raw and perhaps latent potential in humans. While this meaning is not contradicted by Mead's use of the term, he intends a special kind of ability when he uses it. In his view, intelligence is "reflective" in the sense of self-signification developed above. Humans are characterized by the ability to reflect intelligently on the present with respect to the extension of the present into the future, or into other aspects of the present not immediately in view. Reflective intelligence is the "talking to one's self" described in the example of problem solving.

To be able to identify "this as leading to that", and to get some sort of gesture, vocal or other-wise, which can be used to indicate the implication to others and to [the self] so as to make possible the control of conduct with reference to it, is the distinctive thing in human intelligence which is not found in animal intelligence.[24]

In Mead's view of minded behavior, then, the symbolic process is central. We have seen that persons are regarded as being able, through the use of symbolic representations of aspects of their environment, to project their own activities into the future and view their consequences before any overt acts are performed. Also, because of the same symbolic quality, persons are able to adjust their activities mentally to those of others. Through com-munication (using significant symbols) persons mentally view the conse-quences of the acts of others in the same way as they view their own acts. Mentalistic activity is reflective, in that it is the conversational quality of both thinking privately and communicating with others which allows one to make mental extensions of present situations and behaviors. The symbols that enable persons to act mentally capture the essence, or epitomize the nature, of a completed act. That is, symbols represent intentions or the consequences of an act, just the way they signify (stand for) certain aspects of the environment. When reacting to symbols, persons do not react to them directly, but to their interpretation of the act or consequences of the act for which the symbol stands.

For these functions to take place (communication and thinking), it is necessary that the symbols used have shared meanings among those who are using them. Symbolic signification made by one person must "call out" the same response in the other that it calls out in the speaker. This must be so in order that the adjustive and regulative mechanisms associated with the prediction of future states of affairs can operate in similar or compatible ways in each participant in the communication. It is important to note the concept of "significant symbol" as that gesture which calls out the same response in the hearer as it does in the gesturer. This quality of congruence or identity of prediction about a future act derivable from the symbol for that act is at the center of Mead's use of the term "meaning". Meaning arises in the complex including two persons and the environment in which the two communicate. Meaning does not, then, inhere in an object; and in its social connotation, it is not private. It requires the three elements of speaker, hearer and object (part of a situation spoken of).

We have seen that the central mechanism of Mead's theory is the individual's ability to indicate to himself in a way similar to that by which he indicates to others. This means that the individual must be able to understand himself as an object; he must view himself as others do. This ability to respond to one's own gestures implies the possession of a self.[25] Just as in the process of minded behavior, the individual singled out certain aspects of the *environment* by symbolizing them, so too the individual comes to have the ability to single out and symbolize himself as an object.[26] He can stand outside himself for purposes of defining the self as an object and can signify to the self as to another social object. We see, then, that the self is built on the same foundation as that of interhuman communication and mind.

The self is a uniquely social possession, since it is only indirectly that the individual comes to be aware of his self (gains self-consciousness).

The individual experiences himself . . . indirectly from the standpoints of other individual members of the same social group, or from the generalized standpoint of the social group as a whole to which he belongs. For he enters his own experience as a self or individual, not directly or immediately, but only in so far as he first becomes an object to himself just as others are objects to him or in his experience. . . .[27]

Getting outside one's self and viewing it objectively from the standpoint of another person does not imply that such a view is a dispassionate one.

The point Mead makes is that the subject, the individual, must also be object to himself before he can meaningfully experience his self. This is derived from the fundamental proposition about meaning: it arises in the context of the relations of two communicating individuals (or entities, in this case) and the environment. Since the body is physically a unit, the self associated with it must therefore have the facility to be both of the communicating elements at once. That is, signification to the self about the self implies that the self must play the parts of both the signifier and the one signified to. The object about which the internal communication is carried on is also the self. Therefore, the self must become object of the conversation, and its possessor must be both objective and subjective concerning his own self. This facility is utilized in the role-taking experience,[28] in which the individual becomes able to view himself as an object from the standpoint of others in his experience. Thus role-taking is of prime importance in the development of social selves, or in gaining an objective point of view toward the self. This "gaining the objective point of view" is identical to the process of becoming not only a conscious being, but self-conscious.

It can not be stressed enough that Mead views the process of becoming self-conscious in the same terms as the process of attaining minded behavior. It is through the medium of communication that the person becomes able to see himself as an object. The communication process facilitates the individual's taking the attitudes of the other toward himself (i.e., taking the role of the other). From the standpoint of the other's role, the self begins to appear as an object. The process of minded behavior then is trained on the self, so that the internal conversation becomes something like, "What must he think of me when I act thus"? To be successful, this internal process of communication from the standpoint of the other must call up in the individual the same answers that the other would have given if he had been answering the question, "What do I think of him"? Therefore, successful role-taking requires a communication process in which the individual can signify to the self in exactly the same terms as to another.

Taking the role of the other is an activity and ability that must be learned in the social process. It is implied, as we have seen, in the concepts of communication and minded behavior; but the actual development of it in society is dependent on each individual's coming to view himself in the objective sense. Mead gives a two-stage model for the process of acquiring a self which has been extended and made more explicit by others.[29] To begin with, there must be imitation[30] as the basis of language and of role-taking. That is, before successful speech or role-taking can occur, the individual must emit the sounds of speech and emit some behaviors characteristic of the roles of others around him. In this preliminary stage, however, there is no reason to assume that the person is using significant symbols. Rather, he is manipulating the significant symbols of those around him without signifying to himself at the same time. The symbols he is using are not yet significant to him and have no communication value.

Following this stage, after language acquisition has begun, the person starts to take individual roles of others toward the self. From what he sees in the social situation the person comes to abstract the elements of roles played by those around him. He becomes increasingly able to see the continuity concerning the activities of given roles. Thus, for example, a child comes to identify a constellation of activities and attitudes with "mother". This identification is not yet role-taking, but it is preliminary to it. The person who is about to take another's role must have insight into the performances of the role in some rudimentary sense before the name of the role can have any meaning to the person.

After this first insight has been achieved, it is possible for the individual to view the self from the standpoint of the other person's role. That is, in taking the role of the other, it is possible to gain further insight into the role and take on the full complement of attitudes associated with it. In taking the role successfully, a person comes to see that it is not his own role; this differentiation is crucial. The realization that he is not playing his own role, but that of another, makes it possible to see objectively what his *own* role is from the other's point of view. This insight leads to a recognition of the self-in-role, or an insight into self.[31]

After a person has achieved the beginnings of self insight *via* role-taking, he increasingly comes to understand the attitudes of his group. This is a matter of organization as much as simply the compilation of knowledge about various roles. The organization of the roles being played around a person is finally generalized and seen as an organization of roles into which the self is fit as one part. Viewing the self from the standpoint of this generalized unit is different from specific role-taking, since there are attitudes of several roles involved at once. Rather, it is taking the role of the "generalized other". "The attitude of the generalized other is the attitude of the whole community".[32] When the individual has achieved the standpoint of the generalized other toward himself, he is in a position to understand himself completely. He then possesses the ability to see himself in all his various facets, and thus to define his self to himself as it must appear to all those of the community.

Mead argues that the final stage in self insight, and the final stage in the rise of the self, is the self-consciousness which is embodied in insight into the will of the group.[33] As Mead puts it, it is the taking of the attitudes of the generalized other toward the various

phases and aspects of the common social activity or set of social undertakings in which, as members of an organized society or social group, they are all engaged.[34]

That is, the completely formed self not only is able to take the role of the generalized other toward himself, and thus view himself as object, but also he is able to take the generalized other's role toward the group as a whole and toward its tasks. This last phase is not often mentioned in secondary works on Mead's theory of the development of self. But it is important for Mead, since he sees it as the final stage of integration into a community. He views the self as a fundamental aspect of community; in so far as selves attain their last stage of development, the community becomes integrated. Not only does the individual take the roles of others and the generalized other as a standpoint from which to view his self, and thus become self-conscious; he also takes the generalized other's viewpoint toward the group as a whole, gaining insight concerning the place of the self in the larger organization of attitudes and behaviors of which it is one part.

Self understanding and consciousness in terms of the generalized other give the individual a picture of his various "me's".[35] The "me" is the interpretation the individual makes of each of his roles in the social world. There are many "me's", because there are many roles played by an individual. The "me" is the self-incorporated "other" in the individual. That is, it is only by means of taking the role of the other that the self becomes aware of his presentations and aware of his various "me's". Awareness of the "me's" is the awareness of other's attitudes toward the self. The "me" comes into the consciousness of every individual during the internal conversations involving viewing the self objectively. If the individual thinks, "How must the other view me now"? the question implies the consciousness of a certain performance being made by the individual at that moment. These "me's" are the reflections Cooley has in mind when describing the "looking glass self".[36] That is, the various vantage points from which the individual can view his self may be thought of as reflections from others who are "mirrors". But the reflections are mediated through the interpretations made by the individual. Thus the "me's" are the interpretations the individual makes of the responses others make to him.

The self is more than a bundle of "me's", however. Mead also speaks of the "I" as the other part of the social self, a part which is aware of the "me".[37] There is probably more confusion in interactionist literature concerning the nature of the "I" than on any other point. Some interactionists tend to forget the "I" altogether, taking only the insights concerning the "me" for use in research and theoretical development.[38] Mead says it is the "I" that reacts to the "me". In taking the attitude of another, the individual becomes able to view himself objectively. This objective picture of his performances at any one time from any one vantage point gives rise to a "me". This "me" does not, however, react back upon the self directly. We have seen that in symbolic interactionist thinking, it requires a mental act to interpret symbols before they have meaning. Therefore, the self must have another aspect, analytically separate from the "me's", which can become part of the mental act of interpreting the "me's". This is the "I". It seems that Mead meant the "I" as an unconscious unit. Certainly it is "un-self-conscious". In his discussion of remembering, he brings this out.

I talk to myself and I remember what I said. . . . The "I" of this moment is present in the "me" of the next moment . . . [but] I can not turn around quickly enough to catch myself. I become a "me" in so far as I remember what I said. . . . It is because of the "I" that we say that we are never fully aware of what we are, that we surprise ourselves by our own action.[39]

Since the "I" is the response of the organism to the attitudes of others, the "I" is always in the past. That is, the response must be thought of as coming after the experience of the attitude of another, and thus the "I" is always an "historical figure".[40]

The "I" is [an individual's] action over against that social situation within his own conduct, and it gets into his experience only after he has carried out [an] act.[41]

Thus it is the "I" that gives unity to the various "me's" reflected in the attitudes of others toward the self. Rather than the self being a bundle of "me's", the "me's" are mentally reacted to within the symbolic experience of the individual. It is the "I" that so reacts. Since the "I" has this function, it is the aspect of the self that unifies the "me's" by being the standpoint from which all "me's" are interpreted. With reference to these interpretations, it is the agent of action at any given instant. Thus the individual is constantly in a process of acting, viewing his own actions mentally, and acting again according to his interpretations of the acts. At any given instant, it is the "I" that is in action. It is this "I" that acts, but it is the "me" that provides grounds for the interpretations of these acts. The "I" is never left to "run free"; it is always under the check of the reflected "me".

The symbolic interactionist picture of man is now complete. It consists of an individual person with the ability to symbolize aspects of his world and communicate via those symbols with himself as well as his fellows. In communicating, the vocal gesture (or the overt act which may be other than vocal) has a meaning in that it calls out the same reaction in the self as it calls out in the other. When situations are symbolized to the self, the person manipulates symbols for aspects of the environment and thus solves new problems and devises novel solutions to old ones without any overt activity in the environment. This is man's reflective intelligence. The ability to use symbols is the key to the interactionists' picture of man. The process of communication, the symbolic representation of aspects of the individual and his environment to both himself and others, is the paradigm for the view of the mind and of the self.

The mind does not exist as an entity with special attributes. Rather, symbolic interactionism views mind as a process of communication with the self. This is the self-signification process. Through self-signification, the person comes to have insight into a situation and the objects in it. Through the symbolization of objects, the person abstracts them out of the environment. Thus symbolization of the environment structures it for the individual. Therefore man's perception is more than the receiving of stimuli by the senses. It is the interpretation of that stimuli in terms of symbols as it relates to the individual in his special way. For this reason, the interactionist tradition has become very much interested in the Whorf hypothesis concerning the various worlds people "see" as the language used to symbolize that world varies.

Symbolization and communication are related to the idea of the self as a possession of man. *Via* the interpretation of other's attitudes toward the self, the individual comes to have insight into who he is; that is, the self arises in the processes of communication among persons. The individual gains this insight through role-taking, or the viewing of the self from the other's vantage point. Man is viewed as having the facility to symbolize himself as an object as another person might, and treat his self like any other object in a field. By symbolically treating the self as an object, the individual comes to insights about how his performances must appear to others. But this does not mean that the "others" control the individual's self or his self image completely.

There are two aspects of the self that directly interact with each other, giving the self unity and uniqueness as well as reliance on society. These are the "I" and the "me". The "me" is that interpreted reflection upon the self the individual comes to understand through role-taking. By symbolically representing the self in this way, it is possible to change behavior in order to make the other see a different "me". The "I" is the acting entity of the self at any one instant. The "I" and the "me" are in perpetual conversation concerning the actions of the self. Thus, action is constantly being reinterpreted as the "me's" become known and "I's" are being changed accordingly.

To round out the picture of man in symbolic interactionism, it is necessary to comment again upon the nature of the communication process. Communication is the manipulation of meaningful symbols by persons. That is, the symbols used may be vocal gestures, or written or otherwise produced objects, that call forth the same reactions in the person using them as in the person receiving them. The idea of "meaning" of a symbol consists in the fact that a gesture does call forth the same response in another that it calls forth in its user. It is only when this is the case that gestures become "significant". That is, they signify the same thing to the person using them as to the person receiving them.[42]

A symbol, then, is a sign. It may be an "artificial" sign,[43] in that it is contrived by man for his use; but it has the qualities of a sign for symbolic interactionists. That is, the gesture has a meaning by virtue of the consensus about its reference among those that use it. If it had more than one referent, and there was no method of discerning the correct referent from context, there could be no communication, i.e., it would not be "significant".

It is important to keep in mind that the interactionist view of mind and of self depends on this interpretation of symbol. If a symbol did not call out in the other the same response as it calls out in the person using it, there could be no successful role-taking, no communication, and therefore, no self. Similarly, there could be no minded behavior if the individual did not always use the symbols available to him in the same way. It seems more reasonable to suppose that a single individual will signify to himself in terms of his symbols consistently and accurately than to suppose that the *same* reactions will be called out in himself as in others. The extent to which the same reactions are *not* called out in others as in the individual using the symbol must be taken as problematic.

In a later stage of this essay, it will be argued that this view of "symbol" is oversimplified, and a substitute interpretation of it will be advanced. It will be seen that the new interpretation has several consequences for the theory as a whole, especially in regard to the way symbolic interactionists treat the concept of "social structure".

One final point about Mead's view of symbolization must be made. It is unclear in most of his writings and in interpretations of him what it means to "call out" a reaction. The meaning of this term is important, because the difference between sign-function and symbol-function of vocal gestures depends on it. In Mead's example of the bear track in the woods, it seemed that the person seeing the track was not afraid of the track, but of the bear who must have made the track. That is, the reaction was to the *object symbolized*. The "calling out" was of the reaction to that which was symbolized by the track. Blumer puts it this way:

Their [persons'] "response" is not made directly to the actions of one another but instead is based on the meaning which they attach to such actions. Thus human interaction is mediated by the use of symbols, by interpretation, or by ascertaining the meaning of one another's action. This mediation is equivalent to inserting a process of interpretation between stimulus and response in the case of human behavior.[44]

It still seems unclear whether or not the person reacts to the symbol similarly to the way he would react to the thing symbolized. But from Blumer's view it does seem so, since he states that mediation by symbols is equivalent to the insertion of an interpretation between the stimulus and the response. That is, the symbol is reacted to according to the interpretation placed on the *thing the symbol represents*. The reaction is not to the symbol, or to the object directly, but to interpretations. Apparently, the symbol is conceived as standing for the object, and it is the symbol that "calls out" the reaction to the interpretation of the thing it symbolizes. Thus, in the example of the bear track, the reaction is to the interpretation of the bear track as a symbol for a fearsome object (the bear). Presumably, the symbol calls forth the same reaction, that is, the same interpreted reaction, as the object itself. It seems that this is what Mead and the interactionists understand by symbolization. Thus the view of man includes the understanding that he is capable of inserting the interpretation between the stimulus and the response, and of substituting one stimulus for another.

CHAPTER 18

The symbolic interactionist theory of social organization

In dealing with social organization, the process of communication is central for the interactionist just as it was in dealing with minded behavior and the self. Persons have the facility to adjust their behaviors according to their interpretations of the behaviors of others. This is based on the notion of communication among individuals *via* significant symbols. Since the human can be the object of his own actions, as well as the author of actions, he has the ability to take the role of the other and view his actions from the other's perspective. This means that he can imagine the reactions of others (that is, other's interpretations) to his behavior, and he can design his acts accordingly. Thus there is the possibility of constant adjustment among persons in social groups, according to each other's interpretations of the action of each. Action is therefore constructed, or built up, rather than being the release of certain activities as responses to forces or pressures inherent in situations. It is constructed by the individual in the process of constant assessment of his own activities as well as the actions of others, both of which he views as objects.

This leads to the argument that, fundamentally, the action of a group is only the composite of individual actions in it.[45] That is, the group is what the acting individuals make it, and no more. There are no group level phenomena that may not be analyzed in terms of the actions of the persons making up the group. There is no necessity for any action in particular, from the point of view of the group as a whole. While persons may agree to work together in some organized way, and thus give the appearance that the group is directing their activities by more or less assigning each person the tasks which he will perform, it is actually the fact that this group organization is the conscious creation of the individuals and is seen as acceptable, or at least as tolerable, by each person in the group. Group action involves nothing more than getting the meaning of each other's actions and designing one's behavior accordingly.

This model does not rest on either consensus among persons or contention among them. The fundamental assertion that group life is the aligning of individual actions can be applied to both conflict and consensus. Persons can be conceived to align their actions to those of others in circumstances of either competition, conflict, or cooperation. There is no fundamental proposition about the nature of groups[46] in symbolic interactionist thinking that can not be reduced to the basic postulates of the communication process and the fact that persons are seen as having selves. Below we will have occasion to examine the extent to which the postulates concerning communication are actually reductionistic and in what respects they must be seen as describable in terms of laws applying only to them and *not* derivable from the actions of group members.

Symbolic interactionism does not hold that no institutions exist, or that groups do not appear to be characterized by their own activities. But societal level organization is conceived as being ultimately reducible to and explicable in terms of the individuals that make up the social order. Mead understands institutions in terms of "common responses" which come to be built up in community life.

There are . . . whole series of such common responses in the community in which we live, and such responses are what we term "institutions".[47]

The institution is seen as a common response on the part of all the members of the community to a particular situation. Institutionalization is viewed, further, as the predictability of actions on the part of persons made possible by the role-taking process.

There is, for example, an on-going court system because one comes to expect the court's various officials and functionaries to behave in certain ways since one can take their role and make predictions about their behaviors from the standpoint of it. These predictions about the behaviors of others are the expectations that come to be built up in the institutionalization process. That is, one comes to expect a judge to act fairly. The fact that this interpretation becomes general is the basis for the institutionalized expectations about the *role* of the judge. This generalized expectation derives directly from each person's ability to take the judge's role and predict his behavior from knowledge of it. The theoretical result is that the expectations about judges are accounted for in terms of every person's ability to extract more or less the same qualities from his taking of the judge's role as a vantage point from which to generate expectations about possible behaviors toward others, including perhaps, himself.

Institutions and social life also serve to explain the individual. It is not necessarily curious that individual abilities such as role-taking and language use should explain society's formation and existence, at the same time that society explains the individual. In the symbolic interactionist perspective, both these phenomenon (the individual and society) emerge together from the process of social interaction. Without institutions (that is, without organized social attitudes toward certain performances) there could be no fully mature selves. It will be remembered that the final stages in the development of the self were the gaining of the ability both to take the role of the generalized other and to view the self as part of an on-going process within a group of persons acting toward collective goals. It is the institutionalized attitudes toward certain performances that constitute the generalized other in any given context. In this sense, the social order, with its stock of institutionalized attitudes toward certain performances, is what is assumed in the concept of the generalized other. It is the attitude of the generalized other that is finally learned and taken over by the developing self. Therefore, while the society may be explained by the abilities and propensities of individuals to take the role of the other and to communicate intentions and interpretations, the individuals themselves are in turn explained by their mature development of selves in society. Indeed, the interactionist perspective holds that both the individual and the society containing him emerge out of the social life-process.

However, institutions are not seen as defining attitudes or modes of conduct specifically. On the contrary, they define socially responsible modes of conduct only very generally, leaving much room for individual innovation and flexibility. It could be no other way, for Mead's view of the individual is one of a unitary acting person who constructs his behaviors as he goes along according to his reading of the actions of others. There can be nothing rigid about this view, since it relies upon the concept of the person as a bundle of "me's" reflected back to the individual from his comrades and as the "I" which, at any given instant, is the acting, interpreting entity giving the self unity and individuality.

It can not be emphasized enough that the social individual is the one who responds to himself as those of his community respond to him. That is, individual behavior is not seen as the responses of persons to societal "pressures" or to structurally determined circumstances which hem the individual into certain modes of conduct. Conduct is never socially forced; it is always individually constructed. But it is constructed in terms of self evaluations and interpretations which are in general congruent with the interpretations placed on it by others in the community. This accounts for the predictability of actions in situations. It is not the situation that forces the individual to behave in a certain way; rather, it is because a certain community attitude has been internalized by the individual that he designs his actions in given ways in certain situations. He uses as a referent the attitude of the generalized other as a basis from which to understand and evaluate his own actions. Therefore, no real coercion from the social order affects the individual. Social determinism exists only in that the attitudes of the collectivity toward performances in certain situations are taken over by the individual through role-taking. There is no hard and fast determinism here. The fact that the individual normally takes on the attitude of the collectivity accounts for the observation of regularity in social life with respect to certain situations; but it does not follow, in the interactionist view, that this constitutes externally determined action from the individual's point of view.

The maintenance of this kind of social order depends upon the theory of communication and minded behavior developed in interactionism. The individual, to successfully act with reference to the attitudes of the generalized other, must be capable of calling out in himself the same responses to his behavior as would be called out by another member of the same social order as a response to that behavior. That is, he must interpret himself the same way that he is interpreted by others. We saw that the model of minded behavior was that of the internal conversation, in which the individual signified to himself from the viewpoint of the self as an object. The self being an object like other objects, it will be possible to manipulate it mentally via symbolization, just as other objects may be manipulated. This internal manipulation of the symbols for the self and for other objects led to defining "thinking" as mental trial and error in which the "correct" solution to a problem, or the otherwise "appropriate" behavior, could be worked out before any overt behavior was manifested. "Correct" and "appropriate" are conditions placed on the action in the present that have been worked out in past interactions with others in similar situations.

Structural features of the organization of action are not ignored, but they are not accounted for in symbolic interaction theory.

Social systems, social stratification and social roles set conditions for . . . action, but do not determine . . . action. . . . Social organization enters into action only to the extent to which it shapes situations in which people act, and to the extent to which it supplies fixed sets of symbols which people use in interpreting their situations.[48]

It is clear, then, that the symbolic interactionist perspective treats structural features of the social order as direct resultants of individual abilities and ways of acting as social selves. While structural features may "set conditions" for interaction, these conditions are negotiable[49] among the participants in the action. Nothing at the distinctly "sociological" level contravenes this process.

Thus there is a freely acknowledged paradox in symbolic interaction theory concerning the individual and society. The individual needs the social order in which to develop a mature self. He must take on the language in use around him as a basis for making correct interpretations of his own behavior from the viewpoints of others. That is, he needs to rely upon the social order for the attitudes of others so that he can correctly appraise the self. Treating the self as an object presupposes a point of view that is outside the self, but a part of the social order. Coming to understand the self's place in a larger scheme of social interaction presupposes that there *is* this scheme.

But the social order, in turn, relies upon the individuals who make it up. We saw that Mead viewed institutions as very general agreements among persons about how to conduct themselves. He allowed the individual's personal style to bring in considerable innovation and change. Similarly, Blumer sees "social structure" as placing only very wide and amorphous limits on individuals in interaction, and Mead views it as only the "agreements" among persons. The extent to which social organization shapes the conduct of the persons within it, by giving them the symbols with which to symbolize their world, and by giving them set modes of interpreting the situations they confront, is not spelled out. Blumer regards these factors as minor ones. This is clear from the fact that he offers the symbolic interactionist perspective on society as an alternative to what he takes to be social determinism. The paradox in viewing individual and society in the ways just outlined is that they depend on and, in some sense at least, control each other. The proportions in which the one controls the other are left undefined by symbolic interactionists.

Symbolic interactionism does not deal much with societal level phenomena as such. Rather, it tends to take the social order as a backdrop from which to focus on the individual and the interactions he carries out within the broad structure of "society". It is thus more of a micro-sociological theory than a macro one. It is concerned with social-psychological explanation rather than explanation of societal level events or of behavior of groups *qua* groups. While it gives an account of institutions, it does not advance a theoretical reason for their nature or their particulars. Symbolic interactionism uses social structure in its account of individual interactions, but it does not treat social structure analytically. Rather, society is taken as part of the conditions of the interaction situation. The fact that society is seen to change with the impact of individuals and the fact that individuals develop their selves and their minded behavior in the process of social interaction do not alter this view.

Symbolic interactionism thus tends to be a perspective, rather than a substantive social theory. As such, it advances no propositions about human behavior in particular, but only gives insightful suggestions as to the ways in which human interaction is carried out. The fact that the human being is seen as an intelligent organism with the facility for language, and not a bundle of specific propensities, needs, and desires, implies that man could operate successfully in any social arrangement into which he might be born. Human nature is thus everywhere the same. Although the "I" acts at any one instant, and may be unpredictable, the mental check placed upon the "I" by the "me" ensures that as behavior is constructed in the process of social inter-action, it is always dependent upon the interpreted reactions of others.

There may be no reason to quarrel with this kind of formulation, as far as it goes. But as a sociological theory, symbolic interactionism must be seen as a rather loosely arranged collection of insights into how persons get on with each other. The fact that interactionism does not offer a rigorous body of propositions or suggestions concerning human behavior, makes the theory rather difficult to research. Almost without exception, symbolic interaction theory has been applied in small groups, or in areas which may be treated successfully as the aggregation of small group phenomena.

CHAPTER 19

Criticism of interactionism's core ideas— symbol and language

The paradigm for the symbolic interactionist treatment of the mind, the self and society is communication—the signification to the self in the same way as the person signifies to others around him. It will be useful to examine the idea of communication by way of criticism concerning symbols and signification. This will constitute an analysis and critique of the concept of communication in symbolic interactionism. This analysis will point the way toward a resolution of the individual–society paradox, since it will focus directly upon language—the theoretical mechanism which, from the symbolic interactionist perspective, accounts for both society and individual.

Communication is signification to the self and to the other such that the symbols used call out the same reactions in self and other. The *self* is the product which arises from the individual's taking the viewpoint of the other from which to see himself as an object. To accomplish this, he must call out in himself the same attitudes toward himself that the other would call out if the other were to view the individual. The *mind* consists in self-signification, in which the individual holds a conversation with his self, taking an objective view of his possible actions with respect to some problem, and mentally working out how he might or ought to act to solve the problem. *Society* consists in the aligning of each person's activities according to his interpretations of the activities of others. This depends on the individuals' abilities to communicate with each other, to symbolize each other's actions, and to interpret the symbols in terms of the acts which the symbols epitomize.

Each of these three aspects of social life are built up from the view of communication and language spelled out by Mead and others. Communication depends on the use of symbols. Symbols are the contrived or agreed-upon gestures (which may be vocal or otherwise) that call out the same response in each party to the agreement. The symbol does not fetch the reaction directly. The reaction is not to the symbol, but to the thing the symbol is agreed to represent, i.e., the meaning of the symbol. This meaning is the interpretation each person puts on it. Thus, meaning, in the Meadian view of communication (and by implication, minded behavior, self and social interaction) is dependent on the three aspects of symbolization that have already been identified: the gesturer (who is also gestured *to*, since he hears himself make the gesture); the hearer, or the one gestured to; and the vocal gesture itself, as it refers to some event or behavioral object by epitomizing it. The gestures stand for the resultant act to which the individuals give a definite response.

We see in this formulation that it is absolutely necessary for the gesture to have the same "meaning" to both parties,[50] or no communication can result, since the gesture must epitomize the same act to both parties. Further, this meaning is in terms of the resultant behavior that is symbolized by the gesture. It is the behavior that is being interpreted, but has not yet occurred. That is, the symbol is not directly reacted to, but rather, the symbol stands for a certain expectation about behavior which is being reacted to. The "reaction" in each of the parties is not directly to the behavior to come, since it has not yet occurred; it is an expectation, or more accurately, an interpreted expectation. Thus when the master raises his hand, the dog may cower. In the dog, the reaction is not to his interpretation of an expectation, but it is simply the action that comes from being conditioned to cower when the man raises his hand. To the human, a man raising his hand may have a certain meaning, but not in the same way as to the dog. The man interprets the meaning of the raised hand and acts according to the meaning he interprets the raised hand to represent, not to the hand itself, or to the literal situation a raised hand may signify.

This brings up a problem which has not been dealt with in Meadian theory—the idea of the "concept".[51] Clearly, Mead meant that a person dealt with symbols in different ways than animals do. The insertion of the interpretation between the symbol and the behavior in the man indicates this. But the ambiguous expression which Mead used was to "call out" the same reaction in the individual using the symbol as that which was "called out" in the person hearing it. "Calling out" a reaction appears sometimes to mean an uninterpreted reaction and sometimes, an interpreted reaction. In the example of the sight of the bear track in the woods, the individual was not afraid of the track, but of the bear that the track symbolized for him. The track stood for the bear, but there seemed to be no room for the *concept* "bear" in this example.[52] There was no suggestion of a concept "bear" actually being symbolized, and not the particular bear himself. That the example says the track called out the reaction of fear obscures the fact that the symbol was for the *concept* "bear" and not for the particular bear. Thus it is unclear what Mead means when he says that the symbol "calls out" a reaction. Does the symbol call out a concept (which is then interpreted, as it would seem) or does it call out an interpretation of the event or fact symbolized but not a concept of it?

This subtle distinction is most important to the idea of communication in Mead's theory. If the symbol calls out an interpretation of the thing symbolized, then the symbol is really performing a sign-function. That is, it is standing for the thing symbolized, and the party reacting is interpreting the symbol as though it were the thing symbolized. This indeed seems to be what Mead means, at least most of the time. Since the symbol epitomizes subsequent phases of the social act not yet performed, it seems to stand for the act, and not for the concept of the act. In the behavioral terms Mead used, this is expressed as the "calling out" of a reaction in the persons using the symbol. The reaction called out is a behavioral event—albeit an event built up from interpretation, nevertheless a behavioral event. It has no conceptual status.

In the example of the bear track in the woods, the person seeing it conjured up a reaction to the track. That is, the track seemed to set off some kind of mediated reaction in the person. The person did not conceptualize "bear", and then think to himself, using that concept, whether or not the track was made recently, whether it was artificial or real, or try to figure out which way the bear had been moving. The mental activity Mead seemed to have in mind in this example of the bear track was more on the order of the simple mediated reaction taking place as the person saw the track. That is, Mead never used the idea of "concept" when referring to that which is conjured up in the person using the symbol.

Now, if concepts are to be considered the reaction "called up" in persons using symbols, the theory of communication must take on a new dimension. Concepts themselves have no meaning for action. The organizations of concepts and their arrangements according to grammatical rules refer to actions.[53] Opening a dictionary and reading off a list of symbols that stand for concepts has no "meaning" in action. Symbols have "meaning" for action when they are used in conjunction with other symbols according to the rules of grammar; the arrangement of concepts itself has a meaning. This is simply to say that vocabulary alone does not constitute language. Thus, in Mead's example of the bear track, the fact that there was no indication the person seeing the track conceptualized "bear" and used it in mental activity with other concepts indicated that Mead does not view language as conceptualizations symbolized and strung together according to structural rules. His view of language is more concerned with the behavioral reactions to certain signs.[54]

The difference being focused upon here is between the sign-function of a symbol, which may be said to announce the existence or imminence of a thing or event, and the symbol-function of a symbol, which may be said to lead to the conceptualization of an event.[55] It seems that, while Mead may mean both of these at times, his main formulation about communication is in terms of sign-function, since he argues that meaning arises in the context of the symbol user, the symbol hearer and the subsequent event that the symbol epitomizes. Both persons party to the communication must have the same reaction to the sign for it to have meaning. In the symbol-function of a symbol, however, it would be necessary to add a fourth element to Mead's formulation—the concept. Thus, for a symbol to do more than simply announce the imminence of an event or behavior, it would have to include the "concept" phase of meaning. Meaning, then, would arise in the context of four elements, not three: the person using the symbol, the person receiving the symbol, the concept of the thing symbolized, and the thing itself.

The concept of a thing symbolized is the symbol's *connotation*. We think about connotations or concepts, not react toward things and events represented by symbols. This means that, for communication to take place, not only must the symbols conjure up in the communicating individuals the same concepts (or similar concepts), but the concepts must be related together in some way via the structure of language itself. Thus, knowledge of the symbol in a given language does not give one the ability to communicate using those symbols; rather, communicating requires knowledge of the ways in which the symbols are used in conjunction with each other in the structure of the language itself. This view of communication does not ensure that hearer and user will derive the same meaning even when the same concept is conjured up in them by the use of the symbol. If the hearer and user hold different ideas about the use of that symbol, i.e., have different understandings of the structure of language, the symbol alone may be insufficient for successful communication. In other words, communication depends as much upon the structural rules of the language being employed as upon the symbols of that language. It is not the symbols that "say" something; it is the combination of such symbols in linguistic expressions that "says" things.[56]

We have seen that learning the symbols of a language does not lead to communication directly. Symbols in their symbol-function correspond to the definitions of the various words in a language found in a dictionary. While they all have connotations, the connotations themselves do not suffice for communication, since the connotations have to be grouped into assertions or propositions. These propositions do not have "meaning" in the same sense that Mead used the term, since they are not symbols as such, but groups of symbols characterized by a specific structure—grammar.

Now, in human language, it is discourse that has meaning for action. Terms themselves (symbols) make no assertions. They may name things, or call forth concepts, but they do not *say* anything. Without grammar, there could be no propositional language, no literal assertions, and no coherences of meaning transmitted from person to person, or from self to self-as-object. Thus in Mead's example of the bear track, the track must have been the *sign* of the bear. This sign might have alerted the person that a bear could be near, and thus set off a reaction of fright. But if the track was a symbol of "bear" to be used in communication with the self or others, it must have conjured up the concept "bear". The person must then have acted toward an implicit proposition containing that concept, such as, "A bear is near". (Mead leaves this unexamined in his example).

"A bear is near" is a proposition because it states the relationship of two concepts such that the statement conceptually "fits" the empirical facts (or, in this case, may fit the facts, since there was no indication that the bear really was near). The point is that "bear" as a concept was linked with "near" as a concept in the structure of the linguistic expression, "A bear is near". The track as a symbol did not "call out" the reaction of fear but rather, it "called out" the implicit expression of the relationship of "bear" and "near"—that is, it "called out" a *thought*. Thus, in this case, "A bear is near" is a proposition because it fits together two concepts in a pattern. The pattern has a meaning, just as the symbols in it have a meaning, but of a different order. The pattern is conceived to be analogous to the pattern of reality (the bear actually being near), and thus to "fit" reality closely. The "meaning" of this fit (that is, the meaning of the proposition as a whole), was the thing that caused the person seeing the track to manifest fear. Thus, the possibility that the conceptual linking of "bear" and "near" was analogous to the empirical situation of the actual bear and its actual proximity to the person caused the manifestation of fear, not the symbol "bear" alone, and not the track of the bear alone.[57]

The proposition is a picture of reality, then, but it is not a duplicate of it "in the mind". What it shares with reality is a certain proportionality that the concepts share with each other. The concepts "bear" and "near" are related by "is". This proportionality of the two concepts is not a duplication in conceptual form of actual bears being close at hand. It is, rather, a proportionality of the concepts "bear" and "near" that holds a certain supposed congruence with the current location of an actual bear in the "real" world. This means that thought or minded behavior is not the manipulation of symbols alone, and the calling forth of reactions to the meanings of the symbols. Rather, thought is the linking together of concepts using the given structure of a propositional language, i.e., using a set of rules. In minded behavior, then, for thought or internal conversation to exist, there must be the symbol which is associated with a concept, the linking of the concept to some part of "reality" through its representation of it, and a set of rules by which concepts may be linked to form propositions or assertions tying concepts together so that they "fit" the organization of their referents in the real world. This is a considerable divergence from Mead's view of thinking as self-signification using "symbols" as he defined them. Some consequences of this critique of Mead's view of language and meaning will be explored in the next chapter.

CHAPTER 20

Implications of the criticism of the interactionist view of language for the theory as a whole, with special reference to the model of man

It will be appropriate now to examine some of the implications of the foregoing criticism of Mead's theory of communication and minded behavior for symbolic interaction theory as a whole. First, the notion of society as the arrangement of personal lines of action according to individual interpretations will be examined.

It was shown above that in symbolic interactionism, society is seen as that organization of individual actions that takes place through the communication process. Persons come to "agreements" about how to act in certain situations, and it is these agreements which are perpetuated in that they are taught to new members of the society. Presumably, these arrangements could have been anything that happened to be agreed upon initially; there are no necessary conditions or prerequisites concerning society.[58] Group action has nothing inherent in it except the combining of individual lines of action. The "social structures" which exist or have force on the individual were all determined by individuals themselves. They could be changed at will while maintaining harmony and communication. It is the communicative aspect of group life that makes these changes possible, since any organized collectivity can be negotiated about or agreed upon as it is or as it ought to be. In his picture of society from the symbolic interactionist perspective, Blumer argues:

The most important element confronting an acting unit in situations is the actions of other acting units. In modern society, with its increasing criss-crossing of lines of action, it is common for situations to arise in which the actions of participants are not previously regularized and standardized. Correspondingly, the symbols or tools of interpretation used by acting units in such situations may vary and shift considerably. For this reason, social action may go beyond, or depart from, existing organization in *any of its structural dimensions.*[59]

It may be possible to agree with Blumer that the most important element confronting an individual in social life is other individuals, and that in modern society, there are numerous kinds of activity called for that have not been regularized (institutionalized) to some degree. However, it does not follow that because of this, social action may go beyond any of its existing organizational forms and develop new tools of interpretation in order to deal with new situations. It is, rather, precisely because social life is so variable that there is *at least one* institutionalized aspect of life that must remain stable as a condition for the maintenance of all the rest, and as a prerequisite for the controlled change that might take place. This social structural feature is that of the language itself—the key element in symbolic interactionist theory.

We saw that, rather than symbols themselves having meaning and language being built up from the meanings of the symbols individually, there is in fact a structure of the language which alone allows symbols to be arranged so that the total configuration *says* something. That is, all the symbols and all their attendant connotations do not suffice to describe the language completely. Knowing the vocabulary of a language does not allow one to make statements in the language. There is a set of rules that must be followed if one is to communicate. These rules are not subject to negotiation among the persons who use the language (unless, of course, they have another such language to negotiate in) and therefore, the rules constrain the behavior of persons who must communicate. While communication may facilitate the negotiation of some aspects of social organization and become the vehicle through which social organization may be changed, language itself (its structure—that which permits statements), must be considered a constant feature of social life which exists outside of the persons in the society and affects them directly.[60] Thus language must be an institution. Just as institutions are the formalization of the means by which certain crucial activities will be carried out by individuals, so language with its grammatical structure is an institution which lays down rules by which persons must abide. Without adherence to these rules, it would be impossible for persons to make assertions in the language, even if they knew the meanings of the words that make up the language's vocabulary. Thus these rules are not directly negotiable, as all aspects of social order are held to be by interactionists. While it may be possible to agree upon grammatical usage from time to time, it is a precondition of that agreement that the parties to it express themselves according to the grammatical structure in order to make the agreed change.

The view of language as the sum of the meanings of the symbols within it, which appears to characterize the Median position, is therefore inadequate from the viewpoint of the way in which assertions actually are made. This inadequacy has led to the belief that there is no social structure that is out of the control of the individuals making up the society and that there is nothing which may not be negotiated by its participants. Social structures are seen simply as enduring patterns that have been derived directly from individual actions. There are no "sociological" level data that are not accounted for in individual terms.

However, it must be argued that the structure of the language used in a society is a property of that society, and not of the individuals in it, even though those individuals participate in that structure. Language as an institution may be compared to Durkheim's view of the institution of contract.[61] It is his argument that no matter how much the parties to a contract may agree on the particulars of the exchange between them, negotiating the terms and defining the arrangements, it is the pre-existing and constraining institution of contract which makes this possible. That is, rules of fair dealing, of legal redress of grievances, and of the way in which one goes about entering and breaking a contract and so forth have to exist prior to any particular individual's negotiating any contract. Thus the actual elements of all existing contracts can not be summated and exhaust the actual institution of contract. No matter how much negotiation goes on between the parties, there are still the bounds set by the institution of contract that make that negotiation possible. This is a "social fact" for Durkheim, one that is not reducible to psychological facts about individuals. Similarly, it must be argued that the grammatical structure which allows assertions to be made in a language also constitutes a set of "social facts" in the Durkheimian sense.

In Mead's views of mind, and of self, we have seen that the basic process is the ability of the individual to designate things to himself. Man comes to view himself as an object from the viewpoint of others, and from that viewpoint, holds an internal conversation with himself. The view of language as a propositional structure, developed in the last section, is thus relevant to Mead's theories of mind and self. In indicating to himself, and individual must employ the rules of language that are current in his society, in order that the indications he makes take on more than a sign-function significance. The symbols of language may be used to represent aspects of the environment, but to construct a sentence about how another might see the self from his vantage point, it is necessary to come to a *concept* of the other's position. Therefore, it is necessary to first symbolize the self, then symbolize the other and then connect the two symbolizations in a proposition which relates the concepts of self and other in some determinate way, as well as other concepts concerning the situation which might be relevant. Thus the mind and self arising from the simple indication to the self is really the more complex process of symbolization, conceptualization, and manipulation of concepts. This follows from the arguments that (1) symbols refer to concepts, not behaviors present or future, and (2) to say something in a language, it is necessary to relate concepts *via* the grammatical structure of language.

To converse internally with the self in the process of minded behavior is to manipulate conceptions of reality as "pictures" of the environment and the self's relation to it, rather than to manipulate symbols themselves.

This makes the idea of the mediated stimulus-response process seem considerably oversimplified. Rather than the symbols forming the basis for the mediation of the reactive process, the symbols represent elements of formulations that give the person a *conception* of situations and his relationship to them. These organizations of symbols and the connoted concepts then have a relationship to the environment in that the conceptual representation is somehow proportional to its symbolized elements; the two "fit" together; they coincide. It is the apprehension of this fit, and the relation of the individual's self concept to it, that is then interpreted in the mentalistic formulation of actions. It appears that this complex of mental processes is what is actually meant by the assertion that persons interpret the actions of others and act according to the interpretations. Thus, while interactionists may have reached a tenable conclusion about the process of interpretation in its relationship to the outcomes of human action, they have reached this conclusion fortuitously, without examining the process of conceptualization, and without regard for the relevance of the sociological aspect of language as an institution.

It is now clear that symbolic interactionism's view of the relationship of the individual to society is inadequate. It has been shown that the rules of language by which persons communicate are not negotiable in the same way that other social organization might be. This implies that, at the sociological level of analysis, there is a set of facts that are not reducible to the facts about the individuals in the society and the way they think and communicate. This demonstration contradicts the view current in symbolic interaction theory that sociological level data may be reduced to and understood in terms of individual psychology and communication. Since it was shown that the actual mechanism by which persons communicate is influenced by a sociological property (grammar and the structure of language), it must be concluded that persons in fact live within a constraining structure which may not be analyzed or explained in terms of individual psychology, but must be dealt with on the sociological level.

This criticism of Mead's theory suggests an addition that ought to be made to the interactionist model of man. In Mead's theory, man was seen to be a symbolizer and interpreter of symbols, as well as an actor operating on the interpretations of his symbols. The foregoing discussion suggests that he must be thought of as a conceptualizer as well. In conceptualizing, it is necessary to make use of the rules of language laid down by society concerning how symbols are put together into assertions. Thus the mind must be seen as being influenced directly by the social structure in which it matures.

This is a very different formulation from the interactionist assertion that the mind and the self develop in the process of symbolic interaction. While it is true that they do so develop, the crucial distinction is that the interactionists do not see the mind (or the self) as being in any way influenced by aspects of social structure which are not reducible to the individual psychologies of the persons involved in action. In the alternative assertion advanced here, that social structural phenomena influence minded behavior, it is explicitly argued that the structure of the language itself must constrain and control the individual's use of symbols before those symbols can be of use in the internal conversation which Mead argues characterizes minded behavior. Similarly, it is impossible to conceive of a self in other than the terms of reference suggested here. The communication interactionists argue is so important to the development of the self has been shown to depend on sociological level facts that are not related solely to the persons doing the communicating. This means that the self, as well as the mind, develops under the influence of sociological level phenomena which are not reducible to the psychologies of the persons who interact with the developing self.

It follows from the present argument that the symbolic interactionist version of the relationship of man to his society is faulty in two ways. First, the picture of social organization as simply the negotiated arrangements agreed upon by persons must be regarded as inadequate. Rather than an explanation of society resting on the processes of thought and communications among individuals, at least the fundamentals of the required explanation must be sought at the sociological level. Thus the reduction of sociological phenomena to the psychological level must be taken as fallacious and neglectful of some features of the very process through which this reduction is said to be understood.

Second, the model of man which is implied in the symbolic interactionist view of the relationship of man to the social order is entirely too simple. If the interactionist tenet is to be retained to the effect that man is a negotiator with others around him of his own conditions of life, he may not be regarded as only that. As well as a negotiator, he must be seen as a follower of non-negotiable rules. An example of these rules has been indicated in the fact that language consists of more than the symbols current in a language. It consists, too, of the rules by which these symbols are employed. Thus for man to have the hypothesized ability to communicate, and thereby affect his social world, he must be seen as limited and constrained in that world by structures that are outside his negotiation and control.

Notes

1. Mead's work from which sociologists most often quote is the edition of his lecture notes from this class. G. H. Mead, *Mind, Self and Society*, C. W. Morris (ed.) (Chicago: The University of Chicago Press, 1934).

2. The edition of Mead's notes from this course also contains some of the foundations of his sociology. G. H. Mead, *Movements of Thought in the Nineteenth Century*, M. H. Moore (ed.) (Chicago: The University of Chicago Press, 1936).

3. Arnold M. Rose has given his version of symbolic interactionism in systematic form in *Human Behavior and Social Process* (Boston: Houghton Mifflin, 1962), Chapter I.

4. J. G. Manis and B. N. Meltzer (eds.), *Symbolic Interaction* (Boston: Allyn and Bacon, 1967) organizes readings around the three divisions (mind, self and society) of Mead's main sociological text and includes some related theoretical writings. This book also contains some observations on the research implications and applications of symbolic interaction theory.

5. Kuhn notes some nine "types" of symbolic interaction theory, as well as several variations within some of the types in Manford H. Kuhn, "Major Trends in Symbolic Interaction in the Past Twenty-five Years", Manis and Meltzer (eds), *Symbolic Interaction*, p. 50.

6. Since it focuses on the nature of the social order as well as face-to-face interaction, Blumer's influential paper is particularly important to this essay: Herbert Blumer, "Society as Symbolic Interaction", Manis and Meltzer (eds.), *Symbolic Interaction*, pp. 139–55. This article is also printed in Rose, *Human Behavior and Social Process*, 11, 179–92.

7. It was the opinion of at least one reviewer of *Mind, Self and Society* that the editing was done very poorly. It is easy to concur with this judgment. Cf. Wilson D. Wallis' review of *Mind, Self and Society* by G. H. Mead, *International Journal of Ethics*, XLV (1934–35), 456–58.

8. Susanne K. Langer's *Philosophy in a New Key* is an example. This book contains inspiration for the criticism that will be brought to bear on Mead's theory of language in the following pages of this part (Cambridge, Mass.: Harvard University Press, 1942). Other work is under way in this area, but mainly outside sociology. For example, see J. R. Royce (ed.), *Psychology and the Symbol* (New York: Random House, 1965). The philosopher Charles Morris, who edited Mead's *Mind, Self and Society*, has become identified with the pragmatic view of language and signification. Cf. his *Signification and Significance* (Cambridge: The M.I.T. Press, 1964).

9. The term "symbol" was used by Mead. It might be more accurate to speak of "sign" when discussing Mead's theory. But since this would introduce unnecessary confusion into the presentation of his ideas, the term "symbol" will be retained and used in the way Mead used it until the appropriate time to make the distinction between "symbol" and "sign",

10. Bernard N. Meltzer, *The Social Psychology of George Herbert Mead* (Kalamazoo, Michigan: Division of Field Services, Western Michigan University, 1959), p. 11.

11. *Mind, Self and Society*, pp. 68–75.

12.   *Ibid.*, pp. 90–100.

13.   *Ibid.*, p. 75.

14.   *Ibid.*, p. 77.

15.   *Ibid.*, p. 121.

16.   This is a basic point, and one on which Mead is not altogether lucid. As he put it,

"Meaning is thus not to be conceived, fundamentally, as a state of consciousness, or as a set of organized relations existing or subsisting mentally outside the field of experience into which they enter; on the contrary, it should be conceived objectively, as having its existence entirely within this field itself. The response of one organism to the gesture of another in any given social act is the meaning of that gesture. . . ."

Ibid., p. 78. Further, however,

"The symbol is distinguishable from the meaning it refers to. Meanings are in nature, but symbols are the heritage of man".

Ibid., p. 78n.

17.   *Ibid.*, p. 119. This position relative to the source of mind accounts for Mead's popularity in educational psychology. Cf. H. G. Hullfish and P. G. Smith, *Reflective Thinking: The Method of Education* (Toronto: Dodd, Mead. 1964) for an illustration of the applications of Mead's theory of mind to educational practice.

18.   *Mind, Self and Society*, p. 114.

19.   *Ibid.*, pp. 89–90.

20.   *Ibid.*, p. 67.

21.   *Ibid.*, p. 74.

22.   This tends to be the basis on which the symbolic interaction theory of organization is built. See Rose, *Human Behavior and Social Process*, pp. 9ff for a discussion of this proposition.

23.   *Mind, Self and Society*, p. 90.

24.   *Ibid.*, p. 120.

25.   Symbolic interaction theory, especially as it relates to the characteristics of the particular person, is sometimes called "self theory". M. Kuhn's name has come to be associated with the empirical attempt to research self-concepts and their implications.

26.   *Mind, Self and Society*, pp. 152–64.

27.   *Ibid.*, p. 138

28.   *Ibid.*, pp. 375–76.

29.   *Ibid.*, pp. 152–64. Meltzer, in his interpretation of Mead's theory of the self, places the "preparatory stage" before the play stage. This stage is "not explicitly named by Mead, but

inferable from various fragmentary essays". B. N. Meltzer, *The Social Psychology of George Herbert Mead*, p. 15.

30.   *Mind, Self and Society*, pp. 51–61.

31.   *Ibid.*

32.   *Ibid.*, p. 154.

33.   *Ibid.*, p. 158.

34.   *Ibid.*, p. 155.

35.   *Ibid.*, p. 175.

36.   This idea is worked out in Cooley's *Human Nature and the Social Order* (New York: Schocken, 1964) and expanded to a treatment of the larger societal picture in *Social Organization* (New York: Schocken, 1962).

37.   *Mind, Self and Society*, pp. 173–6. Mead may have taken his cue from Cooley here, who reflects about the "I" in Descarte's famous phrase, "*Cognito, ergo sum*". Cf. Cooley's *Social Organization*, pp. 6–12.

38.   Cf. Glaser's explanation of differential-association theory in criminology. Daniel B. Glaser, "The Differential-Association Theory of Crime", *Human Behavior and Social Process*, Rose (ed.), pp. 425–42. Disregard for Mead's "I" may also lead to a position of social determinism, in that the person is seen as characterless, and completely formed by those around him. This seems to be the position called into question in Dorothy Emmet's *Rules, Roles and Relations* (London: St. Martin's Press, 1966), Chapter 6, "Sociological Explanation and Individual Responsibility".

39.   *Mind, Self and Society*, p. 174.

40.   *Ibid.*, p. 174.

41.   *Ibid.*, p. 175.

42.   The interesting argument brought against this kind of reasoning about symbols by Cassier and others concerns the problem of analytic statements. According to this view,

"If by analytic statement be understood a formula the validity of which is independent of the truth-values of its components ... or ... as not designative of things but significant only with respect to (the syntax of) language, it must indeed be empty in the sense of not naming events".

Carl H. Hamburg, *Symbol and Reality* (The Hague: Martinus Nijhoff, 1965), p. 154. The question of whether or not Mead is dealing with *statements* in his view of communication will be confronted presently, but even if we assume he is, it is not clear whether his pragmatist view of language could accommodate analytic statements. The closest Mead seems to come to confronting this problem is in his essay, "The Function of Imagery in Conduct", which seems to treat "images" as concepts, some of which he treats as based on "experiences which are necessarily confined to the particular individual, and which can not in their individual character be shared ... and *incapable of reference to an object*".

It seems from this that Mead is on the verge of describing how the view he has of language could accommodate analytic statements, but he later says of these images that "they either have, or are assumed to have, objective referents". The Function of Imagery in Conduct", reprinted in *Mind, Self and Society*, pp. 337–46; quote taken from p. 339.

43. For a discussion of the differences between sign and symbol see L. Von Bertalanffy, "On the Definition of the Symbol", *Psychology and the Symbol*, J. R. Royce (ed.), pp. 26–72. Also see Susanne K. Langer, *Philosophy in a New Key*, Chapter 3, "The Logic of Signs and Symbol".

44. Herbert Blumer, "Society as Symbolic Interaction", p. 139.

45. This is Blumer's view. Cf. Herbert Blumer, "Society as Symbolic Interaction", pp. 139–48. Cooley views societal level phenomena as manifestations of the "public mind", by which he means to indicate that the group operates through communication like the mind does, through communication internally. Institutions, to him, are simply the conventions to which persons have agreed. Cf. Cooley, *Social Organization*, Chapter XXVIII.

46. For example that group life is necessarily characterized by conflict, or that group life is the manifestation of a natural harmony.

47. Mead, "The Community and the Institution", *George Herbert Mead on Social Psychology*, A. Strauss (ed.) (Chicago: The University of Chicago Press, 1964), p. 249.

48. Blumer, "Society as Symbolic Interaction", pp. 146–47.

49. For an example of the idea of negotiated order, see A. Strauss, *et al.*, "The Hospital and its Negotiated Order", *The Hospital in Modern Society*, E. Friedson (ed.) (New York: The Free Press, 1963), 147–69.

50. Cf. C. W. Morris, *Signs, Language and Behavior* (New York: Prentice-Hall, 1946), pp. 32 ff. for a more complete treatment of meaning and language, as well as a definition of language as sign-behavior which is derived from Mead and the pragmatist tradition.

51. Langer, *Philosophy in a New Key*, p. 61.

52. Mead did speak of the "image". But this was always in behavioral terms, concerning the behaviors of objects represented by the signs. Cf. G. H. Mead, "The Function of Imagery in Conduct", *Mind, Self and Society*, pp. 337–46.

53. Langer, *Philosophy in a New Key*, pp. 66 ff.

54. It is probably more correct to say Mead had a *view* of language rather than a fully worked out *theory* of it. For him, language came into his larger scale theory at several points, as has been indicated.

55. Langer, *Philosophy in a New Key*, pp. 66 ff.

56. *Ibid.*

57. The question of purely analytic statements calls Mead's view of language further into question. It would seemingly require a behavioral event which could not be present for Mead's view to apply to analytic statements.

58. Dewey argues that it is not unreasonable for persons to agree so widely, since the problems they face in life are so similar. Cf. John Dewey, "Communication, Individual and Society", *Symbolic Interaction*, Manis and Meltzer (eds.), pp. 149–52.

59. Herbert Blumer, "Society as Symbolic Interaction", p. 147 (emphasis mine).

60. Von Bertalanffy has reached a similar conclusion about symbol systems. He makes the same general point concerning these systems, in a more sweeping manner:

"Symbol systems, so to speak, are self-propelling. They therefore have an autonomy or inner logic of development. Myth, Renaissance painting from Giotto to Titian, music from Bach to Richard Strauss, physics from Galileo to Bohr, the British Empire, or the evolution of Indo-Germanic languages—they all follow their respective immanent laws, which are not psychological laws that characterize mental processes in their creators".

Ludwig von Bertalanffy, *Robots, Men and Minds* (New York: George Braziller, 1967), p. 30.

61. Emile Durkheim, *The Division of Labor in Society*, translated by George Simpson (New York: The Free Press, 1964), pp. 200–33.

Conclusion

This study has been concerned with models of man in sociological theory and how these models relate to sociological explanation. The justification for such an investigation becomes apparent when one considers the task facing modern sociology. Sociological theory is concerned to explain behaviors of groups and the behaviors of persons in groups. That is, a sociologist must achieve a perspective which relates man and society. Sociology does not deal with groups alone or individuals alone; it deals with the relationship of the two. This is why it is not reasonable to speak of groups and societies while neglecting individuals in social theory. Even if societies were thought to have lives of their own as well as their own laws and movements independent of the persons who comprised them, these societal level phenomena could not out-run the bounds placed on them by the nature of man. On the other hand, it is clear that persons exhibit regularized, routinized, and formalized modes of conduct. It is an open question to what degree and in what ways one can attribute the cause of this kind of conduct to the society in which such persons live.

Thus in the theoretical sense, it seems necessary that models of man in sociological theory be compatible with models of society, and vice versa. This has led the present investigation in two directions at once. First, the models of man in the theories under consideration had to be identified; then, the model of society and its force upon the individual had to be worked out. Each of the three theories considered in this book attempted an acceptable solution to the problem of relating the individual and the society. Each of these solutions will be briefly summarized before we proceed to a comparative discussion of some aspects of them. In the comparative portion of this chapter, the discussion will be organized around the determinants of conformity found in the three theories. We will see that the voluntaristic-deterministic dimension which figured into Parsons' work so prominently has counterparts in the other theories. Similarly, the theoretical motivations to conform in society may be examined over an internal–external dimension, from the viewpoint of the actor.

We saw that Homans' theory was based upon individuals exchanging one kind of service or reward for another. This led to the formulation of the model of man in terms of the idea of exchange and raised certain problems connected with conceptualizing man in this way. First was the problem of what was to be exchanged. We saw that Homans' propositions about exchanges between persons were in terms of the values held by individuals

177

in the exchange relationships. Homans suggested that, to understand what things an individual considers of worth in exchange (i.e., what he values), we should examine that person's history of exchange relationships. We would thereby discover patterns of exchange and inductively build up a generalization about that person's values.

It was seen that this exchange model implied certain problems for conceptualizing the exchange relationship unless a norm of rationality, or a kind of regulation about how to exchange, was introduced. Persons must be capable of agreeing as to what is a "good deal". Assumptions must be made, therefore, concerning each person's maximization of gratification from an exchange relationship. These assumptions entered Homans' theory as the norm of intrinsic rationality. For the theory to be of any use as a device with which to understand interhuman exchange, it had to be assumed that each person behaving according to this norm maximized his gratifications and minimized his efforts and outputs.

Both the problems of what things were to be exchanged and how they were to be exchanged raised questions about exchange theory that are solved in terms of its model of man. Concerning what things are to be exchanged, initially it was hypothesized that the values of men could vary infinitely. That is, for theoretical purposes the assumption was that men's values and activities were not regulated by anything besides man's own desires. We found, upon analysis, that this proposition was not supportable within the context of exchange theory, since as a fundamental postulate it was also argued that persons exchanged with each other according to what was termed the norm of rationality. Thus there appeared to be at least one norm outside man's own desires, by which persons are governed in their exchange relationships with each other.

Similarly, if one considered the concept of "institution", it was found that Homans' theoretical infinity of values among men broke down. Either some kind of theoretical consensus had to be inserted about what things were to be exchanged, and by whom, or a further limiting assumption had to be made about the nature of man. This further assumption would have had to contradict the postulate that individuals might value anything at all, replacing this with some propositions about the natural uniformities of values among men. Homans actually took both of these alternatives, depending upon the level of explanation he was attempting. His view of "equilibrium" on the personal interaction level may be seen as an agreement among those in the exchange relationship that the existing exchange was mutually acceptable. This could be accounted for by Homans, since all participants could be thought of as maximizing their rewards. But when Homans took the long view and considered institutions, we saw him making the assumption that institutions were what they were because men were similarly constituted and disposed. This theoretical similarity of man's basic values or needs ensured that every society would exhibit similar institutional arrangements. Of course, when treating man this way, Homans violated his assumption that values could vary infinitely among men, and called into question the need for formulating exchange theory at all. If men could be viewed as similarly disposed and rational, there was an explanation of social order implicit in these assumptions. Another was made unnecessary.

Thus we saw Homans' theory fail at two crucial points as he attempted to reason from the nature of man toward an explanation of social order. If order was to be conceptualized as simply the exchanges between persons, agreements would have to be reached concerning what would be exchanged, and how the transactions would be governed. These problems led Homans to contradict his postulate that individually, human values could be anything, and thus, to violate his proposal that institutional arrangements theoretically could be derived from an analysis of the interactions of discrete persons. While the difficulties of exchange theory do not prove in a positive sense that society is qualitatively a different phenomenon from the individuals in it, such difficulties do beg the question of the individual and his relation to society. It does not seem that Homans' *animal rationale*, with his values on exchanging rewarding behaviors at the least possible cost to himself, is sufficient basis on which to build a theory of society and of man's interactions.

Similar problems arose when symbolic interaction theory was examined. Homans attempted to base his theory of social order on the transactions of individuals as they went about exchanging rewarding behaviors. The interactionist position, too, was characterized by the view that society was the fitting together of individual actions which were negotiable among society's participants. This view implied the central place of communication and language in the nature of man. To align actions to other men's, individuals theoretically had to be able to communicate so that mutually adjusted possibilities obtained. However, we saw that individuals could not have negotiated the language with which they gained each other's perspective in their mutual adjusting activities. This fact compared directly to Homans' failure to account for the totality of social arrangements in individual terms. It did not seem possible, therefore, to reason that social order was nothing more than the aligning of individual actions through either negotiation or conflict among discrete persons. It seemed, rather, that the structure of language itself, the fundamental building block of interactionist theory, had to be considered out of the control and beyond the possibility of negotiation by individuals.

Thus we see symbolic interactionism failing to account sufficiently for social organization internally. It was shown that it was necessary to draw upon assumptions concerning the nature of an order outside the control of individuals to account for how social organization is possible. Thus, as in the case of exchange theory, it seemed that this failure pointed toward the conclusion that accounts of social organization in terms of a model of man alone are insufficient, and encounter difficulties concerning the conceptual basis on which such an order could be grounded.

Exchange theory and symbolic interaction theory are similar in that basic propositions about the nature of social order are not compatible with the propositions implicit in the theories concerning man himself. Man can not be the negotiator of all social order, in which individuals come to control their behaviors according to individual value systems, if certain fundamental properties about the nature of that order are demonstrably outside the negotiation and control of individuals.

In the discussion of Parsons' functional theory, a fundamental dualism concerning the relationships of the model of man and the explanation of social order was brought out in several ways. It was observed that Parsons sees man as having fundamental desires and propensities that were shaped according to the interests and values current in the society. To this extent, Parsons' theory seems to indicate a model of man which is basically socially determined. However, Parsons also sees man as the volunteer for his own actions. That is, Parsons' man is not a näive robot, performing those functions set for him by society. Rather, man has certain socio-culturally formed dispositions to act in situations toward certain objects in specific ways. Thus, Parsons concludes that while society has a hand in forming the individual's dispositions to act, it is always the individual who formulates and carries through the action. To this extent, man must be seen as a conceptualizer and the formulator of his own activities.

Thus we see that Parsons did not make the mistake of trying to explain social order by a model of man; neither did he attempt to explain man wholly in terms of a model of social order, as he is sometimes accused of doing. Rather, his account of the relations of the two (social order and model of man) is not wholly in terms of one or the other. Thus arises the fundamental dualism in Parsons which begs certain questions concerning the theoretical relation of the model of man to the explanation of social order.

It was shown that in Parsons' voluntaristic emphasis, in which he derives a model of man from his theory of systems, there is considerable room for choice on the part of the individual and self determination of action. The model of man is definitely constructed in terms of alternatives and modes of choosing between alternatives. In Parsons' deterministic emphasis, it was seen that a second model of man is implied, one which is essentially derived from the functional requirements of societies. In this second model, Parsons' man is almost wholly determined by the social order, and is virtually sub-servient to it. Hence the dualism: Parsons' work includes two models of man from which he draws selectively according to the kind of analysis under way.[1] It was then concluded that a means for specifying the relations of the two models was imperative if Parsons' theory was to be considered consistent on this point. Parsons was shown to have tried out and rejected a pattern variable which, if it had worked, would have related the two models of man. It was seen that the failure of this pattern variable was related directly to the implicit duality in the assumptions about man in Parsons' theory. As an alternative, Parsons has proposed a cybernetic model of the relationship between man and society, by which it is perhaps possible to specify the conditions under which man ought to be seen as dominated by the larger social order, and those under which individual choice and self determination theoretically obtain. It was noted that Parsons' work has been concerned more with the specification of society's bearing on the individual than the other way around. This leads to the conclusion that Parsons' theory as a specification of the relationship of man to his social organization is still inadequate.

Concerning the internal–external dimension of determinants of conformity, Parsons' theory is a blend of the internal and the external aspects of determination from the point of view of the individual. In terms of motivation, it is the problem of Parsons' theory to show that the acting person is motivated internally to perform certain acts spontaneously, as well as motivated externally by selective reward and punishment given by others. In Parsonian social action, then, the same act is the result of both these kinds of motivation.

Exchange and symbolic interaction theories can be contrasted and related to Parsonian theory over this internal–external dimension. Exchange theory argues that internally-rooted needs are gratified externally in the exchange relationship. The exchange between persons is in terms of those sentiments and activities that gratify the parties to the exchange. The reason for acting, in any individual's case, is in order to satisfy some want. The satisfaction of that want is either held or controlled by the individual with whom the exchange takes place. Thus, the interaction procures the other's good or service that is satisfying the individual's internal want. Motivated behavior is seen as internally determined (persons have wants) and externally rewarded. The objects of action are all seen as lying outside the self and only indirectly under the control of the acting individual. This corresponds to Parsons' external gratification from role behavior. A person entering a role relationship with another is rewarded by the other for correct performance. In exchange theory terms, correct performance would consist of playing the role according to expectations of the person having the power to reward the role player. However, Parsons and exchange theorists part company at this point. Parsons also postulates that internal motivation to play the role will give rise to the same behavior as the external reward would. Exchange theorists do not argue that the performance of a role is internally gratifying as well as a possible necessity for being rewarded.[2]

That is, exchange theory contains no postulation of a learned or inherent set of needs or dispositions to act which would lead one to behave in a certain way in the absence of external gratifications.

Symbolic interaction theory compares to Parsonian theory concerning the external–internal polarity and the question of motivation in another way. It will be remembered that the final phase in the development of self was acquiring the attitudes of the generalized other. As the self became fully formed, the community became organized; the attitudes of the generalized other came to characterize each self. Thus, paradoxically, the self acted in accord with the attitudes of the generalized other, which in turn was made up of the attitudes of members of the community. Thus individual action was seen as dependent upon the attitudes of the larger group of which the self was a part. There was no postulation in symbolic interaction theory of external sanctions and rewards.[3] The individual designs his own actions according to his own motivations; but these motivations are with special reference to the generalized other. Since this is the case, there is no *need* to be concerned with external sanctions. The actions that are the result of this kind of process will be organized and predictable, since they will be influenced by the generalized other as a standpoint from which to judge for oneself the appropriateness of actions for the community.[4]

Thus, exchange and symbolic interaction theories contrast with each other and with Parsons' theory over the theoretical determinants of conforming behavior (i.e., of social organization) in the following way. Exchange theory sees the conforming behavior of individuals as a result of external forces, but in response to internal wants. Other, who has the power to reward ego in an exchange relationship, rewards him if he is in a position to produce some behavior which is gratifying to other. The variability of wants among persons is problematic and also can account for change, since the changing nature of individual wants can explain the changing nature of associations. It is definitely not the case in exchange theory that the external nature of the reward mechanism is identified with a uniquely sociological level entity or abstraction. The external–internal dimension refers only to the location of the reward in interpersonal exchange.

In symbolic interaction, theory, the situation is somewhat the reverse. It is not the external reward of other persons that leads to conforming behavior, but the internalization of the attitudes of the generalized other that has this result. The fact that the theory does not specifically describe conditions under which persons will wish to conform and under which they will wish to deviate indicates that the generalized other might be seen as incorporating a set of societal values and ends of action, as well as a set of attitudes toward performances. Reference group theory leads one to this conclusion; it is the central tenet of this approach that persons will see themselves, and thus act, in terms of the group, person, or idea to which they refer and from which they take their self image.

Parsonian theory employs both internally and externally determined wants and rewards in accounting for conforming behavior. It is Parsons' notion that the individual internalizes a set of values and highly generalized prescriptions for conduct that lead him to make certain evaluations of situations as they arise and to act accordingly. In this, the individual is internally motivated; his actions are entirely voluntary. However, somewhat in the manner of exchange theory, the individual is also rewarded or punished according to whether or not he performs up to Other's expectations. In the latter case, performances are externally controlled and rewarded by those to whom Actor's duties are expectations and rights. Parsons thus employs both sides of the internal–external scheme in his discussion of the social act. It follows directly from this that he employs both sides of the internal–external scheme also in his theoretical account of what action will be taken. It is part of the individual's internalizations that he will wish to act in certain ways. That is, certain values will be inherent in the individual by virtue of his socialization. Since the same thing is also true of Other, the actor will want to act according to Other's expectations and values, which will be based on Other's internalizations. Thus, the actor's particular acts will be internally determined by his own value system, and externally determined by that of Other with whom the actor interacts.

We have seen that in accounting for conforming behavior, Parsonian theory combines the outlooks of both exchange and symbolic interaction theory. Combining these leads to certain problems concerning the model of man in Parsonian theory. We saw in Part II of this work that, depending upon which side of the coupled voluntarism-determinism (internal–external) polarity was emphasized, different formulations about the nature of man were implicit in Parsons' theory. When it seemed necessary to see the individual as submitting to the wishes of society, the individual was viewed as "plastic" and willing to act according to society's wishes. When the emphasis was on voluntarism and internal processes, we saw that man was an evaluator, cognizer, and conceptualizer who based his activities on an internal set of need-dispositions, desires and propensities. In Parsons' voluntaristic emphasis, to be sure, it was the socio-cultural milieu which set the limits and general outlines of the nature of man; but these were seen as being at a very high level of generality and allowing wide latitude concerning performances. In his deterministic emphasis, these limits were seen to narrow and choke off the voluntarism of individuals, making individual need-dispositions and idiosyncratic aspects of value systems irrelevant. The correct proportions of voluntarism and determinism in each individual act were not made explicit.

The theoretical nature of the relationship between the model of man and social organization in symbolic interaction and exchange theory is problematic. The problem is disguised because these viewpoints on the problem of social order take only one half of the internal–external polarity as a point of departure. Symbolic interaction theory sees institutional arrangements as very highly general and loosely organized "agreements" between persons. This seems to follow from the fact that this perspective depends completely upon internal processes in the formulation of individual actions. It is the individual who fits his action to that of the persons around him. With the generalized other as a basis from which to view the social scene objectively, each person constructs his own activities according to his views of what is appropriate.[5] The fact that others do the same ensures that order will be maintained, but there is no coercion, no external control of persons. Similarly, exchange theory views ordered social action as the permanent arrangements which are rewarding to individuals. If an individual's values change, he must find another social organization in which he can gratify his new wants through different kinds of exchanges or the values of the others must change to become compatible with those of that individual. The difference here lies in the fact that, in exchange theory, the inducement to individual social acts is external to the acting individuals, whereas in symbolic interaction theory, it is internal.

We have seen that the internal–external polarity with reference to the determinants of social order corresponds to the voluntaristic-deterministic dimension identified in Parsonian theory. We can now examine some issues in relation to the problem of determinism and voluntarism with respect to the other two theories dealt with in this paper. In voluntarism, the emphasis was found to be on the individual himself, operating in society according to his own set of values and needs. Determinism was identified with the "wishes" of a greater society in which the individual was sometimes, due to system requirements, obliged to act contrary to his wishes. That is, voluntarism was identified with the individual while determinism was identified with society as the agent of choice in actions. We are now in a position to show the relevance of the facts that exchange theory was found to depend on a norm of rationality and symbolic interactionism was found to depend upon the structure of language.

Both the norm of rationality and the structure of language were shown to be prior conditions of successful social action, from the particular viewpoints of the theories involving them. That is, to use comparative terminology, they were identified with the entity which "determines" in Parsons' deterministic emphasis. Both the norm of rationality and the structure of language were seen as institutions which made the rest of social action theoretically possible. Without these, no amount of exchanging or wielding of symbols could have produced ordered social action. Similarly, in Parsons' theory it was seen that social action depended both on individually contrived action and socio-cultural determination.

This implies a criticism of both exchange and symbolic interaction theories as they relate to sociological explanation. By failing to recognize their implied reliance on assumptions about the deterministic aspects of social order, they reach the conclusion that the social order can be accounted for in terms of the psychology of individuals alone, without reference to uniquely sociological level phenomena. They thus mistakenly conclude that the social order can be fully explained on the basis of assumptions about the nature of man. We saw in exchange theory that the model of man was said to include all that was necessary to explain social order. These characteristics included man as a valuing creature who acted in society in ways calculated to gain him the things he valued. In symbolic interaction theory we saw that the theory of the self and of minded behavior became the paradigm for the explanation of social order. These two aspects of man were characterized by the central place of the symbol and communication (both to the self, and to others). However, when analyzed, these major features of the two theories were seen to rely on other factors that could not be accounted for in terms of the nature of man alone. Since this was the case, the attempts to account for social organization in terms of a model of man alone must be regarded as failures.

It was seen that Parsons recognizes the impossibility of reasoning directly from individual to society and vice versa. But his theory was seen to be indeterminate regarding the porportions of socio-cultural determinism and voluntarism concerning any given act. His use of cybernetics in relating individual and society-level abstractions is promising; however, only the hierarchy of controlling factors (from cultural system through social system to personality) has been worked out to date. It remains for Parsons to detail the hierarchy of conditioning factors, in which the individual will be seen as placing certain demands and limits on the social and cultural systems.

The problem of voluntarism *vs.* determinism is related to the question of how sociological theory ought to deal with the concept of motivation. Homans' theory confronts this problem through the concepts of value and reinforcement. Homans saw that the means–ends schema ought to be the basis for an individualistic theory of social behavior; individuals had to be seen as having ends, and contriving means to realize them. The question of whether this kind of thinking was appropriate for a sociological theory was raised, and a positivist critique of the concept "value" in Homans' theory was made. It seemed that, if "value" was to be considered the basis of motivation to action, this disqualified the theory as a scientific work, since "values" do not seem to be operationalizable by other than the behavior "values" were meant to explain. This logical difficulty placed the value-behavior propositions outside scientific discourse, since they were not falsifiable.

A similar problem arises in Parsonian theory, except that it is more complex, since the values that underlie behavior are also tied in with the system of action and the culture. Whereas Homans wishes to base a theory of social motivation on individually held values, Parsons' theory of action is based on a conception of values held in common which characterize the whole society. Parsons shows that there is a sense in which necessary action (i.e., action determined or highly desirable from the viewpoint of the society) is also chosen action on the part of individuals. This point arises in Parsons' work in the identification of logical action as being also the manifestation of sentiment (and thus, individually chosen action).

We saw that the definition of the social system was in terms of its solutions to the system's problems. The system is in this sense "defined into existence" in terms of roles played in it. The persons are, by definition, playing roles according to the system's demands. Thus Parsons' theoretical point that persons play roles because they are internally motivated to do so as well as externally motivated from the system point of view is as much a logical point, dependent on the definition of the system of action, as an empirical problem. Indeed, there appears to be no method for determining when and if action is *not* the result of system demands. Action is by definition satisfying some system exigency, since it is intrinsic to the definition of "system" that behavior fulfills functional requirements. Thus, while Homans' use of the term "value" as explanatory of behaviors ran into difficulty because empirically the behaviors and the values said to underlie them were inseparable, Parsons meets equal difficulty in his account of motivation of action. Since by definition action is confined in systems that are solving their problems (otherwise no system exists), it was logically impossible to conceive of action that was not so confined. We see then, that the definition of "system" and its implication that actions fulfill system problems require that action be seen as motivated by the system. By definition there is no other kind of action. It is logically impossible to separate internally and externally motivated actions. As much as any other theoretical point, the definition of "system" by the behaviors in it make it necessary to see motivated behavior in this way.

It is notable that symbolic interaction theory does not offer a clear theory of motivation. To begin with, the doctrine of parallelism in social behaviorism holds that what happens in individual consciousness runs parallel to what takes place in the nervous system. The roots of action, and the center of consciousness, where sensory stimulation is registered, are to be taken as physiological. Thus conduct, from the point of view of motivation, is not seen as a product of deliberation. Rather, this doctrine holds that deliberation comes into the picture only after an act has been performed.[6] It is true, once an act is begun, deliberation begins. After action is started, deliberation about it is constant, so that at any one moment, both the act and minded behavior about it follow very closely on each other. It is in this sense that Mean meant the "I" as an "historical figure", coming into the consciousness only after the person has acted. It is also in this "after the fact" sense that the generalized other influences action. It is quite outside symbolic interaction theory to speak of a general theory of motivation, since ultimately, action springs from the physiological nature of the body, and is only later (even if later is *instantly*) brought to consciousness. This point of view brought Mead's colleague, William James, to his theory of emotions, which is the reverse of the theories of Parsons and Homans on this point. James argues that it is because we exhibit certain behaviors that emotions grow up around them. That is, we must run away before we feel the emotion of fear. We must act before we can value, and not vice versa. This fits in with Mead's theory of symbols as the epitomization of *acts* and not thoughts, since acts are required before they can come to mind and be associated with the self.

Symbolic interaction theory, then, gives no theory of motivation in the same sense that Parsonian and exchange theory do. It argues only that acts which occur influence those that come after through deliberation. Whereas both Parsons and Homans would argue that action is in response to some value or need component in individuals that precedes the action, Mead would contend, with James, that the psychological states identified with certain actions come in after the action has occurred. Thus symbolic interaction theory must be regarded as incomparable with the other two theories on the point of motivation.

The symbolic interaction position on motivation entails problems, especially with regard to a sociological theory of why certain actions are taken as opposed to others which seem at least logically possible. The fact that a generalized other exists for the individuals in a group does not solve this problem completely, since it is with reference to the generalized other that a person evaluates his action once it is taken (and adjusts his following actions), but it is not with reference to it that a person initially takes action. Thus, in the logical sense, if we are to follow symbolic interaction theory to its roots in psychological parallelism, it is impossible to account for acts taken initially. Rather, it is only possible to account for how those acts, once taken, are evaluated and how those evaluations translate into physiological states that go, in the next instant, into physiological motivation of the next act, and so on. It must be emphasized that this does not amount to a theory of motivation. Stating that acts are adjusted and evaluated with reference to the generalized other, and that selves are formed by the individual's becoming aware of his place in the larger system, is not to give a theory of why the self is seen in relation to the generalized other in particular ways, why acts are influenced by it in patterned ways, or indeed, why individuals should take account of the generalized other at all.

At present, both the means–ends schema and the point of view of social behaviorism on the problem of motivation seem rather unresearchable. If they are truly not falsifiable in the sense that Popper[7] means the term, then the whole notion of motivation must be considered rather outside the purview of a scientific account of social action. We may investigate the concept of motivation using scientific means, but the possibility of empirically identifying the links between "value" and action still seems rather remote.

The conclusion to be drawn is that motivational categories ought to be included in a sociological theory. While it is perhaps possible to detail the structural aspects of society, this activity does not make a theory. Theory requires the demonstration that these structural features have some impact on the persons living in that society. That is, this demonstration has to be in the form of an account of how sociological features influence human action. Since action is assumed to be motivated, the inclusion of the concept of "action" implies the inclusion of "motivation" as well. It has been shown, however, that attempting to construct sociological theory on psychological principles alone is unrewarding, since the question of exactly why certain actions are taken ultimately comes down to either an assertion that it is in man's nature to take such actions, or that certain actions are somehow determined for individuals.

One can argue, therefore, that no matter what the claims of these three theories concerning their status as productive of empirically falsifiable hypotheses, each one examined in this book is essentially what Zetterberg has called "dimensionist". Each relates a group of more or less general insights together such that the total theory suggests the dimensions in which social behavior may be examined. It is notable that in each theory, the model of man has implicitly, if not explicitly, played a large part in defining these dimensions.

Thus we see again the problem of the nature of man in sociological theory. If man is taken as necessary and sufficient for the explanation of social order, a variety of metaphysical assumptions concerning his needs, desires, wants, propensities and so on have to be introduced to account for the particular social actions he takes, or else faulty reasoning must be employed to obscure the fact that such assumptions are actually being made. On the other hand, if the nature of man is taken as a minimal starting point from which assertions are made concerning the nature of societies themselves, similar metaphysical assumptions have to be made concerning the nature of societies. We saw that it is possible to combine these approaches so that both man and society are considered as separate "levels" of systems, and fitted together in terms of the desires and needs of man as well as those of society.

When examining a representative of this approach, we found that this solution entailed its own problems. Agreement had to be reached concerning the attributes of the system which related man and society in this way, as well as concerning the metaphysical assumptions to be taken about the nature of man and of society.

This book has demonstrated that, in several different ways, the relationship of models of man to sociological explanation in the three theories examined has been inadequate. This is perhaps partially due to the strain placed on these perspectives to become full-blown general theories, with explanations implicit in them for all sociological questions. This may result from the fact that, one way or another, certain theoretical perspectives become ideologically charged. For instance, functionalism tends to be identified, especially by its opponents, as the theory of the Right. This gives rise to the need to offer an alternative to the objectionable theory which can explain just as much, and perhaps more, in a more "acceptable" way. But if the three theories examined in this book are not considered to have achieved the full status of general theory, in that they have run into logical or other difficulties at some levels, they may yet be complementary, even though they are based on widely differing assumptions and assertions.

It seems that symbolic interaction theory has been crucial to sociology, especially regarding its insight into the way roles become known, and the way man comes to an understanding of the social system. While the account of exactly how man plays his roles, for whatever reasons, may be considered somewhat thin, the fact that interactionism has offered a perspective from which to view the bringing to consciousness of the idea of role must be regarded as a considerable positive step. It is true that the awareness of role as an abstract collection of duties and rights connected with a status is absolutely essential to every person's understanding of himself and his place in the larger social organization into which he is born. The concept of role-taking and the insights concerning the central place of language and the objectification of the self appear to be fundamental contributions.

If the interactionist perspective on role-taking and the development of self consciousness is taken as a point of departure, it is clear that the next step in developing sociological understanding is the detailing of how roles fit together, and how these roles may be thought of as parts of larger systems containing differentiated roles. This kind of consideration is still at a high level of generality, since the actual content of roles may be left largely undefined. But the insights concerning the complementarity of role structures and the arrangements of roles into larger units (which may be viewed as having an organization of their own) are fundamental to the understanding of the relationship of man to his society. Viewing the interlocking nature of roles in this way may be considered an advance over the insights of interactionism concerning the individual's basic understandings of his roles. The idea of larger systems as the aligning of individual actions may be enlarged and viewed from another perspective. Parsons has shown how roles may be thought to have attributes that make them complementary or incompatible, and how roles interlock in role systems. The Parsonian approach, while at a very high level of generality, may be seen as a framework into which the basic insights of Mead concerning how persons come to see their roles may be fitted.

In exchange theory, more detail still is achieved, but at a lower level of generality. If in Parsons and Mead one finds an adequate account of the idea of roles and how they may be thought to fit together, the exact nature of the fit has not been spelled out. Homans has attempted an elaboration of one aspect of this problem in his description of the complementarity of roles in terms of the exchanges which actually take place between persons. In achieving this detail, however, Homans was forced to focus on one aspect of a greater problem. We saw above that whereas Parsons viewed the complementarity of roles as being based on both internal and external gratifications with respect to some end, Homans has seen fit to develop the external aspect of this complementarity while neglecting the internal. On a different level of analysis, Parsons and Shils have explored the exchanges between other aspects of the role structure in *Economy and Society*. The analogy between the exchanges at the individual level and those at the institutional level is really rather close, and it must be concluded that Parsons and Homans are talking about the same thing in regard to exchange. While exchange theory is not functionalism, there is a sense in which it may be seen as clearly complementary to it.

It may be concluded, then, that each of the three major branches of North American sociology examined in this book have contributed to the understanding of the relation of man to his society. But none of these theories alone can be taken as giving full account of the matter. In fact, it appears that the three taken together are still inadequate, if the logical possibilities opened up by any one are to be fully explored. Perhaps, since exchange theory has focused on the external nature of the rewards for acting and the relations of these to the exchange process, it would be fruitful to examine in as much depth the ways in which exchange may be conceptualized when the rewards are seen as internal. This view of exchange theory seems to resurrect the problem of the nature of culture, since it would surely be to cultural uniformities as well as to the model of man that theorists would look to find the nature of internal reward. Similarly, the lead offered by *Economy and Society* regarding institutional level exchanges ought to be followed with respect to other institutions and their relationships. Mead's insight concerning the ways in which persons become conscious of a social reality around them may prove to be too general; instead, it may be the case that different structural aspects of social life impinge on the consciousness in different ways. The comparative study of role structures from the viewpoint of how one becomes aware of his role and motivated to play it should shed light on this matter.

Clearly it seems that a new theory of social order and man's relationship to it is not what is called for. Rather, the inroads that have been made on the understanding of some aspects of this problem ought to be followed up by working out the theoretical links between these insights. Thus, it seems that until some larger theory comes along to update and subsume current theories under it, the next phase in theoretical work ought to be more modest theories of special phenomena. This has actually been the history of the development of North American sociology. Merton has called for theories of the "middle range" mainly in this sense.

The danger of this kind of approach, however, is that the links between the more modest theories may become so obscured by the sheer mass of material that the greater theoretical work of making sense of the parts will be virtually impossible. If this problem becomes too great, sociological theory will never see itself reunified at a higher level of sophistication. While specialization and reunification of theoretical schemes is a constant process which is never finished, it is also true that one half of the process ought not to be allowed to outrun the other. If the problem of theoretical unification is deemed so great that it is neglected, the resulting emphasis on "middle range" theory will certainly threaten the significance of sociological theory as a whole.

Notes

1. The voluntarism and inherent dilemmas for choice of the first model of man may be understood in the following way. Since any action implies a range of consequences, the contradictory nature of the system of action must be considered by the actor as he acts. For example, an adaptively oriented act will be characterized by universalism, specificity, performance and neutrality. But the problem raised by an adaptive act is the integration of the system, especially relative to that act. Integration is characterized by the opposites of the above choices of pattern variables. Thus the "voluntarism" of action in Parsons' first model may be thought of as the actor's balancing out of the degrees to which he will pursue each of the polar ends of the pattern variables, or the degree of inefficiency he can tolerate while acting in ways that do not maximize the returns of any given act for a specific functional problem.

2. Although it may be that playing a role is in itself gratifying, this possibility is not developed in exchange theory.

3. Although it is presumed these could exist, they are not crucial to the theory of ordered social behavior.

4. In this discussion, the concept of the "I" has been deliberately omitted. This is not because it is not important. In the following pages, the "I" will be discussed in the context of the way in which the generalized other influences motivated action.

5. "Appropriate" behavior is left undeveloped theoretically in interactionism.

6. It must be understood that by an "act", Mead means both overt and mental activity. Since Mead's "symbol" is the telescoped act and its consequences, the conduct spoken of here may be taking thought, in the Meadian sense. Mental and overt "activity" are subject to the same behavioral analysis.

7. Karl R. Popper, *The Logic of Scientific Discovery*, Chapters I–IV.

Bibliography

Bales, R. F. *Interaction Process Analysis*. Cambridge, Mass.: Adison-Wesley, 1950.

Banton, Michael. *Roles*. London: Tavinstock Publishers, 1965.

Barron, M. L. (ed.). *Contemporary Sociology*. New York: Dodd, Mead, 1964.

Barth, Fredrik. *Models of Social Organization*. (Royal Anthropological Institute of Great Britain and Ireland, Occasional Paper No. 23.) London: 1966.

Baumrin, Bernard (ed.). *Philosophy of Science*. New York: Interscience Publishers, 1963.

Bertalanffy, L. Von. "On the Definition of the Symbol", *Psychology and the Symbol*. Edited by J. R. Royce. (New York: Random House, 1965), 26–72.

————. *Robots, Men and Minds*. New York: George Braziller, 1967.

Bierstedt, R. "The Means–ends Schema in Sociological Theory", *American Sociological Review*, **III**, No. 5 (October, 1938), 665–71.

Black, Max. "Some Questions About Parsons' Theories", *The Social Theories of Talcott Parsons*. Edited by Max Black. Englewood Cliffs, New Jersey: Prentice-Hall, 1961), 268–88.

————. (ed.). *The Social Theories of Talcott Parsons*. Englewood Cliffs, New Jersey: Prentice-Hall, 1961.

Blau, Peter M. *Exchange and Power in Social Life*. New York: John Wiley and Sons, 1964.

Blumer, Herbert. "Society as Symbolic Interaction", *Symbolic Interaction*. Edited by J. Manis and B. Meltzer. (Boston: Allyn and Bacon, 1967), 139–49.

Braithwaite, Richard Bevan. *Scientific Explanation*. New York: Harper and Row, 1953.

Bridgman, P. W. *The Logic of Modern Physics*. New York: Macmillan Company, 1961.

Cambell, Norman Robert. *Foundations of Science*. New York: Dover Publications, 1957.

Carnap, Rudolf. *Philosopical Foundations of Physics*. New York: Basic Books, 1966.

Cassier, E. *The Philosophy of Symbolic Forms*. Vol. I. Translated by Ralph Manheim. New Haven: Yale University Press, 1953.

Cooley, C. H. *Human Nature and the Social Order*. New York: Schocken, 1964.

————. *Social Organization*. New York: Schribner's, 1909.

Dahrendorf, Ralf. "Out of Utopia: Toward a Reorientation of Sociological Analysis", *American Journal of Sociology*, **LXIV**, (September, 1958), 115–27.

Davis, A. K. "Social Theory and Social Problems", *Philosophy and Phenomenological Research*, **XVIII**, (December, 1957), 190–208.

Davis, Kingsley. "The Myth of Functional Analysis as a Special Method in Sociology and Anthropology", *American Sociological Review*, **XXIV**, No. 6 (December, 1959), 737–71.

Demerath, N. J. and R. A. Peterson. (eds.). *System Change and Conflict*. New York: The Free Press, 1967.

Deutsch, M. and R. M. Krauss. *Theories in Social Psychology*. New York: Basic Books, 1965.

Devereux, E. C., Jr. "Parsons' Sociological Theory", *The Social Theories of Talcott Parsons*. Edited by Max Black. (Englewood Cliffs, New Jersey: Prentice-Hall, 1961), 1–63.

Dewey, John. "Communication, Individual and Society", *Symbolic Interaction*. Edited by J. Manis and B. Meltzer. (Boston: Allyn and Bacon, 1967), 149–52.

Dubin, Robert. "Parsons' Actor: Continuities in Sociological Theory", *Sociological Theory and Modern Society*. Edited by Talcott Parsons. (New York: The Free Press, 1967), 521–36.

Duncan, H. D. *Language and Literature in Society*. New York: Bedminster Press, 1961.

Durkheim, E. *Essays on Sociology and Philosophy*. Edited by Kurt Wolff. New York: Harper, 1964.

————. *The Division of Labor in Society*. Translated by George Simpson. New York: The Free Press, 1964.

Emmet, Dorothy, *Rules, Roles and Relations*. London: St. Martins Press, 1966.

Faris, E. Review of *The Social System* by Talcott Parsons. *American Sociological Review*, **XVIII** (February, 1953), 103–6.

Faris, R. E. L. (ed.). *Handbook of Modern Sociology*. Chicago: Rand-McNally, 1964.

Feigl, Herbert and Michael Scriven (eds.). *Minnesota Studies in the Philosophy of Science*. Vol. I: *The Foundations of Science and the Concepts of Psychology and Psychoanalysis*. Vol. III: *Scientific Explanation, Space, and Time*. Minneapolis: University of Minnesota Press, 1956, 1962.

Foss, Daniel. "The World View of Talcott Parsons", *Sociology on Trial*. Edited by M. Stein and A. Vidich. (Englewood Cliffs, New Jersey: Prentice-Hall, 1963), 96–126.

Friedson, Elliot. (ed.). *The Hospital in Modern Society*. New York: The Free Press, 1963.

Glaser, Daniel. "The Differential-Association Theory of Crime", *Human Behavior and Social Process*. Edited by A. M. Rose. (Boston: Houghton Mifflin, 1962), 425–42.

Hamburg, Carl H. *Symbol and Reality*. The Hague: Martinus Nijhoff, 1956.

Homans, George C. "Bringing Men Back In", *American Sociological Review*, **XXIX** (December, 1964), 809–19. (Presidential Address delivered at the annual meeting of the American Sociological Association, at Montreal, September 2, 1964.)

————. "A Conceptual Scheme for the Study of Social Organization", *American Sociological Review*, **XI** (September, 1946), 13–26.

————. "Contemporary Theory in Sociology", *Handbook of Modern Sociology*. Edited by R. E. L. Faris. (Chicago: Rand-McNally, 1964), 951–77.

————. *The Human Group*. New York: Harcourt, Brace and World, 1950.

————. *The Nature of Social Science*. New York: Harcourt, Brace, and World, 1967.

————. "Social Behavior as Exchange", *American Journal of Sociology*, **LXIII** (May, 1958), 597–607.

————. *Social Behavior: Its Elementary Forms*. New York: Harcourt, Brace and World, 1961.

————. "A Theory of Social Interaction", *Transactions of the Fifth World Congress of Sociology*, IV (Louvain: International Sociological Association, 1964), 113–25.

————. *Sentiments and Activities*. New York: The Free Press, 1962.

Hullfish, H. Gordon and Philip G. Smith, *Reflective Thinking: The Method of Education*. Toronto: Dodd, Mead, 1964.

Kantor, J. R. Review of *Mind, Self and Society* by G. H. Mead. *International Journal of Ethics*, **XLV** (1934–35), 459–61.

Kaplan, Abraham. *The Conduct of Inquiry*. San Francisco: Chandler Publishing Co., 1964.

Koch, S. (ed.). *Psychology: A Study of a Science*. Toronto: McGraw-Hill, 1959.

Kolb, W. L. "Images of Man and the Sociology of Religion", *Journal for the Scientific Study of Religion*, **I**, No. 1 (October, 1961), 5–22.

Kuhn, Manford H. "Major Trends in Symbolic Interaction Theory in the Past Twenty-five Years", *Symbolic Interaction*. Edited by J. Manis and B. Meltzer. (Boston: Allyn and Bacon, 1967), 46–67.

Laing, R. D. *The Divided Self*. London: Tavinstock Publications, 1960.

————. *The Self and Others*. London: Tavinstock Publications, 1959.

Langer, Susanne K. *Mind: An Essay on Human Feeling*. Vol. I. Baltimore: Johns Hopkins Press, 1967.

————. *Philosophical Sketches*. New York: Mentor Books, 1964.

————. *Philosophy in a New Key*. Cambridge: Harvard University Press, 1942.

Levy, M. J., Jr. *The Structure of Society*. Princeton: Princeton University Press, 1950.

Louch, A. R. *Explanation and Human Action*. Berkeley: University of California Press, 1966.

MacIver, R. M. *Social Causation*. New York: Harper and Row, 1962.

Manis, J. G. and B. N. Meltzer. (eds.). *Symbolic Interaction*. Boston: Allyn and Bacon, 1967.

Martel, Martin U. "Some Controversial Assumptions in Parsons' Approach to Social Systems Theory", *Alpha Kappa Deltan*, **XXIX** (Winter, 1959), 38–46.

Matson, F. (ed.). *Being, Becoming and Behavior*. New York: George Braziller, 1967.

McCall, G. J. and J. L. Simmons. (eds.). *Identities and Interactions*. New York: The Free Press, 1966.

McKinney, John C. *Constructive Typology and Social Theory*. New York: Appleton-Century-Crofts, 1966.

Mead, G. H. *George Herbert Mead on Social Psychology*. Edited by A. Strauss. Chicago: University of Chicago Press, 1964.

Mead, G. H. *Mind, Self, and Society*. Edited by Charles W. Morris. Chicago: The University of Chicago Press, 1934.

——————. *Movements of Thought in the Nineteenth Century*. Edited by Merritt H. Moore. Chicago: University of Chicago Press, 1936.

——————. *The Definition of the Psychical*. Chicago: The University of Chicago Press, 1903.

——————. "The Function of Imagery in Conduct", *Mind, Self and Society*. Edited by C. W. Morris. (Chicago: The University of Chicago Press, 1934), 337–46.

Meisel, J. H. (ed.). *Pareto and Mosca*. Englewood Cliffs, New Jersey: Prentice-Hall, 1965.

Meltzer, B. N. "Mead's Social Psychology", *Symbolic Interaction*. Edited by J. Manis and B. Meltzer. (Boston: Allyn and Bacon, 1967), 5–24.

——————. *The Social Psychology of George Herbert Mead*. Kalamazoo, Michigan: Division of Field Services, Western Michigan University, 1959.

Mills, C. Wright. *Images of Man*. New York: George Braziller, 1960.

Mitchell, W. *Sociological Analysis and Politics*. Englewood Cliffs, New Jersey: Prentice-Hall, 1967.

Moore, Barrington, Jr. *Political Power and Social Theory*. New York: Harper, 1958.

——————. "The New Scholasticism and the Study of Politics", *Political Power and Social Theory*. Edited by B. Moore, Jr. (New York: Harper, 1958), 89–110.

Morris, C. W. *Signification and Significance*. Cambridge: The M. I. T. Press, 1964.

——————. *Signs, Language and Behavior*. New York: Prentice-Hall, 1946.

——————. *Six Theories of Mind*. Chicago: The University of Chicago Press, 1932.

Nagel, Ernest. (ed.). *John Stuart Mill's Philosophy of Scientific Method*. New York: Hafner Publishing Co., 1950.

——————. *The Structure of Science*. New York: Harcourt, Brace and World, 1961.

Natanson, Maurice. (ed.). *Philosophy of the Social Sciences*. New York: Random House, 1963.

Ogles, Richard. "Programmatic Theory and the Critics of Talcott Parsons", *Pacific Sociological Review*, **IX**, No. 2 (Fall, 1961), 53–56.

——————. "Some Methodological Issues in Sociological Theory", Unpublished Ph.D. dissertation, Department of Sociology, Washington State University, 1961.

Park, Peter. "Some Methodological Problems of Homans' Theory of Social Behavior", (Paper presented at the annual meeting of the Canadian Sociology and Anthropology Association, at Calgary, Alberta, June, 1968.)

Parkinson, G. H. R. (ed.). *The Theory of Meaning*. London: Oxford University Press, 1968.

Parsons, Talcott. "An Approach to Psychological Theory in Terms of the Theory of Action", *Psychology: A Study of a Science*. Edited by S. Koch. Vol. III. (Toronto: McGraw-Hill, 1959), 612–711.

——————. "Comments on Kolb's Paper", *Journal for the Scientific Study of Religion*, **I**, No. 1 (October, 1961), 22–29.

————. *Essays in Sociological Theory*. New York: The Free Press, 1949.

————. "Pareto's Central Analytical Scheme", *Pareto and Mosca*. Edited by J. H. Meisel. (Englewood Cliffs, New Jersey: Prentice-Hall, 1965), 71–88.

————. "The Pattern Variables Revisited: A Response to Robert Dubin", *Sociological Theory and Modern Society*. Edited by Talcott Parsons. (New York: The Free Press, 1967), 192–219.

Parsons, Talcott. "The Place of Ultimate Values in Sociological Theory", *International Journal of Ethics*, **XLV**, (1934–35), 282–316.

————. "The Point of View of the Author", *The Social Theories of Talcott Parsons*. Edited by Max Black. (Englewood Cliffs, New Jersey: Prentice-Hall, 1961), 311–63.

————. "The Present Position and Prospects of Systematic Theory in Sociology", *Essays in Sociological Theory*. Revised Edition. (New York: The Free Press, 1954), 212–237.

————. "Psychoanalysis and the Social Structure", *Essays in Sociological Theory*. Revised Edition. (New York: The Free Press, 1954), 336–47.

————. *Social Structure and Personality*. New York: The Free Press, 1964.

————. *The Social System*. New York: The Free Press, 1951.

————. *Societies*. Englewood Cliffs, New Jersey: Prentice-Hall, 1966.

————. (ed.). *Sociological Theory and Modern Society*. New York: The Free Press, 1967.

————. "Some Comments on the State of the General Theory of Action", *Contemporary Sociology*. Edited by M. L. Barron. (New York: Dodd, Mead, 1964), 572–89.

————. *Structure and Process in Modern Societies*. New York: The Free Press, 1965.

————. *The Structure of Social Action*. New York: The Free Press, 1949.

————. "The System of Modern Societies", (Mimeographed, n. d., n. p.)

Parsons, Talcott and R. F. Bales. "The Dimensions of Action-space", *Working Papers in the Theory of Action*. Edited by Talcott Parsons, Robert F. Bales and Edward Shils. (New York: The Free Press, 1953), 63–110.

Parsons, Talcott and R. F. Bales. *Family, Socialization and Interaction Process*. New York: The Free Press, 1955.

Parsons, Talcott, R. F. Bales and E. A. Shils. "Phase Movement in Relation to Motivation, Symbol Formation, and Role Structure", *Working Papers in the Theory of Action*. Edited by Talcott Parsons, Robert F. Bales, and Edward Shils. (New York: The Free Press, 1953), 163–269.

Parsons, Talcott, R. F. Bales and E. A. Shils. *Working Papers in the Theory of Action*. New York: The Free Press, 1953.

Parsons, Talcott and E. A: Shils (ed.). *Toward a General Theory of Action*. New York: Harper, 1951.

Parsons, Talcott and N. J. Smelser. *Economy and Society*. London: Routledge and Kegan Paul, 1957.

Parsons, Talcott, *et al. Theories of Society*. 2 vols. New York: The Free Press, 1961.

Popper, Sir Karl. *The Logic of Scientific Discovery*. New York: Harper and Row, 1959.

Rose, A. M. (ed.). *Human Behavior and Social Process*. Boston: Houghton Mifflin, 1962.

Ross, Ralph. *Symbols and Civilization*. New York: Harcourt, Brace and World, 1962.

Royce, J. R. (ed.). *Psychology and the Symbol*. New York: Random House, 1965.

Rudner, Richard S. *Philosophy of Social Science*. Englewood Cliffs, New Jersey: Prentice-Hall, 1966.

Ryle, Gilbert. "Use, Usage and Meaning", *The Theory of Meaning*. Edited by G. H. R. Parkinson. (London: Oxford University Press, 1968), 109–16.

Scheff, Thomas. *Being Mentally Ill*. Chicago: Aldine, 1966.

Schrag, Clarence. "Comments on the General Theory of Action", *Alpha Kappa Deltan*, **XXIX** (Winter, 1959), 46–52.

Simon, Herbert. *Models of Man*. New York: Wiley, 1957.

Skidmore, W. L. *Theoretical Thinking in Sociology*. New York: Cambridge University Press, 1975.

Smith, Adam. *An Inquiry Into the Nature and Causes of the Wealth of Nations*. 2 vols. Homewood, Illinois: Richard D. Irwin, 1963.

Sorokin, P. A. *Contemporary Sociological Theories*. New York: Harper, 1928.

Stein, M. and A. Vidich. *Sociology on Trial*. Englewood Cliffs, New Jersey: Prentice-Hall, 1963.

Strauss, Anselm *et al.* "The Hospital and its Negotiated Order", *The Hospital in Modern Society*. Edited by Elliot Friedson. (New York: The Free Press, 1963), 147–169.

Tiryakian, E. A. *Sociological Theory, Values, and Sociocultural Change*. New York: Harper, 1963.

Wallis, Wilson D. Review of *Mind, Self and Society* by G. H. Mead. *International Journal of Ethics*, **XLV** (1934–35), 456–58.

Weber, Max. *The Protestant Ethic and the Spirit of Capitalism*. Translated by Talcott Parsons. New York: Scribners, 1958.

————. *The Theory of Social and Economic Organization*. Translated by Talcott Parsons. New York: The Free Press, 1947.

Whorf, B. L. *Language, Thought and Reality*. Cambridge, Mass.: M. I. T. Press, 1956.

Winch, Peter. *The Idea of a Social Science*. New York: Humanities Press, 1958.

Wrong, Dennis. "The Oversocialized Concept of Man in Modern Sociology", *American Sociological Review*, **XXVI**, No. 2 (April, 1961), 183–93.

Zetterberg, H. L. Review of *Modern Sociological Theory in Continuity and Change* by H. Becker and A. Boskoff. *American Sociological Review*, **XXIII** (February, 1958), 95–96.

————. *On Theory and Verification in Sociology*. Totowa, New Jersey: The Bedminster Press, 1954.

Author Index

Subject Index